WAYS AND MEANS

FOR THE YOUNG PEOPLE'S
SOCIETY OF CHRISTIAN
ENDEAVOR

A book of suggestions for the prayer - meeeting, the committees, and all lines of Christian work adopted by Christian Endeavor Societies.

by

Rev. F. E. Clark, D.D.

First Fruits Press
Wilmore, Kentucky
c2015

Ways and means for the Young People's Society of Christian Endeavor: a book of suggestions for the prayer-meeting, the committees, and all lines of Christian work adopted by Christian Endeavor Societies, by Rev. Francis E. Clark, D.D.

First Fruits Press, ©2015
Previously published: Boston : D. Lothrop Company, ©1890.

ISBN: 9781621713432 (print), 9781621713449 (digital)

Digital version at http://place.asburyseminary.edu/christianendeavorbooks/36/

First Fruits Press is a digital imprint of the Asbury Theological Seminary, B.L. Fisher Library. Asbury Theological Seminary is the legal owner of the material previously published by the Pentecostal Publishing Co. and reserves the right to release new editions of this material as well as new material produced by Asbury Theological Seminary. Its publications are available for noncommercial and educational uses, such as research, teaching and private study. First Fruits Press has licensed the digital version of this work under the Creative Commons Attribution Noncommercial 3.0 United States License. To view a copy of this license, visit http://creativecommons.org/licenses/by-nc/3.0/us/.

For all other uses, contact:

First Fruits Press
B.L. Fisher Library
Asbury Theological Seminary
204 N. Lexington Ave.
Wilmore, KY 40390
http://place.asburyseminary.edu/firstfruits

Clark, Francis E. (Francis Edward), 1851-1927.
    Ways and means for the Young People's Society of Christian Endeavor : a book of suggestions for the prayer-meeting, the committees, and all lines of Christian work adopted by Christian Endeavor Societies / by Rev. Francis E. Clark.
    340, [9] pages; 21 cm.
    Wilmore, Ky. : First Fruits Press, ©2015.
    Includes indexes.
    Reprint. Previously published: Boston : D. Lothrop Company, ©1890.
    ISBN: 9781621713432 (pbk.)
    1. Church group work with youth. 2. International Society of Christian Endeavor.. I. Title.
BV1425 .C52 2015

Cover design by Jonathan Ramsay

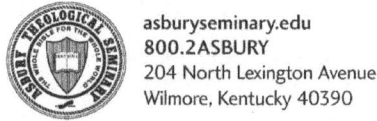

asburyseminary.edu
800.2ASBURY
204 North Lexington Avenue
Wilmore, Kentucky 40390

First Fruits Press
The Academic Open Press of Asbury Theological Seminary
204 N. Lexington Ave., Wilmore, KY 40390
859-858-2236
first.fruits@asburyseminary.edu
asbury.to/firstfruits

WAYS AND MEANS

FOR THE YOUNG PEOPLE'S SOCIETY OF CHRISTIAN ENDEAVOR.

A book of suggestions for the prayer-meeting, the committees, and all lines of Christian work adopted by Christian Endeavor Societies.

BY

REV. F. E. CLARK, D. D.

President of the United Society of Christian Endeavor.

Author of "The Mossback Correspondence," "Young People's Prayer-meetings," "The Children and the Church," etc.

BOSTON
D LOTHROP COMPANY
WASHINGTON STREET OPPOSITE BROMFIELD

COPYRIGHT, 1890,
BY
D. LOTHROP COMPANY.

INTRODUCTION.

THIS book in every line has been dictated by experience. There are no mere theories in it. Every plan suggested has been tried successfully in some society of Christian Endeavor. It is given to the public in response to a very generally expressed desire for such a publication. For several years past many correspondents have suggested that among the growing Christian Endeavor Societies, with their hundreds of thousands of members, such a book had become well nigh a necessity. Most of the suggestions herein contained have appeared in the columns of *The Golden Rule*, but in the cumbrous files of a weekly newspaper they cannot readily be found, and the fact that they have thus appeared has created a demand for their publication in book form. The editor wishes to express his sincere thanks to the many friends who have contributed to these pages, whose names will be found in the index, and he regrets that it has seemed necessary to include so many of his own articles; but the fact that he has had occasion during the last ten years to write upon almost every phase of the work of the Christian Endeavor Society, while others have written only on special features of the organization, must be his excuse for including in this compilation so much of his own work. When the "familiar letters" have been reproduced he has deemed it best to retain their "familiar" correspondence style, thinking that in this informal form they would be quite as useful as if rewritten in more didactic style. Though this book deals largely with methods it is hoped that the earnest spiritual purpose underlying all these methods will not be overlooked. The editor fully realizes that methods and plans and organizations are of no avail without the informing and pervading presence of the Spirit of God, but that God has wonderfully and graciously used these methods of the Christian Endeavor Society, the history of the movement makes plain, and the editor devoutly prays that this volume, which details and emphasizes these plans, may also be used for the further advancement of the Kingdom of God among the young people of this generation.

F. E. CLARK.

BOSTON, Oct. 1, 1890.

WAYS AND MEANS.

A SHORT HISTORY OF THE CHRISTIAN ENDEAVOR MOVEMENT.

BY REV. F. E. CLARK, D. D.

I HAVE been frequently requested by friends to give some authentic account of the origin of the Young People's Societies of Christian Endeavor. I have hesitated somewhat to do this, feeling that such an account might savor of self-gratulation; also, that a movement which is still so young as is this could hardly have much history worth recording. Of late, however, these calls for a chapter of history have been more numerous than ever, and certain misrepresentations concerning the origin of the society have appeared, which make it more necessary to give a succinct account of the earliest years of the movement. I hope, also, to make it plain that for this society, which is assuming such large proportions throughout the world, no special credit is due to any one man, but rather to a large number of faithful ministers and laymen, who were eager for some means of developing the religious life of their young people. Most manifest has been the leading of the Spirit of God in all this work from its inception.

In the winter of 1880–81 a precious revival spirit visited the Williston Church, of Portland, Me., and many, especially among the young people, gave their hearts to God.

The pastor and older church-members were naturally anxious concerning these young disciples, and felt that great wisdom and care were necessary to keep them true to the Saviour during the first critical years of their discipleship. The problem weighed heavily upon their minds, for they felt that neither the Sunday-school, nor the church prayer-meeting, nor the young people's prayer-meeting, though all well sustained and admirable in their way, were sufficient to hold and mould the Christian character of these young converts. There was a gap between conversion and church-membership to be filled, and all these young souls were to be trained and set at work. How should these things be done? These were the pressing problems. After much prayer and thought, the pastor of the church invited the recent converts, as well as the young church-members, to his house, on the evening of February 2, 1881, and after an hour of social intercourse presented a constitution, which he had previously drawn up, of the "Williston Young People's Society of Christian Endeavor." This constitution is essentially the same as that adopted by the great majority of Societies of Christian Endeavor at the present day.

Some three years later, at the request of one of the national conventions, with the aid of Rev. S. W. Adriance, the writer revised the constitution and framed the by-laws, adding various committees as they now appear in the "Model Constitution." But the essential features of the work were in the first constitution. The definition of the object, the two classes of members, the "prayer-meeting pledge" (the most important part of the constitution), the consecration or experience meeting, the roll-call, the provision for dropping members, and the three main committees, are provisions which are all found in the first constitution.

Thus it will be seen that the Society of Christian Endeavor was born of a revival, and was the outcome of a real, felt necessity, the necessity of training and guiding aright the young Christians who might otherwise stray away. It will be also seen that it was a mere experiment, in the first place, and that little credit is due to the originator except for an effort to train his own young people in the Christian life, an effort which is always made by every true pastor. To his delight, and somewhat, also, it must be confessed, to his surprise, nearly all the young people who assembled at that pastor's house on the second of February signed the constitution containing the stringent prayer-meeting clause, and, to his still greater delight, they lived up to it. The young people's meeting took a fresh start; the spiritual life of the members was intensified; their activities were very greatly enlarged; and, so far as they were concerned, the problem of leading them to confess Christ with their lips, of setting them at work and keeping them at work, seemed to be solved. When that pastor also found that in many other churches the same efforts accomplished the same results, he began to feel that the hand of the Lord was in it.

The first knowledge of this experiment given to the world was contained in an article published in *The Congregationalist*, of Boston, in August, 1881, entitled, "How One Church Cares for its Young People." This article, and others which followed it, at once brought letters from pastors and Christian workers in all parts of the country. First they came singly, then in pairs, and then in scores, almost every day, and they have kept coming, in constantly increasing numbers, ever since. One of the first pastors to introduce this system of Christian nurture among his young people was Rev. C. A. Dickinson, then pastor of the Second Parish Church, of Portland, and no small share of the success of the movement has been due ever since to his wisdom and counsel. The second society, however, was established in Newburyport, Mass., by Rev. C. P. Mills, in the same year that the movement originated. He has also ever since been one of the stanch friends of the cause; while another gentleman, who soon threw himself into the movement with characteristic energy, was Rev. James L. Hill, then of Lynn, and now of Medford. The first President of the United Society, Mr. W. J. Van Patten, of Burlington, Vt., was one of the first to recognize the potency of the movement, and, in several long letters, suggested plans for future growth which have since been carried out, and have demonstrated his wisdom and sagacity. The first man who signed the constitution, at his pastor's house, on that winter evening in 1881, was Mr. W. H. Pennell, teacher, in the Williston Sunday-school, of a large class of young men. He took this step, perhaps, as much to help his boys as for any other reason. His whole-souled support has never been wanting from that day to this, and the National Convention honored his early devotion to the work by choosing him for three successive years its president. Among others conspicuous in the early history of the movement were Rev. S. W. Adriance, of Woodfords, now of Lowell; Mr. J. W. Stevenson, of Portland; Eli Manchester, Jr., of New Haven, Conn., and others whose names we cannot mention, but who will not soon be forgotten.

Since this short history is given in part to correct misapprehension, it may be well to add that the writer was quite surprised to learn from a Western paper, that he obtained the Christian Endeavor idea from Rev. Edward Eggleston. This talented author once was the pastor of a church called "The church of Christian Endeavor," as is well known, but no organization, I think, like the present societies ever existed in his church. This society has also been said to have been modeled after a young people's society in Dr. Cuyler's church, in Brooklyn. This most wise and eminent pastor, who has done so much to endear him to the young people of America, does, indeed, have a vigorous young people's organization in his church, and the success of this effort was an inspiration to the writer to believe that young people could be effectively organized for Christian work. But what the special characteristics of this society are he does not, even now, know. So far as careful search reveals, the distinctive features of the Christian Endeavor movement, the strict prayer-meeting pledge, the consecration-meeting, the roll-call, the variety of committee work, and the duties of these committees, are characteristics of this organization alone. At first, as has been shown, the Society of Christian Endeavor grew apparently as it were by chance, if it is ever right to use such a word. Wherever one of the winged seeds of information was wafted, it usually "struck" and took root, and a little Christian Endeavor plant was the result; or, as some one wittily expressed it at one of our National Conventions: "The society was contagious, like the measles; if one church had it, the church next it was pretty sure to catch it also."

For some months, in fact for years, little was done in a systematic or organized way to establish societies. As letters were received they were answered as fast as possible, and so it came about, that in different parts of the country were those who had heard of and tried and believed in the organization, long before any "United Society" was proposed. One of the first developments of the new work was naturally in the line of annual conventions. Those interested were not content to work out the problem for themselves, they must come together and tell each other what great things the Lord had done for them. The first of these conferences was held June 2, 1882, in the Williston church, Portland, Me. A glowing newspaper report, which lies before me, shows that even in the early days, when societies were few and numbers small, enthusiasm and devotion were not lacking. There were but six societies recorded then, though doubtless there were others (as the one in Newburyport, Mass.), which were not then known to the conference. These six societies were in the Williston, Second Parish, West and St. Lawrence Street Churches, of Portland, in one of the churches of Bath, and one in Hampden, Me. These six societies, except the one in Hampden, were represented, and gave encouraging reports of the work done.

The programme consisted of discussions in the afternoon, of "The Prayer-Meeting," "The Experience-Meeting," "The Sociables" and "The Lookout Committee Work," and of addresses in the evening by Rev. C. A. Dickinson, Rev. A. H. Wright and Rev. F. E. Clark. At this meeting, Mr. W. H. Pennell was chosen President of the Conference, and Mr. J. W. Stevenson, Secretary, offices which they filled for three years, to the great benefit of the society. In these six societies were 481 members, the Williston Society leading off with 168.

Small as this meeting was, in comparison with the great gathering of recent years, when churches are crowded with delegates and the societies are many thousand strong, there was, nevertheless, power and promise in this conference, as is shown by the prayer of faith offered by one who recorded in print the chronicles of this Convention: "May the time speedily come when every church in our land shall cherish in its midst one of these societies of earnest Christian Endeavor." With only six or seven societies to point to, this wish seemed, perhaps, wild and extravagant. It is only a few years since that conference was held, and already it seems far from improbable that the prophetic prayer may yet be fulfilled.

The next annual conference was held in the same city of Portland, June 7, 1883, but in another church, the Second Parish. A large growth over the preceding year was noted, though statistics were obtained from only fifty-three societies with 2,630 members. Of these fifty-three societies the report says five were organized in 1881, twenty-one in 1882, and twenty-seven in the first five months of

1883, showing what an impetus to the work was given by the little Convention of the year before. Seventeen of these societies were found in Maine, eleven in Massachusetts — forty-one in all New England; while of the other twelve, five were in New York, and the rest scattered through-out the West, a very large one being found in the First Congregational Church of Oakland, Cal. At this Convention the questions which have since become so familiar were discussed, and the usual business performed. Mr. W. J. Van Patten, afterward our President, was chosen Treasurer, and Vice-Presidents were selected from various States where any societies existed. Among the latter was the Rev. C. L. Goodell, D. D., the late revered pastor of the Pilgrim Church, St. Louis, who threw the generous weight of his influence on the side of this, as every good cause, declaring that "The society transplanted from Maine to Missouri had survived all injury," and, changing the figure, that "it was feet for him to run all over the city on God's errands."

Other gentlemen who were prominent and useful in this Convention were H. H. Burgess, Esq., Granville Staples, and Rev. J. M. Louden, of Portland, and Rev. J. J. Hall, of Auburn. After this Convention the society held on the even tenor of its way, growing rapidly and steadily, but did not call another National Convention until October 22, 1884, when it convened in Kirk Street Church, Lowell, the church of which Rev. C. A. Dickinson had become pastor. This was a two days' session, and was a large, enthusiastic meeting, though only 150 delegates from out of the city were in attendance. The Secretary reported that the society had nearly trebled during the past year, having grown to 151 societies, with 6,414 members. Notable addresses were made at this Convention by Rev. Drs. A. H. Plumb, Michael Burnham and Alexander McKenzie.

The next National Convention convened July 9th and

10th, at Ocean Park, a charming seaside resort near Old Orchard Beach, Me., and was by far the largest and most important of all conventions yet held. It was considered by the committee to be a doubtful experiment to go to a summer resort so far from a large city and church; but the success of the meeting proved their wisdom, and the society there adopted a most important principle: never to be dependent on private hospitality for entertainment.

Not only was this Convention notable for good speeches, but for the inauguration of wise and far-reaching plans. The idea of securing a General Secretary who should give all his time to the work was here broached; $1,200 was raised to pay, in part, the salary, and, perhaps more important than all, the "United Society of Christian Endeavor" was founded and incorporated under the laws of Maine. At this Convention Mr. Van Patten was chosen President in place of Mr. Pennell, who had served the society so faithfully and acceptably for three years past.

This Convention was also notable for the advent of several earnest workers who were soon to become prominent in the society, notably: Rev. H. B. Grose, of the first Babtist Church, Poughkeepsie, Rev. R. W. Brokaw, of the Reformed Church, Belleville, and Rev. N. Boynton, of Haverhill, who are now among the Trustees of the United Society. Rev. E. Blakeslee, who has done so much for our society in Connecticut, was also prominent in this Convention, as were also Dr. Hawes, of Burlington, and Rev. O. P. Gifford, who gave excellent addresses, and Messrs. Shumway, Hobbs and Manchester, besides many other earnest workers.

It seems, however, almost invidious to mention names when so many were active and efficient. Rev. J. L. Hill demonstrated his power as a money-raiser at this Convention. As one of the correspondents remarked, in a letter to the Chicago *Advance* about this Convention: "Mr.

Kimball, the debt-lifter may well look out for his laurels when Mr. Hill, of Lynn, is about."

The society had now grown to 253 societies, with 14,892 members in all parts of the country. They had begun to be reported in foreign lands, also, and news came of flourishing Christian Endeavor societies in Foochow, Honolulu, and other foreign lands. From this Convention the work received a marvelous impulse, and everywhere the churches began to establish societies. The serious question of who should be the Secretary now agitated the Trustees of the United Society. At last, Rev. S. W. Adriance was chosen, and though at first he thought he should be able to accept the place permanently, he found, after a month or two, much to the regret of the trustees, that the claims of his church were too strong to resist, and Mr. Geo. M. Ward, of Lowell, who had been previously chosen Treasurer at the Ocean Park Convention, was elected by the Trustees to fill the vacant office in the fall of 1885.

In the spring of 1890 Mr. J. W. Baer, of Minnesota, was chosen to fill the general secretaryship which, because of ill health, Mr. Ward was compelled to resign.

Mr. William Shaw, of Boston, was then chosen the efficient Treasurer of the society. Headquarters of the United Society were established at No. 8 Beacon Street, Boston, but were soon removed to more commodious rooms at No. 50 Bromfield Street. The Fifth Annual convention was held at Saratoga Springs, N. Y., July 6-8, 1886, and was a large and enthusiastic gathering. In the summer of 1887, at the Saratoga Convention, Rev. F. E. Clark was chosen President of the United Society and editor of Christian Endeavor literature, a position which he accepted in the following autumn, resigning the pastorate of Phillips Church, Boston, to accept the position. The recent history must be dismissed in a few words, for it is so fresh in our minds that it need not be dwelt upon at length.

Some of the prominent features of the recent growth have been the establishment of State Unions in nearly all the States of the Union, many of these patterning after Connecticut, which led the way in the State organizations; the establishment of local unions in hundreds of places, the adoption of *The Golden Rule* as the representative of the societies, have been some of the causes which, under the blessing of God, have increased the one society of 1881 to the growing myriads of the present time, with their hundreds of thousands of members in America, and many added thousands in Great Britain and all missionary lands. It would be pleasant to speak of the recent great National Conventions, so grandly sustained in numbers and spiritual earnestness, of the large State Conventions scarcely less inspiring, and to mention by name the hundreds of earnest workers who have made the present growth possible. But space forbids, and the rapid growth makes all statistics untrustworthy. We can only say, "The Lord hath done great things for us, whereof we are glad."

It remains to be said, that in his letter of acceptance the President of the United Society formulated certain principles which he presented to the societies as conditions on which he accepted their call. These principles have been adopted by many influential State Conventions and local unions in all parts of the country, and may fairly be considered the platform of principles on which the society stands.

PLATFORM OF PRINCIPLES.

1st. The society of Christian Endeavor is not, and is not to be, an organization independent of the church. It is the Church at work for and with the young, and the young people at work for and with the Church. In all that we do and say, let us bear this in mind, and seek for the fullest co-operation of pastors and church officers and members in carrying on our work. The society of Christian Endeavor can always afford to wait rather than force itself upon an unwilling church.

2d. Since the societies exist in every evangelical denomination, the basis of the union of the societies is one of common loyalty to Christ, common methods of service for Him, and mutual Christian affection, rather than a doctrinal and ecclesiastical basis. In such a union all evangelical Christians can unite without repudiating or being disloyal to any denominational custom or tenet.

3d. The purely Religious features of the organization shall always be paramount. The Society of Christian Endeavor centers about the prayer-meeting. The strict "prayer-meeting pledge," honestly interpreted, as experience has proved, is essential to the continued success of a Society of Christian Endeavor.

4th. The society of Christian Endeavor sympathizes with temperance and all true moral reforms, with wise philanthropic measures, and especially with missions at home and abroad; yet is not to be used as a convenience by any organization to further ends other than its own.

5th. The finances of the society shall be managed economically in accordance with the past policy of the Board of Trustees, and the raising of funds to support a large number of paid agents or Christian Endeavor missionaries, either in connection with the United Society or the State Unions, is not contemplated. In winning our way we can best depend in the future as in the past upon the abundant dissemination of our literature, and on the voluntary and freely-given labors of our friends, rather than upon the paid services of local agents.

The expenses of the central office will be largely for the publication of literature, and for the expenses of our General Secretary in the field. In raising very large sums and employing many agents for whose work the United Society will be responsible, and yet which it cannot to any great extent control, we shall run the risk of losing the sympathy of the churches. There is little danger that the society will not grow with sufficient rapidity if every member does his best to make known our principles. Let it be our chief concern that our growth shall be as strong and substantial as it is rapid. In all State and local work the society can best rely upon the zeal and generosity of its friends, hundreds of whom, both laymen and ministers, are willing freely to lend their aid to our cause.

The past three years have been the most remarkable in the history of the society.

1st. On account of the marvelous increase in the number of societies. In July, 1887, there were 2,314; in July, 1889, 7,672; in June, 1890, 11,013.

2d. For the increasing favor with which they are being received by the pastors and churches. The young people by their earnest endeavors, have convinced the doubters of their loyalty to both Christ and the church. One of the most interesting developments of the society has been along the line of work for the children, and Junior Societies are increasing in numbers and efficiency.

The great Convention held in Battery D. Armory Hall, Chicago, Ill., July 5th, 6th, 7th and 8th, was a remarkable gathering. Over five thousand delegates were present from thirty-three States and Territories. The addresses and papers were of a high order of merit. Rev. James W. Brooks, D. D., of St Louis; Rev. John H. Barrows, D. D., of Chicago; Bishop Samuel Fallows, of Chicago; Rev. Arthur Mitchell, D. D., Prof. W. R. Harper, and Miss Frances Willard, were a few of the many eloquent speakers who addressed the Convention.

The Eighth Annual Convention, which was held in the 1st Regiment Armory Hall, Philadelphia, July 9th, 10th and 11th, was, in numbers and influence, the greatest Convention we have held. Over six thousand, five hundred delegates were present, representing thirty-one States and Territories, Germany, Turkey, Canada, Ontario, Quebec and Nova Scotia. Among the many noted speakers were Rev. A. T. Pierson, D. D., Rev. J. W. Hamilton, D. D., Rev. O. P. Gifford, D. D., Rev. Geo. H. Wells, D. D., Major-General O. O. Howard, and Hon. John Wanamaker. President Harrison sent a telegram of greeting to the Convention. The work is growing steadily in England, and from all mission lands comes the news of the formation of societies that are proving very helpful in training the young people in Christian service.

The Ninth Annual Convention, held at St Louis June 12–15, 1890, was the greatest and in many respects the best of the series. The throngs attending the meeting were enormous, over 8,000 delegates being registered and fully 11,000 people being present at the principal meeting and the four overflow meetings held on the last evening of the session. The spiritual power was not inferior to the size of the convention, and it was pronounced by competent judges to be, undoubtedly, the largest religious convention ever held in America. Several new trustees of the United Society, representing all the evangelical denominations, have recently been elected. At the present writing, October, 1890, there are nearly 12,000 societies known to exist, with fully 700,000 members. The United Society, since 1889, has not asked any contributions for its support. It has become wholly self-sustaining by the sales of its literature, and because of the fact that its expenses are very small, most of the workers giving their services freely for love of the cause.

PART II.

YOUNG PEOPLE'S SOCIETY OF CHRISTIAN ENDEAVOR.

WHAT IT IS AND HOW IT WORKS.

BY REV. F. E. CLARK, D. D.

ORGANIZED EFFORT.

The Young People's Society of Christian Endeavor is simply an organized effort to lead the young people to Christ and into His church, to establish them firmly in the faith, and to set them at work in the Lord's Vineyard. The main point upon which the Constitution insists, is the weekly prayer-meeting, which each active member pledges himself or herself to attend (unless detained by some absolute necessity) and to participate in, in some way, if only by the repetition of a verse of Scripture.

Once each month a special meeting of reconsecration to Christ is held, at which special pains are taken to see whether every active member is faithful to his pledge and true to Christ. The society may, and as an actual fact often does, branch off into many other departments of Christian effort, adapting itself to the local needs of each Church, but these rules concerning the prayer-meeting are imperative; without them there cannot be a true Society of Christian Endeavor.

It cannot be insisted on too strongly that the society of Christian Endeavor is first and last and always a Religious Society. It has social and literary and other features, but it is neither a social nor literary society.

In the Platform of Principles set forth by the President

of the United Society when he accepted the position, and since very generally endorsed by the societies and adopted by their Conventions, is the following:

"The purely religious features of the organization shall always be paramount. The Society of Christian Endeavor centers about the prayer-meeting. The strict prayer-meeting pledge, honestly interpreted, is essential to the continued success of a society of Christian Endeavor."

A society thus organized among the young people has proved itself to be in many cases

A TRAINING SCHOOL IN THE CHURCH.

It gives the young Christian something to do at once.

It accustoms him to the sound of his own voice in the prayer-meeting.

It causes him to understand that he has a part to perform in the activities of the church as well as the oldest Christian. It sends him upon a hundred errands for Christ. Very soon he learns that he has a duty in the general church prayer-meetings, and he becomes naturally and easily one of the pastor's trusted helpers. We are speaking from actual experience in this matter and are not theorizing.

A generation of Christians trained from early boyhood and girlhood in this way, patiently, persistently, kindly, would be a generation of working Christians.

This society is also a

WATCH-TOWER FOR THE CHURCH.

The pastor ought always if possible to attend the prayer-meetings and the social gatherings, and, unseen, keep his hands on the reins of the organization. If he does so, wisely and constantly, he cannot help knowing how the young converts are progressing in the Christian life. If they are faithful to their voluntary vows he knows it, and can mark with joy their growth in grace. If they are negligent he knows that, and can at once look after and reclaim the unfaithful ones.

No month need ever go by without the pastor knowing the religious status of each of his young people.

THE COMMITTEES.

The various committees are very important features of the Young People's Society of Christian Endeavor. With faithful, earnest, intelligent committees, the work can scarcely fail to succeed. Perhaps the most important committee is the "Lookout Committee." This committee has for part of its work to introduce new members to the society, and it should take great pains that only those who have begun the Christian life are thus introduced as active members. But its most delicate, and at the same time important duty, is the reclaiming of those who have grown lax and indifferent to their vows. If any Active Member is away from the monthly Consecration Meeting, the Lookout Committee should know the fact, and should find out the reason for the absence. The very fact that this committee is on the "Lookout" will prove a salutary restraint upon many. There are but few young people who stay away who cannot be reclaimed and brought back to their allegiance by a wise and faithful Lookout Committee.

The other committees, especially the Prayer-Meeting and Social Committees, are scarcely less important, but their duties are easily understood as defined in the Consitution,* and their work will be defined and explained on other pages.

All these committees, according to their zeal and devotion, can make much or little of their office. Each one of them affords a grand opportunity for efficient service if it is rightly used.

WHO MAY BECOME MEMBERS?

Should there be an age limit? These are questions which are often asked. We are not in favor of a strict age limit, since youth and age are such variable terms. Many a man is old at twenty-five. Many a man at fifty is still

---

* See Model Constitution, ART VI., and By-Laws, ART. XII.

young. This matter can usually be left to the sanctified common sense of Christian men and women. As a general rule the older church members will feel that they can do more good by praying for the young people's meeting at home. Their presence in large numbers would embarrass, and perhaps silence, many timid young Christians. Still there are exceptions to this rule. It is very essential that there should be in the society a number of older young people, say those between twenty and forty, to give stability to the work and to take the lead in the committees. While the children should always be welcomed and encouraged to come, yet a society composed wholly of chilren will hardly succeed. On the younger side the age limit easily takes care of itself. Children whom their parents allow to be out in the evening are not too young to become members. The Junior Societies are being formed in large numbers and with excellent results for the training of the boys and girls under thirteen and fourteen years of age.

THE CONSECRATION MEETING.

This meeting is one of great importance. It may be called by various names: "Consecration," "Experience," "Progress," or simply the "Monthly Meeting," but by whatever name it is called it should and may be made a real power. At this meeting, in some way, some expression of renewed loyalty to Christ should be obtained from every active member. When the roll is called it should be made a very serious matter, and the mere response to the name should be considered a reconsecration. Most societies have found it best to call the roll, not at the close, but during the progress of the meeting, so that each may respond to his name with a prayer, or a word of testimony, or a passage of Scripture. This plan for many reasons is the best.

THE ASSOCIATE MEMBERS.

The duties of the active members are plain enough — humble Christian living, constant attendance upon the meetings, and constant participation. The duties of the

Associate Members are less easily defined. They are the young people who, while they are not willing to avow themselves active Christians, are willing to put themselves under Christian influences, and are willing to receive the prayers of the Active Members. That they owe something to the society is plain. Habitual attendance upon the meetings should be required from the Associate Members, but not participation in the meeting. At the Consecration Meeting in some societies their names are called, for the purpose of finding out if they are present, not for the purpose of obtaining a renewed consecration. Every good influence should be kept around such members, and every effort made to bring them to Christ. The invitation to the prayer meetings should be of the broadest and most cordial character to embrace not only the members, but all the young people of the community.

THE RELATION OF THE PASTOR AND THE CHURCH.

The society is a part of the church. One of its principal objects is to bring all the young people into the work of the church. In this respect it differs from all other organizations. Its motto is: "For Christ and the Church." Each society is connected with some one individual church, and its efforts are directed to her upbuilding. The Platform of Principles before alluded to says: "The society of Christian Endeavor is not and is not to be an organization independent of the church. It is the church at work for and with the young, and the young people at work for and with the church." Testimonies from hundreds of prominent pastors relate how this society has brought back their young people from desultory and unproductive work outside of the church, and has concentrated their efforts in church channels. In the Church Prayer-meeting, the Sunday School, the Musical Services, the social life and missionary efforts of the church, the young people thus organized can be of untold usefulness.

The Pastor should, if possible, attend all their meetings,

aid their efforts and show himself in fullest and most hearty sympathy with the young life of his church, otherwise he cannot hope for large success. See Article IX., Model Constitution.

THE SOCIETY INTERDENOMINATIONAL, NOT UNDENOMINATIONAL.

The best proof of this is found in the fact that it exists in all evangelical denominations, and is found equally useful in all denominations. In some sections it prevails more largely in one denomination, in other sections in another.

The Platform of Principles says on this point: "The basis of the union of the societies is one of common loyalty to Christ, common methods of service for Him, and mutual Christian affection rather than a doctrinal and ecclesiastical basis. In such a union all evangelical Christians can unite without repudiating or being disloyal to any denominational custom or tenet."

BUSINESS FEATURES.

The business features of the society should not be accorded very much prominence. Sharp parliamentary practice and long or heated discussion should be discouraged. The society of Christian Endeavor is not a debating society. If questions requiring debate are brought only before the Executive Committee (as provided in Article VI., 4), and reported favorably or otherwise by this committee to the society for adoption, much trouble may be avoided. But little money is required for the society, and this can be raised by a monthly pledge of five cents, by an unobjectionable entertainment of which the church shall approve, or in any other simple way.

HOW TO FORM A SOCIETY.

Begin with as many earnest active young Christians as are available for this work. Do not be anxious for numbers. Think more of quality than quantity. Half a score of those who are earnest and consecrated are worth in this work ten score of half-hearted ones. A very few young people of the right sort can make a strong society of Christian Endeavor. If the society begins right it is sure to grow. Do not lower the standard or cater to the worldly laxness of the average Christian by making the way in easy. The great danger is just in this line — that many will rush in at first who have no proper conception of their obligations, and who will prove a positive source of weakness to the society. Make sure that every one who joins fully understands his duties and obligations, and is willing in Christ's strength to undertake them. Call together the earnest young Christians who are thus willing to pledge themselves to this work; let them adopt and sign the Constitution, which act solemnly pledges them to a performance of these duties; let them choose their officers and committees, and the society is formed ready to go forward with its work.

SUMMARY.

The essential features, then, of the Young People's Society of Christian Endeavor are: pledged and constant attendance upon the weekly prayer-meetings; Pledged and constant participation therein by every Active Member; pledged and constant work for others through the Committees, and in any way which may be suggested. A few living up to these pledges faithfully will, with the blessing of God, soon become a powerful host in any church. There is no danger that the rules will be too strictly enforced. There is great danger that they will be regarded too loosely. The society that looks to God for all blessings and strictly observes its vows, voluntarily assumed by each young person, cannot fail. More can be learned concerning the society from a careful study of the Constitution printed herein, than in any other way.

THE MODEL CONSTITUTION.

This Constitution, which, in its important features is substantially the same as that adopted by the first society in Portland, Feb. 2, 1881, has been prepared with great care, and met with the very hearty indorsement of the Fourth National Conference, to which it was presented. It has been revised and approved by the Trustees of the United Society at a meeting held October, 1887.

It is not necessarily binding upon any local society, but is to be regarded in the light of a recommendation, especially for the guidance of new organizations and those unacquainted with the work of the society of Christian Endeavor. It is hoped, however, for the sake of uniformity, that the Constitution, which deals only with main principles, may be generally adopted, and that such changes as may be needed to adapt the society to local needs will be made in the By-laws. Even if the language of the Constitution of some local societies should vary from this Model Constitution, it should be borne in mind that only those societies that adhere to the prayer-meeting idea, as embodied in Article VII, and the main features of committee work, can properly claim the name of Christian Endeavor Societies. The specimen By-Laws which are here appended, embrace suggestions for the government of the society, which have been found successful in many places. Each one is approved by experience.

MODEL CONSTITUTION.

Article I. — Name.

This society shall be called the ——————— Young People's Society of Christian Endeavor.

Article II. — Object.

Its object shall be to promote an earnest Christian life among its members, to increase their mutual acquaintance, and to make them more useful in the service of God.

Article III. — Membership.

1. The members shall consist of three classes — active, associate, and affiliated or honorary.

2. ACTIVE MEMBERS. The active members of this society shall consist of all young persons who believe themselves to be Christians, and who sincerely desire to accomplish the objects above specified. Voting powers shall be vested only in the active members.

3. ASSOCIATE MEMBERS. All young persons of worthy character who are not at present willing to be considered decided Christians, may become associate members of this society. They shall have the special prayers and sympathy of the active members, but shall be excused from taking part in the prayer-meeting. It is expected that all associate members will habitually attend the prayer-meetings, and that they will in time become active members, and the society will work to this end.

4. AFFILIATED OR HONORARY MEMBERS.* All persons who, though no longer young, are still interested in the society and wish to have some connection with it, though they cannot regularly attend the meetings, may become affiliated members. Their names shall be kept on the list under the appropriate heading, but shall not be called at the roll-call meeting. It is understood that the society may look to the affiliated members for financial and moral support in all worthy efforts. (For special class of honorary members see Article IX.)

5. These different persons shall become members, upon being elected by the society, after carefully examining the Constitution and upon signing their names to it, thereby pledging themselves to live up to its requirements.

---

*This class of membership is provided for Christians of mature years, especially for those who have been active members, and who desire to remain throughout their lives connected with the society. Young persons who can be either active or associate members should in no case be affiliated members.

Article IV. — Officers.

1. The officers of this society shall be a President, Vice-President, Recording Secretary, Corresponding Secretary, and Treasurer, who shall be chosen from among the active members of the society.

2. There shall also be a Lookout Committee, a Prayer-Meeting Committee, a Social Committee, and such other committees as the local needs of each society may require, each consisting of five active members. There shall also be an Executive Committee as provided in Article VI.

Article V. — Duties of Officers.

1. PRESIDENT. The President of the society shall perform the duties usually pertaining to that office. He shall have especial watch over the interests of the society, and it shall be his care to see that the different committees perform the duties devolving upon them.

2. VICE-PRESIDENT. The Vice-President shall perform the duties of the President in his absence.

3. CORRESPONDING SECRETARY. It shall be the duty of the Corresponding Secretary to keep the local society in communication with the United Society and with other local societies, and to present to his own society such matters of interest as may come from the United Society, from other local societies, and from other authorized sources of Christian Endeavor. This office shall be permanent, and the name shall be forwarded to the United Society.

4. RECORDING SECRETARY. It shall be the duty of the Recording Secretary to keep a record of the members, and to correct it from time to time, as may be necessary, and to obtain the signature of each newly-elected member to the Constitution; also, to correspond with absent members, and inform them of their standing in the society; also, to keep correct minutes of all business meetings of the society; also, to notify all persons elected to office or to committees, and to do so in writing, if necessary.

5. TREASURER. It shall be the duty of the Treasurer to safely keep all moneys belonging to the society, and to pay out only such sums as shall be voted by the society.

ARTICLE VI. — DUTIES OF COMMITTEES.

1. LOOKOUT COMMITTEE. It shall be the duty of this committee to bring new members into the society, to introduce them to the work and to the other members, and to affectionately look after and reclaim any that seem indifferent to their duties as outlined in the pledge. This committee shall also by personal investigation, satisfy itself of the fitness of young persons to become members of this society, and shall propose their names at least one week before their election to membership.

2. PRAYER-MEETING COMMITTEE. It shall be the duty of this committee to have in charge the prayer-meeting, and to see that a topic is assigned and a leader appointed for every meeting, and to do what it can to secure faithfulness to the prayer-meeting pledge.

3. SOCIAL COMMITTEE. It shall be the duty of this committee to promote the social interests of the society by welcoming strangers to the meetings, and by providing for the mutual acquaintance of the members by occasional sociables, for which any appropriate entertainment, of which the church approves, may be provided.

4. EXECUTIVE COMMITTEE.* This committee shall consist of the pastor of the church, the officers of the society, and the chairmen of the various committees. All matters of business requiring debate shall be brought first before this committee, and by it reported either favorably or adversely to the society. All discussion of proposed measures shall take place before this committee and not before the society.

* The object of this committee is to prevent waste of time in the regular meetings of the society, by useless debate and unnecessary parliamentary practice, which are always harmful to the spirit of a prayer-meeting.

Recommendations concerning the finances of the society shall also originate with this committee.

Each committee, except the Executive, shall make a report in writing to the society, at the monthly business meetings, concerning the work of the past month.

ARTICLE VII. — THE PRAYER-MEETING.

1. All the active members shall be present at every meeting, unless detained by some absolute necessity, and each active member shall take some part, however slight, in every meeting. To the above all the active members shall pledge* themselves, understanding by "absolute necessity" some reason for absence which can conscientiously be given to their Master, Jesus Christ. The meetings shall be held one hour, and at the close some time may be taken for introduction and social intercourse, if desired.

2. Once each month a consecration or experience meeting shall be held, at which each active member shall speak concerning his progress in the Christian life, or renew his vows of consecration. If any one chooses, he can express his feelings by an appropriate verse of Scripture or other quotation.

3. At each consecration or experience meeting the roll shall be called, and the responses of the active members who are present shall be considered as a renewed expression of allegiance to Christ. It is expected that, if any one is obliged to be absent from this meeting, he will send a request to be excused by some one who attends.

4. If any active member of this society is absent from this monthly meeting, and fails to send an excuse, the Lookout Committee is expected to take the name of such a one, and in a kind and brotherly spirit ascertain the reason for the absence. If any active member of the society is absent and unexcused from three consecutive monthly

---

* For form of pledge see By-Laws, ART. V.

meetings, such a one ceases to be a member of the society, and his name shall be stricken from the list of members.

ARTICLE VIII.— BUSINESS MEETINGS AND ELECTIONS.

1. Business meetings may be held at the close of the evening prayer-meeting, or at any other time in accordance with the call of the President.

2. An election of the officers and committees shall be held once in six months. Names may be proposed by a Nominating Committee appointed by the President.

ARTICLE IX.— RELATION TO THE CHURCH.

This society being a part of the church, the pastor, deacons, elders or stewards, and Sunday-school superintendent shall be *ex officio* honorary members. Any difficult question may be laid before them for advice.

ARTICLE X.— WITHDRAWALS.

Any member who may wish to withdraw from the society shall state the reasons in writing to the Lookout Committee and pastor, and if these reasons seem sufficient, they may be allowed to withdraw.

ARTICLE XI.— MISCELLANEOUS.

Any other committees may be added and duties assumed by this society which in the future may seem best.

AMENDMENT.

(The following amendment was proposed by Rev. F. E. Clark, and recommended to the societies by vote of the National Conference held in Chicago, July 5–8, 1888.)

Since it would in the end defeat the very object of our organization if the older active members, who have been trained in the society for usefulness in the church, should remain content with fulfilling their pledge to the society only, therefore it s expected that the older members, when it shall become impossible for them to attend two weekly prayer-meetings, shall be transferred to the honorary membership of the society, if previously faithful to their vows as active members. This transfer, however, shall be made with the understanding that the obligations for faithful service shall still be binding upon them in the regular church prayer-meeting. It shall be left to the Lookout Committee, in conjunction with the pastor, to see that this transfer of membership is made as occasion requires. Special pains shall also be taken to see that a share of the duties and responsibilities, both of the prayer-meeting and of the general work of the society, shall be borne by the younger members.

SPECIMEN BY-LAWS GIVEN AS HINTS FOR THE REGULATION OF LOCAL SOCIETIES.

If it is thought that these rules and regulations are unnecessarily long, it should be borne distinctly in mind that these specimen By-Laws are simply suggestions. It is not recommended that they be adopted entire, as in the case of the Model Constitution, for all of them would not be adapted, perhaps, to the need of any one society, but from them all valuable hints may be derived for the government of local organizations. The fundamental principles of the society are exceedingly simple, and only so many of these By-Laws need be adopted as seem necessary to the easy working of this plan for Christian nurture. Undue attention to rules and parliamentary law is to be deprecated, and the fundamental fact that the object of this society is solely for Christian work and growth should never be lost sight of.

BY-LAWS.

ARTICLE I.

This society shall hold a prayer-meeting on ——————— evening of each week. The last regular prayer-meeting of the month shall be a consecration or experience meeting, at which the roll shall be called.

ARTICLE II.

METHOD OF CONDUCTING THE EXPERIENCE OR CONSECRATION MEETING.

At this meeting the roll may be called by the leader during the meeting, instead of at its close. After the opening exercises, the names of five or more may be called, and then a hymn sung or prayer offered. Thus varied, with singing and prayer interspersed, the entire roll may be called.

ARTICLE III.

This society shall hold its regular business meeting in connection with the first regular prayer-meeting in the month. Special business meetings at the call of the President.

ARTICLE IV.

The election of officers and committees shall be held at the first business meeting in ──────────

A Nominating Committee shall be appointed by the President, of which the pastor may be a member *ex officio*. The following clause of the By-Laws may be read to the society before each semi-annual election of officers:

While membership on the board of officers or committees of this society should be distributed as evenly as the best good of the society will warrant, among the different members, the offices should not be considered places of honor to be striven for, but simply opportunities for increased usefulness, and any ill-feeling or jealousy springing from this cause shall be deemed unworthy a member of the society of Christian Endeavor. When, however, a member has been fairly elected, it is expected that he will consider his office a sacred trust, to be conscientiously accepted, and never to be declined, except for most urgent and valid reasons.

ARTICLE V.

Applications for membership may be made on printed forms, which shall be supplied by the Lookout Committee, and returned to them for consideration.

Names may be proposed for membership at the close of the consecration meetings, and shall be voted on by the society at the following business meeting. The Lookout Committee may also, in order to satisfy itself of the Chrisitan character of the candidate, present to all candidates for active membership the following card to be signed:

Trusting in the Lord Jesus Christ for strength, I promise Him that I will strive to do whatever He would like to have me do; that I will make it the rule of my life to pray and to read the Bible every day, and to support my own church in every way, especially by attending all her regular Sunday and mid-week services, unless prevented by some reason which I can conscientiously give to my Saviour, and that, just so far as I know how, throughout my whole life, I will endeavor to lead a Christian life.

As an active member, I promise to be true to all my duties, to be present at, and take some part, aside from singing, in every Christian Endeavor prayer-meeting, unless hindered by some reason which I can conscientiously give to my Lord and Master. If obliged to be absent from the monthly consecration meeting of the society I will, if possible, send at least a verse of Scripture to be read in response to my name at the roll-call.

Signed,

Article VI.

Persons who have forfeited their membership may be readmitted on recommendation of the Lookout Committee and pastor, and a two-thirds vote of the members present at any regular business-meeting.

Article VII.

New members shall sign the Constitution and By-Laws within four weeks from their election, to confirm the vote of the society.

Article VIII.

Any who cannot accept the office to which they may be elected shall notify the President in writing before the next business-meeting, at which the vacancy shall be filed.

Article IX.

Membership tickets may be furnished to all members of the society, admitting them to all the socials. The Social Committee may furnish tickets to members for their friends, providing they are suitable persons, admitting them to the socials dated on the ticket.

Article X.

The Lookout Committee shall read the names of any

who may cease to be members, and give the reason why their names should be taken off the list.

ARTICLE XI.

Letters of Introduction to other Christian Endeavor societies shall be given to members in good standing who apply to be released from their obligations to the society; this release to take effect when they shall become members of another society; until then their names shall be kept on the absent list. Members removing to other places or desiring to join other Christian Endeavor societies in the same city or town, are requested to obtain letters of Introduction within six months from the time of their leaving, unless they shall give satisfactory reasons to the society for their further delay.

ARTICLE XII.

Other committees may be added according to the needs of local societies, whose duties may be defined as follows:

SUNDAY SCHOOL COMMITTEE. It shall be the duty of this committee to endeavor to bring into the Sunday School those who do not attend elsewhere, and to co-operate with the superintendent and officers of the school in any ways which they may suggest for the benefit of the Sunday School.

CALLING COMMITTEE. It shall be the duty of this committee to have a special care for those among the young people who do not feel at home in the church, to call on them, and to remind others where calls should be made.

MUSIC COMMITTEE. It shall be the duty of this committee to provide for the singing at the young people's meeting, and also to turn the musical ability of the society into account, when necessary, at public religious meetings.

MISSIONARY COMMITTEE. It shall be the duty of this committee to provide for occasional missionary meetings, to interest the members of the society in all ways in missionary topics, and to aid in any manner which may seem practicable, the cause of home and foreign missions.

FLOWER COMMITTEE. It shall be the duty of this committee to provide flowers for the pulpit, and to distribute them to the sick at the close of the Sabbath services.

TEMPERANCE COMMITTEE. It shall be the duty of this committee to do what may be deemed best to promote temperance principles and sentiment among the members of the society.

RELIEF COMMITTEE. It shall be the duty of this committee to do what it can to cheer and aid, if possible and necessary, by material comforts, the sick and destitute among the young people of the church and Sunday School.

GOOD LITERATURE COMMITTEE. It shall be the duty of this committee to do its utmost to promote the reading of good books and papers. To this end it shall do what it can to circulate the religious newspaper representing the society among its members, also to obtain subscribers for the denominational papers or magazines among the families of the congregation as the pastor and the church may direct. It may, if deemed best, distribute tracts and religious leaflets, and, in any other suitable way which may be desired, introduce good reading matter wherever practicable.

ARTICLE XIII.

Members who cannot meet with this society for a time are requested to obtain Leave of Absence, which shall be granted by the society on recommendation of the Lookout Committee and pastor, and their names shall be placed on the Absent List.

ARTICLE XIV.

——members shall constitute a quorum.

ARTICLE XV.

These By-Laws may be amended by a two-thirds vote of the members present, provided that notice of such amendment is given in writing and is recorded by the Secretary at least one week before the amendment is acted upon.

THE BEST WAY OF TRAINING YOUNG CHRISTIANS.

BY WAYLAND HOYT, D. D.

I am frank to confess I have become an enthusiast in the Christian Endeavor movement, and the more I know of its principles and workings the more fervent is my enthusiasm. And for reasons like these:

1. Because of the emphasis the movement puts upon the local church. Its beating heart and center is the special church with which the young Christian is in personal relation. The steady song of the movement concerning the local church is:

> "For her my tears shall fall;
> For her my prayers ascend;
> To her my cares and toils be given,
> Till toils and cares shall end.
>
> "Beyond my highest joy
> I prize her heavenly ways,
> Her sweet communion, solemn vows,
> Her hymns of love and praise."

No pastor, especially in the large cities, but must have often felt that there are frequent and great temptations, nowadays, presented to his young people for main service at some other center than their own particular church home. Young Men's Christian Associations, mission halls, general evangelistic enterprises — I have no word to say against any of these things; I say, rather, God bless them and God speed them! They must be, and they are accomplishing vast good; but I am quite sure a pastor must often come to see that the danger of these is that they are too apt to cut, or at least paralyze, the nerve of attachment to that whence all evangelizing agencies must get their spring, and where they must gather their impetus, viz., the local church. The possession of the very gifts which would make a young Christian most useful in his own church is too commonly urged as the chief reason why he should exercise his gifts elsewhere. The church becomes the fringe, these other ways and places of work the focus. Now, a high advantage of the Christian Endeavor plan is this, that it furnishes an offset to this tendency. It does not tell the young Christian that he is not to use himself in these directions, but it does tell him that the eminent place of love and loyalty and religious attempt is his own church, to which he has sworn personal allegiance. This is healthful. This is according to the New Testament. This concentrates service and prevents sporadic and frequently aimless scatterings of power. For Christ and the church is the inspiring motto of the Christian Endeavor movement. As a pastor I utterly rejoice in such a marshalling of the young Christians of the churches.

2. That it is so thoroughly a religious movement is another reason for my enthusiasm. It is not mainly literary nor is it mainly social; it is supremely religious. The hearth where its fires are to kindle is the prayer-meeting. The end of the holy striving of the members of the Christian Endeavor Society is to make the prayer-meeting — the place of religious converse with the Lord Christ and with each other — alive, alert, interesting, edifying. A Christian Endeavor organization without a prayer-meeting, would be like a body without a heart; it could not live an hour.

3. A third reason for my glad endorsement of this movement is the specific pledge of service it exacts. Sometimes there comes a deadness of feeling, a lax grasp on endeavor, to all Christians. To be sure, the highest motive is a fervid love. But sometimes ashes gather above its heat. Just here the pledge comes in — the right appeal to personal honor. The ashes of indifference are swept away and the coals of love begin to glow again. The pledge inculcates the formation of a Christian character, not by the unsteady hand of sentiment, "of feeling

like it," but by the strong, tense hand of duty. So the young Christian is armed against the dissuasions of a rainy night, a cold state of the church, the enticement of social engagements, and what not. He has promised to be present at his Christian Endeavor meeting and to take part in it. He is taught to steer by duty and not by the aurora flashings of feeling. Who cannot see that a Christian character growing thus, amid the inspirations of duty, must get girded, pithy—like an oak on the hillside, able to withstand the winds.

4. Another reason for my deep interest in this movement is, that it takes equal grasp on the young women as well as on the young men. It tells them that their speech, also, is to be consecrated to Christ. It strikes the shakles from their "liberty of prophesying."

5. Still another reason why I so rejoice in this movement is its tender management of young Christians. It adjusts itself to their youth and inexperience. It does not set before them too great things to do at first. It says, if you can do no more, come with the Scripture you have found nutritious to yourself, and simply tell that. It teaches young Christians to search the Scripture for this special end, thus finding food for the religious life.

6. Still an added reason for my gladness in this movement is the delightful inter-relations it brings about between the various evangelical denominations. This movement has no word or hint of dissuasion from the particular truth the particular denomination believes itself set to guard. It does not say, in joining yourself to us, become less a Congregationalist or a Methodist or a Presbyterian or a Baptist. It insists rather on the most steadfast loyalty to the special tenets of the special church. But it does, by its grand marshalling of the young Christians in all churches, give the inspiring feeling of union with a great host of Christian Endeavorers the land through. I am heartily in favor of the badge to manifest this feeling. So,

too, the State and city and town meetings of the members of the Society minister to this consciousness of membership in a noble host, and the discussions there, and the acquaintances formed, tend to wider religious vision and more earnest purpose and larger plans for service.

I believe, from my heart, that this Christian Endeavor movement is of God. We see, as yet, only the edges of its fair leaves as they are bursting from the calyx; it is a most lustrous and fragrant bloom these last years of our century are to behold. Let me say again what I have said before, the best thing that has ever come to the church of which I have the honor to be pastor, is its Society of Christian Endeavor.

SEVEN REASONS FOR COMMENDING THE YOUNG PEOPLE'S SOCIETY OF CHRISTIAN ENDEAVOR.

BY REV. J. Z. TYLER, D. D.

First, Because it makes the religious element dominant. The societies organized on the plan presented in the model constitution are not for social enjoyment or literary culture — although these have their place — but they are organized to promote an earnest Christian life among their members, to increase their mutual acquaintance, and to make them more useful in the service of God. Every true Christian Endeavor Society centers in its prayer-meeting.

Second, It exacts a definite pledge. The young Christian especially needs definiteness of purpose and aim. Vague dreaming will not do. Every one, on becoming an active member, promises to attend the meetings regularly and to take some part in the services. The society becomes the training school. It takes the new convert, with all the glow of enthusiasm which marks the beginning of Christian life, and gives him something definite to do.

Third, It enjoins daily private study of the Bible and

daily private prayer. It thus feeds the fountains of life and prevents Christian activity from degenerating into what has been well called a mere spectacular Christianity. The need, in this day of public enterprise and activity, is to see to it that private devotion is nourished. Bible study and prayer, in the secrecy of the closet, need to receive special emphasis just now, and the Christian Endeavor plan gives it.

Fourth, It blends worship and work. They must be joined together for the health of each, and to form a well-balanced character. Sentiment should find expression in service, and service needs the inspiration of sentiment. The devotions of the closet should prepare for living for Christ in the world. To develop activity without devotion, or to nourish devotion without active duty, is abnormal and unscriptural. The need is to blend them, and this the Christian Endeavor does.

Fifth, Its methods of work are flexible, so that it easily adjusts itself to the necessities of every field. It has no plan as to details of work, but leaves these details to the sanctified common-sense of the members of each society. Whatever may be the work that is needed for the prosperity of the church, the members of the Christian Endeavor Society are expected to be earnest helpers. It is a society in the church and for the church. It aids the regular prayer-meeting, it helps build up the Sunday School, it assists the pastor — in brief, it is expected to be ready for any and every good word and work. It is flexible as to methods.

Sixth, It is a great force working toward Christian union. For this reason, especially, it should receive a hearty welcome among our churches. The trend of these societies is away from the doctrinal basis of fellowship to that which is found in personal love and loyalty to the personal Saviour. This is the line among which we must look for union. This is the New Testament idea of union.

The nearer we come to the personal Christ, the nearer we come to each other. Then, too, the fellowship of service and the mingling of the young Christians in local and State unions and in the great annual conventions, all tend to bring them nearer together. It seems to be one of the providential agencies of our times given to aid in the practical solution of the union problem.

Seventh, It affords an excellent means of reaching the unconverted. Its constitution provides for associate members, and these are generally those who are interested in the church but have never publicly accepted Christ as their personal Saviour. The active members are expected to aim at their conversion. The pastor finds in the associate membership material at hand for his attention. The last report from the general secretary says, " Probably not less than forty-five thousand were converted last year." What a magnificent work! What possibilities for future work! I would that the young people in all our churches were organized into Christian Endeavor societies.

SOME ELOQUENT INDORSEMENTS.

It is not often that we find so many eminent ministers of so many denominations uniting in such hearty indorsement of the same methods of work, but this is what they say from their experience of the Christian Endeavor Society. Rev. John Henry Barrows, D. D., of Chicago; Rev. J. S. Niccolls, D. D., LL. D., of St Louis; Rev. T. S. Hamlin, of Washington, and Rev. Geo. H. Wells, D. D., of Montreal, leading ministers in the Presbyterian church, write in a circular letter to the pastors of Presbyterian churches, in which they say:

" We are glad of an opportunity of addressing to the Presbyterian pastors of the country a few words of earnest testimony with regard to the working of the Christian Endeavor Societies in our churches. From the experience which we have had with them in our own congregations, and from a wide observation of the work elsewhere, we most heartily commend these organizations as contributing to the Christian development of the young people and the spiritual life of the whole church. The uniform success of the new organizations, which are made vertebral and vigorous by the pledge, have convinced us that the Christian Endeavor idea is peculiarly adapted to meet a universal want, and we expect from it a world-wide blessing. We should rejoice to see such societies established in all churches."

Dr. J. W. Hamilton, of Boston, writing to Methodist pastors, says:

"The Society of Christian Endeavor is one of the most remarkable inspirations of the mordern church. I view the importance of the society both from its relation to the local church and from its interdenominational relations in the great international body. The society must be what the church is in which it is organized. It may be Methodist, Presbyterian, Baptist or Congregational, at home. In the great convention it is what all would have it to be — Christian; the members there see Jesus only."

"The plan was a great conception of the founder, but eye hath not seen, nor ear heard, neither have entered into the heart of man the things which God hath prepared for these young people that love Him."

Rev. J. Z. Tyler, D. D., of Cincinnati, a leading minister of the Christian Church, says:

"I find that wherever these societies have been formed and nourished they have worked well. They bring new life into the prayer-meeting, awaken fresh interest in the Sunday School, and enlist the young people more heartily in all the enterprises of the church. They lay emphasis upon the private daily reading of the Scriptures and daily private prayer, and they train all their active members to take part in the prayer-meeting."

Rev. W. J. Darby, D. D., General Manager of the Publishing Work of the Cumberland Presbyterian Church, writes:

"It is useless to attempt to describe the good it has done. Suffice it to say, that as I now look back over a pastorate of more than eighteen years, the scenes and experiences connected with the Y. P. S. C. E. are among the brightest and happiest, by reason of the precious results accomplished with that class, from whom many of the most efficient workers of the church have come."

Rev. J. B. Helwig, D. D., Pastor of the First English Lutheran Church of Springfield, Ohio, writing to his Lutheran brethren, says:

"Two years ago I organized a Young People's Society of Christian Endeavor in my church, and as far as I can secure the attention of our Lutheran ministry of the General Synod, I desire to say that after an experience of that length of time, myself and the young people comprising the society can give it our hearty indorsement, not only as a most excellent incentive to Bible study, but as a most excellent help, also, to the use of the Bible after study; and, next to prayer, we believe, also, one of the best constant means of grace for the advancement of Christian nurture and the steady growth and progress of the spiritual life of the soul."

A PASTOR'S OBJECTIONS ANSWERED.

1. "I fear the Society will prove a church within a church."

Ans.— Experience has not proved this to be a valid objection. The young people, through this Society, learn allegiance, not to the Society, but to Christ and His church.

2. "I fear the young people will not come to the regular prayer-meeting."

Ans.— Again experience proves that those who are most faithful to the society meeting are usually the most faithful to the church prayer-meeting. All may not go to both, but, as a rule, the regular prayer-meeting has been greatly reinforced.

3. "I fear it will make the young people uppish and forward."

Ans.— Nine years experience proves the reverse. This Society has increased their vital piety, and true piety is humble.

4. "I do not like any society plan. It detracts from the individual responsibility."

Ans.— Again experience proves that the exact reverse is true. This plan singles out the members; gives them each something definite to do, and thus increases the individual responsibility.

5. "We are organized to death already. I can't add another organization to those existing."

Ans. — There are organizations that are unto life and not unto death. This is one of them. It saves a multiplicity of organizations among the young, by having one central body (of which the prayer-meeting is the heart), and many arms, in the shape of committees which do the work, if it is thought best, of a dozen societies.

6. "All these pledges are included in the church covenant — why renew them?"

Ans. — True; but they are not made definite and specific there, and cannot be. The young Christian needs to have definite and specific duties pointed out, and thus he will learn to keep all his vows.

7. "This Society will cost too much money."

Ans. — It need cost very little money. None at all, in fact, unless you choose.

8. "An attempt was made to start such a society without my knowledge or approval."

Ans. — If that is so, it was contrary to the principles and wishes of the Society at large. No one is authorized to start societies. This movement should always originate with the pastor.

9. "My young people are not like others. They will not take the pledge."

Ans. — Try it and see.

10. "My young people will not hold out."

Ans. — Try it and see.

11. "The whole movement is ephemeral."

Ans. — Wait and see.

DISTINGUISHING FEATURES.

The Society of Christian Endeavor is extremely flexible and capable of adapting itself to any church or community.

The necessary rules are few and simple, but there are some distinguishing characteristics which cause it to differ from all other similar organizations.

1. It is in and for the church. It has no life aside from the local church. Each society does its work for some individual church. It exists for no other purpose.

2. It is interdenominational. It inculcates neither sectarianism nor undenominationalism. It seeks to make every young person loyal to his own church, the church of his fathers and of his own choice.

3. It insists on making the religious features paramount; the prayer-meeting pledge, promising attendance and participation in every meeting, unless hindered by some reason which can conscientiously be given to the Master, is essential.

4. It makes much of the consecration-meeting, the purely spiritual element.

5. It supplements and balances confession by work, through the committees, which are very important.

HOW TO START A SOCIETY.

Call together the Christian young people of the church and congregation. Explain to them the object of the Society, just what it is for, how important the religious element is, how subordinate is everything else to this one idea. Read the constitution, dwell upon the prayer-meeting clauses until they are thoroughly understood. Explain their reasonableness as well as their strictness. Show that this is nothing but what any young Christian should be willing to subscribe to. Appoint a committee to adapt the by-laws to local needs. Receive the signatures to the constitution of all who are ready to sign it understandingly and willingly. Accept no others for active members, and you have a strong society, whether it numbers ten or two hundred.

PART III.

THE MEMBERSHIP.

PRACTICAL QUESTIONS CONCERNING ACTIVE MEMBERSHIP.

Question. What is to be done with a member of a Christian Endeavor society, who takes no part whatever in the meetings, and at consecration-meetings, though present, he does not respond to his name when called, nor does he take any part in them? Of course, if he were absent from three consecutive consecration-meetings, he would, by reason of such absence, be dropped from the rolls. But this seems to be a different case.

Ans. He should be "labored with" by the Lookout Committee, kindly but persistently, after every such neglect of duty. Before many weeks he will probably either withdraw or fulfil his pledge.

Ques. Do you consider it fulfilling the obligations that active members have taken to respond at roll-call or at consecration-meetings the word "Present"? Does this meet the requirements of the constitution?

Ans. Certainly not, unless those who thus answer have previously taken a real part, by testimony, prayer, or Scripture recitation. To answer "present" at the roll-call, and to do nothing else, is a mere "get off," unworthy of an active member of our societies.

Ques. Should a member be retained on the active list who, although he has a good excuse each time, can never possibly be at the prayer-meeting?

Ans. No, if it is true that he can never attend. If he cannot attend for six months or even a year, place his name on the absent list.

Ques. Cannot a person who tries to live a Christian life, but who does not belong to any church, be an active member as long as he conforms with our constitution?

Ans. That is for each society to decide. Every earnest Christian, however, will wish to join some church just as soon as possible. If one has a good reason for not joining the church (such as prohibition of parents, or unwillingness of the church to receive him) we do not think he ought to be debarred from membership in the society.

Ques. One of our active members wishes to withdraw from the society and asks for an honorable discharge, but offers no reason and apparently has no excuse for the step. Should such an honorable dismissal be given?

Ans. Every person thus wishing to withdraw ought to give some reason for the step. The Lookout Committees have no right to go behind this reason. If it seems to satisfy the conscience of the one who gives it, that is sufficient, even though it appears lame and weak to the society. We have no right to meddle with or question another's conscience. If, however, no reason is assigned, and after kindly interviews, none is given, we should say the rules of the society ought to take their course, and such a person dropped for three consecutive absences from the consecration-meetings. Let him thus put himself out.

Ques. Who ought to judge when an active member should leave the active membership and join the affiliated list?

Ans. The person who makes the change, after conscientious deliberation. Of course he may consult with friends, but his conscience alone is the final criterion.

FOR ASSOCIATE MEMBERS.

A familiar letter from the President of the United Society.

DEAR ASSOCIATE MEMBERS:

For many months I have been writing a letter each week to your friends in the active membership of our society.

Allow me to say a few earnest words to you. Let me ask this personal question: Why are you not an active member? Will you not repeat it to yourselves— "Why am I not an active member?"

For every important matter that largely effects our lives we ought to be able to give a good and sufficient reason. Here is a matter of the very utmost importance to you and to others. Have you any good reason to give for not being an active member?

TAKE THE NEXT STEP.

I am very glad that you are not outside of our society altogether. It is much better to be an associate member than to have no connection with us at all. You have made at least one move in the right direction. But still the question returns: Why are you not an active member? Since you have taken one important step, why not take the next, which is still more important? Perhaps you say, "I am afraid I am not a Christian, and on that account I am not become an active member." That, after all, is only saying the same thing in another form, and the same question must be asked again: "Why, then, are you not a Christian?"

A POSSIBLE REASON.

Because of some one in the active membership whom you do not believe in? Do you say: "To do as he does is a pretty way for a Christian to act"? After all, that is a poor excuse, and you will acknowledge that it is, I believe, when you stop to think of it. Your salvation in no way depends upon that unfaithful or thoughtless member. Besides, if every one else was perfect, there would be much less reason why you should become a Christian than there is now. In that case you would only have yourself to save; others would not need the help of your earnest life. But now Christ asks for your service, not only for your own soul's sake, but for the sake of that very one whom you criticise as "a pretty sort of a Christian."

THE EXCUSE TURNS INTO AN ARGUMENT.

Come into the Christian life and into the active membership for the sake of helping him who is so far from perfect, by letting him see how a Christian should live.

Or perhaps you say: "I am a little afraid of all those duties that are expected of active members — the prayer-meeting pledge and the consecration-meeting and all that." But if these are a Christian's duties, they are just as much your duties now as they will ever be, for it is your first duty to be a Christian. The child cannot get rid of the duty of obedience by running away from home and hiding in the woods. It is just as much his duty to obey his father when he stands outside the door of his father's house as when he stands within. You cannot get rid of any real duty by remaining outside the family circle. You are only failing in two things instead of one, for the first duty is to enter in.

WAITING FOR A STARTLING EXPERIENCE.

Or is it possible you are waiting for a startling, wonderful experience? Do you expect to see a fiery cross in the sky, or to hear such a voice as Paul heard? You will wait a long while if you wait for that, I fear. There was only one Paul, and only one man with Paul's experience. It is just as needless to wait for that experience as it would be to wait until you could journey from Jerusalem to Damascus for the sake of being converted on the exact spot where Paul heard Christ speak to him. Just as really as though the heavens were opened can you hear Him speak to you while you read this letter. It is just as much His message, and just as important that it should be obeyed, when it is printed on this page, as if written across the face of the sky. Here is His message:

Come unto Me, Repent and Believe.

POSITIVE REASONS.

I have spoken of the most important reason — " For

Christ's sake"; but here are some other very urgent and positive reasons, I think, why you should become an active member, which means simply, to become an active Christian.

First, you need to do it for your own sake. Get into the best company. These young Christians are not perfect, by any means, but they are most of them doing their best, and you will not find any better company. Every day you stay outside the ranks of God's people is in some sense a wasted day.

Again, the church and the society need you as much as you need them. They are both weaker than they should be, because you are not active in them, and you are responsible for the weakness. They are not doing so much work, nor such good work, as if you were doing your best in their ranks, where you belong.

Still again, the other associate members need your influence as an active member. Some of them stay out, very likely, because you stay out. Do you dare to be responsible for their loss?

Will you not listen to all these voices and accept their many invitations? There is no reason that any one can give for remaining an associate member; there is every reason for becoming an active member and an active Christian now. Let me urge you once more, dear friend — Give your heart to Christ to-day, and to-morrow ask the Lookout Committee to propose your name as an active member, and just as soon as you can appropriately do so, join the church in which you have been brought up, and whose pastor, I know, is longing to welcome you as one of its members.

Your Friend,
FRANCIS E. CLARK.

HOW CAN WE HELP OUR ASSOCIATE MEMBERS?

Report of the Conference led by Rev. D. R. Lowell, D. D., Pastor of the M. E. Church, Rutland, Vt., at the Eighth National Christian Endeavor Convention.

The large church was full, and all seemed eager to speak or to catch every word.

Not a moment was lost, many being on their feet at the same time, to make suggestions, ask questions, or to give information.

After singing "All Hail the Power of Jesus' name," in which all joined heartily, the leader briefly said: This Christian Endeavor movement attempts two things — first, to establish and develop Christian character; and second, to reach out after the unsaved. We are concerned in this conference only with the latter — "How can we help our associate members?"

The Christian Endeavor individual or society lacking this spirit of a burning desire for the unsaved is not possessed of the real Christian Endeavor spirit.

Now, mark, we are to confer as to methods. The fundamental principles of the plan of salvation are settled; God has settled them; they abide forever and may not be changed by us. But methods are human, and we are here to confer as to the best methods of helping our associate members.

Now, while I am on my feet, let me suggest:

First, Use live and persistent efforts to secure their attendance at the weekly meetings.

Second, When there, let them be surrounded by a warm, spiritual, stimulating atmosphere.

No unsaved person can, as a rule, long stand out against such a spiritual meeting. Now, how to secure such a meeting:

First, Be warm and spiritual yourself.

Second, By frequent, hearty and spiritual singing.

Third, By prompt speaking, praying, etc. Let no time be wasted in the meeting.

Another and the chief means of reaching and helping them will be by tender, loving, wise, personal appeals.

Remember that they will be very quick in discerning between real and spurious interest; the former will win, the latter will disgust and repel.

In the conference many questions were asked and answered, and much valuable experience was elicited.

The prevailing sentiment seemed to be that kindly and personal effort was the most important and successful agency. Many illustrations of this were given, several delegates telling how a large proportion of the associate members in their societies were brought into the active membership in this way. In some cases an active member would take an associate member, and personally pray for and labor with that member, and in nearly every case, in a very short time, the associate became an active member. Sometimes two active members would unite for an associate member; sometimes one of the committees would divide up the associate-member list and give a portion to each active member. In all these cases, the same result followed, and the associate members were reached and saved. One society could get more associate members than they could care for, but most societies found difficulty in getting enough associate members, because they were so easily and constantly being transferred to the active list.

Several delegates gave their experience in securing associate members. The most successful method was to divide up the lists of eligible persons, and give them to active members to be looked after. In most cases such efforts were successful.

Several cases were reported where persons who were members of the church had been admitted as associate members. This was conceded to be wrong. How to prevail on them to become active members was discussed. In some cases it was easy to persuade them to the change, in others very difficult. Personal appeal seemed the most effective agency here.

The sentiment prevailed very strongly that when the society was faithful and really spiritual there was no trouble in reaching the associate members.

The whole conference revealed a most earnest desire to reach out after and help the associate members. It was an hour memorable to those who were present.

PRACTICAL QUESTIONS CONCERNING ASSOCIATE MEMBERS.

Question. Has an associate member any right to lead a meeting, or be chairman of any committee?

Ans. According to the constitution of most societies, these are the duties of active members. It is important that such matters should be in the hands of those "who believe themselves to be Christians."

Ques. Our pastor objects to the Y. P. S. C. E. on the ground of 2 Cor. iv: 14–18, and says that by having associate members we are unequally yoked with unbelievers. How would you answer him?

Ans. We would say that the associate members are yoked together, neither equally nor unequally with the active members. They are in a different relation to the society from the active members. If we keep unconverted persons out of the associate membership, we should, to be consistent, keep them out of the Sunday School and the prayer-meeting, also.

Ques Is it best to allow any who are Christians to become associate members?

Ans. No; never. A professing Christian ought never to join the Christian Endeavor Society as an associate member. It confuses all distinctions, and, after a while, makes the associate list a retreat for unfaithful Christians, and even those who are not Christians will not wish to join such ranks.

Ques. What shall we do with associate members who very seldom attend the prayer-meeting and who never attend our consecration and business meeting, which we hold on a week evening?

Ans. Strive in every way to hold them and by personal influence to bring them into the Christian life and the active membership.

CONCERNING AFFILIATED MEMBERS.

A Familiar Letter from the President of the United Society.

My Dear Friends:

There is one class of members of our Christian Endeavor Society about whom we hear little, but who, nevertheless, are very important factors in the successful working of the societies. I refer to the affiliated or honorary members. I do not care what they are called, and I do not much care whether they are formal members of the society even, but I sincerely hope that every society has some who do for it what the affiliated membership was designed to do for the society. In fact, I think that comparatively few societies have such members regularly enrolled; but most, I am glad to know, have those who are in reality affiliated members. As the boys in blue during the late war would have been comparatively powerless had they not been heartily supported by the affiliated army of fathers and mothers, and brothers and sisters, who had to stay at home, so our Christian Endeavor army can accomplish comparatively little without the support and sympathy of thousands who cannot go to their meetings or serve on their committees, but who can vastly help them in their work.

WHO SHOULD BE AFFILIATED MEMBERS?

The Constitution says:

"All persons who, though no longer young, are still interested in the Society, and wish to have some connection with it, though they cannot regularly attend the meetings, may become Affiliated Members. Their names shall be kept upon the list under the appropriate heading, but shall not be called at the roll-call meeting. It is understood that the Society may look to the Affiliated Members for financial and moral support in all worthy efforts."

And concerning honorary members:

"This Society being in closest relation to the Church, the Pastor, Deacons, Elders or Stewards, and Sunday School Superintendents shall be *ex officio* Honorary Members. Any difficult question may be laid before them for advice."

Some of our friends have objected to that phrase, "who, though no longer young," as if it drew an invidious "dead line" between the affiliated members and the others; but the design of that phrase is simply to exclude from this lot young Christians who ought to be active members, but who might seek to be affiliated members, because it gave them a chance to have some connection with the society without giving them much to do.

But it is very evident who are intended to come within this definition. The busy deacon, who carries a good share of the burden of the church; the Sunday School superintendent, the elder of the church, who rejoices in the work of the young people, but cannot meet with them; the mothers and fathers, who thank God daily that the society is training for usefulness their sons and daughters; the older Sunday School teachers, whose other duties forbid their regular attendance at the meetings — all these are fit candidates for the affiliated or honorary list. Whether they are called by this name or not, I hope every society has such a company of friends and backers.

WHAT CAN THE AFFILIATED MEMBERS DO FOR THE SOCIETY?

They can sympathize with it in all its laudable efforts. They can give it a moral support and recognition, without which no society can do its best work. They can defend it if unjustly accused. They can create a public sentiment in the church favorable to it. They can restrain it from wrong courses, if they see any tendencies in those directions. They can occasionally, at least, drop into the meetings, and can speak an encouraging word (if they will only be brief) to their younger friends. Here is something very specific which the affiliated members of one society promise to do. It is a beautiful idea, and I hope all will adopt it. They agree, whenever the notice of the Christian Endeavor prayer-meeting is given out, to offer a silent, earnest prayer for the meeting and the society. Such a custom is worth italicising. How strong would every society feel if the members thought, when the notice of the meeting was given every Sunday, " Scores are praying now for our meeting." I do not see how such a society could have a poor meeting.

WHAT THEY WILL NOT DO.

The affiliated members will not expect perfection in the society all at once. They will not unduly magnify or criticise little faults. They will not make long speeches in the Christian Endeavor prayer-meetings. Nor will they offer long prayers there. They will not forget that it is a young people's prayer-meeting. They will not seek to take the burden of responsibility from the younger shoulders, by bearing which alone can they learn to bear heavier burdens.

HOW THE OTHER MEMBERS WILL TREAT THE AFFILIATED MEMBERS.

They will treat them with the utmost consideration, respect and love. They will remember that the view-point of the older person is not always the same as that of the younger, and that it is more than probable that the older person is right. They will always welcome them to their gatherings, and will seek their advice on difficult questions. They will be guided by the wisdom of these older persons, even when their own judgment might differ. They will show them that they care not only for their society and its meetings, but just as much for all the services of the church. Once in a while they will have a prayer-meeting to which all the affiliated members will be especially invited, though of course they will always be welcome to all the meetings; and occasionally, perhaps, at the anniversary time, there will be a social gathering especially in honor of the affiliated members, when the society can take particular pains to show how much they are esteemed, and when the bonds of cordial good fellowship between older and younger can be knit more closely than ever.

Your friend,

FRANCIS E. CLARK.

THE RECEPTION OF NEW MEMBERS.

A Familiar Letter from the President of the United Society.

MY DEAR FRIENDS:

The complaint is often heard that, however warmly and cordially Christians may feel toward the new members of the church, few of them express their welcome. There is too much truth in this charge, and perhaps some of our societies are guilty of the same lack of cordiality toward new members.

I am sure that no indifference is felt, just as I am sure that there is no lack of real hospitality on the part of church-members when they receive new members, but we ought to manifest our hospitality more frequently and more warmly than we do.

A NATIONAL CHARACTERISTIC.

I think this same want of expressed appreciation is characteristic of American life generally. We have too little expressed affection in the family. The boy is afraid to kiss even his mother, except on the sly, and when it comes to his father, nothing would induce him to make such an exhibition of himself, if anybody was looking on. So it is between husbands and wives, and dear friends, oftentimes. We suppress our emotions and take altogether too much for granted in regard to the feelings of the heart. In our public audiences it is the same. How rarely any applause gets started, even when we intensely enjoy and thoroughly appreciate the speaker's positions, while our English friends, under similar circumstances, clap their hands sore, and shout "Good, good," "Hear, hear," until they are hoarse.

GREETING NEW-COMERS.

But I have wandered away from my subject a little, which relates to our reception of the new members who join our Christian Endeavor societies.

If we never show our affection on other occasions, we surely should do so at such a time. Not only ordinary politeness, but Christian courtesy demands this. No newcomer should ever be admitted as an active or associate member, or should be transferred from the associate to the active list, without receiving from every other member at least a hearty hand-grasp and word of welcome.

After the meeting, when new members have been received, they should be asked to wait for a few minutes; the president and secretary or the members of the Lookout Committee should resolve themselves into a reception committee, and should introduce them to all the others; thus the ice would be broken and (to mix figures a little) the way would be paved for future acquaintance. At least, no stranger could say he was not welcomed.

REMINDING THEM OF THEIR DUTIES.

I think, too, that there might be much improvement made in the form of receiving new members. As it is in most societies, their names are read one week and voted upon the next, and thus, when they have signed the constitution, they become members. I do not believe in having much ceremony about the reception of new members, but I think that at such times we might well call to mind our obligations. I would advocate having the new members receive once a month, at the close of the consecration-meeting, perhaps, or, possibly, at the close of the monthly business-meeting; have the names read distinctly, so that all can understand who is about to join. Then let the president read the definition of active members from the constitution, if active members are received, or the definition of associate members, if associate members are received; and then, in the case of active members at least, let the president read the prayer-meeting pledge, or let all the members read or repeat it together. This will not only impress it upon the new members, but will recall it to the minds of any who are in danger of forgetting it, and, it seems to me, can have only a good effect.

Some societies already do this, and I can see no possible objection to it. While I would carefully avoid anything that might seem like overdoing what should be a very simple service, at the same time it may wisely be made an impressive matter. At any rate, do not forget the cordial hand-grasp after the meeting.

Let the new-comers feel that since we all have a common Father and the same Elder Brother, we are indeed brothers and sisters with them, and from the first they will be glad that their lines have fallen in such pleasant places, and they will be not only happier but more useful members of our society.

Your friend,

FRANCIS E. CLARK.

PART IV.

THE PRAYER-MEETING.

THE NEW PRAYER-MEETING.

BY REV. WAYLAND HOYT, D. D.

The new prayer-meeting is the prayer-meeting of Christian Endeavor, and the reason why the new prayer-meeting of Christian Endeavor is the best is because it is a reversion to the old typical prayer-meeting of the New Testament.

In the gallery at Bergamo there is a fascinating picture of the Virgin mother and the Holy Child, by Raphael. That picture has a history. When Napoleon the Great was conquering Italy, Milan fell before him and with it Bergamo. Napoleon was taking all the rare and precious pictures and sending them to adorn Paris. Lest this picture should be seized and lost to Italy, someone painted on its face a coarse and ugly picture, which, of course, Napoleon, not knowing the treasure underneath, did not desire. When he was dethroned, the rifled pictures were sent back to Bergamo, and among them hung this treasure of Raphael, but, in the painter's hurry, there had been no mark left upon it and so it could not be identified, and where it hung among the other great and beautiful pictures no one could tell. At last, in the year 1868, the daub began to scale away, and then reverent hands set about to clean the picture, and at last the long-lost treasure shone forth again.

DISFIGURATIONS OF THE IDEAL PRAYER-MEETING.

Now, over the fair ideal of a real prayer-meeting presented to us in the New Testament, have come many disfigurations; long prayers that take in the Jews and the uttermost parts of the earth, and stiff routine and hard formalism and awfully long pauses, and only now and then a new voice, too much bench and too little people. These things and things like these have made too often the sad simile, "As dull as a prayer-meeting," too full of the miserable truth, and have frequently generated the idea that convenience and enjoyment in the typical New Testament prayer-meetings was something that could not be seen and was impossible to obtain. All these things have been blotting the fair vision, in the New Testament, of a genuine prayer-meeting. Thank God, in these days of ours, these hindering blotches are made to scale away through powerful influences, and among the instruments working toward this end, Christian Endeavor has had and is having a very supreme part.

Consider a little that typical New Testament prayer-meeting, that we may see how closely the new prayer-meeting of Christian Endeavor is approximating unto it, and that we may also be stirred with holy and enthusiastic zeal, every one of us, to bring our Christian Endeavor new prayer-meeting into the exact likeness of that New Testament ideal, for we wish no other ideal than that of the New Testament. There is no deeper purpose in our hearts than the purpose of, so far as possible, making that ideal actual.

A painter was once toiling at a picture; wearied, he left his brush and his color for a little, the picture remaining on the easel. When he returned he saw swept around that picture a perfect circle, the most difficult thing to do in art, and the pupil, beholding, could only exclaim, "The Master has been here! The Master has been here!" We wish no higher and no nobler ideal than the touch and sweep of the Holy Ghost.

THE TYPICAL PRAYER-MEETING.

Consider, then, that typical New Testament prayer-meeting. Remember the first few verses of the second chapter of the Acts, and you have it before you. It was an attended prayer-meeting; they were all with one accord, in one place; Peter was not absent because it happened to be a little hot, and James was not away because it happened to be a little cool, and Bartholomew was not away because it happened to be a little wet, and Matthew was not away because his toga was a little worn, and Mary was not absent because her veil had gotten to be a little out of style, and Salome and Bartholomew did not refuse to fill their places because just then there happened to be a party in Jerusalem, and James the Less was not away because he thought that Peter was taking a little too much on himself and was just a little officious. Not for any reasons like these or for any other reasons imaginable, was any one away. It was an attended prayer-meeting. They were all with one accord, in one place. Oh, the enthusiasm of numbers! Oh, the holy contagion of religious elbow touch! Oh, the power of presence! And this typical prayer-meeting had all these. It was an attended prayer-meeting.

THE PLEDGE.

How does the new prayer-meeting of Christian Endeavor conform to the old type? Very closely, I think; for Christian Endeavor lays steady insistence on attendance. That is the meaning of the pledge. Christian Endeavor makes a sacrament of attendance in the true sense of sacrament.

When a Roman soldier swore fealty to the Senate and people of Rome, he lifted up his right hand and took the pledge, the sacramentum, and Christian Endeavor makes a sacrament of attendance. That is the first thing it does. Whether anybody else is there or not, Christian Endeavor must be there. Not feeling, duty; not convenience, duty; not another engagement, but an engagement with the Lord.

Somebody asked an old Waterloo soldier, who at the Battle of Waterloo was in charge of a gun holding an important summit, what he could see when the battle was going on. "See!" he said; "nothing but dust and smoke." "What did you do?" "Do! I stood by my gun." What a Christian Endeavor says is, "Whether you can see anything going on or not, whether you know the day is against you or for you, whether this thing is true or that other thing is true, stand by your gun of attendance anyhow."

A MEETING ACCORDANT.

Also, this typical prayer-meeting was a meeting accordant, and they were all with one accord, in one place.

I have no time to go into the philosophy of the matter. It is enough to say that our Lord Jesus tells us that accordant prayer is prevailing prayer. "Wherever two or three are gathered together in my name, there am I in the midst of them." If two of you agree on earth in regard to anything, it shall be done unto you; and a new Christian Endeavor prayer-meeting is also an accordant prayer-meeting, because it takes upon itself the pledge and promise of attendance and participation. Nothing is more philosophical than the Constitution of Christian Endeavor toward securing the feeling of accord, for feeling always follows action and does not precede it. Why, when a man rises to speak to such an assembly as this, if he is at all my sort of a man, he is pretty badly scared. Suppose that man indulges himself in a scared gesture, suppose he means to get scared, suppose he stands every which way and trembles about; he will be scared worse and worse. The feeling of scare will come on with surprising increment, and pretty soon he will have to sit down. But suppose a man scared determines to act as if he were not, puts on the gesture of self-control, stands firmly, maintains, so far as he may, his self centre, it does not take very long before the feeling of not being scared comes, and the man, before he knows it, is master of himself, and perhaps, to some extent, master of those who are listening to him.

It is always action that precedes feeling and never feeling that precedes action; and when Christian Endeavor sets before young Christian people the action of taking of a definite pledge for prayer and service, it does not take very long before the action draws after itself a train of appropriate accordant feeling. So again, Christian Endeavor is in accord with the old type. Its prayer-meeting is a prayer-meeting accordant.

A MEETING OF PROMISE-PLEADING.

Also, that old typical New Testament prayer-meeting was a prayer-meeting of promise-pleading. Thus our Lord told the disciples that in a little time the power of the Spirit should come upon them, and those disciples were all of one accord, in one place, to plead that promise. There is a mighty principle there, which I leave you to think through. There are all sorts of wonders in it, this mediating place which prayer holds between promise on the one hand and fulfillment on the other. Pray for what God has promised to give you and you will get what God has promised to give you, for prayer is a condition of fulfillment. This typical prayer-meeting was a prayer-meeting of promise-pleading. They said: "O Thou Risen and Ascended Christ, Thou hast promised. Be true to Thy promise." How in this regard does the new prayer-meeting of Christian Endeavor find accordance with the old type? Ah, how delightful it is! Ah, how spiritually comforting it is in the new prayer-meeting of Christian Endeavor to hear one and another and another and another rise and utter another and another and another of the unchangeable promises of our God in Holy Scriptures!

THE PRAYER OF FAITH.

Do you know that service has deeper relation than you perhaps think, for it makes possible the prayer of faith? What is the prayer of faith? A prayer of strain? A prayer of result, misinterpreting utterly a famous passage of Scripture? A prayer of rapture? A seeking to pull one's self up or to push one's self up into a kind of ecstasy? What is the prayer of faith? The prayer of faith is a prayer springing out of great grip on the promises and pleading the promises. That is the prayer of faith.

I asked Mr. Spurgeon once how he prayed, and he said to me, "I always find a promise appropriate to the need, and then in the name of the Lord Jesus and for His sake I simply plead that promise."

The old, typical, New Testament prayer-meeting was a prayer-meeting of promise-pleading, and the new prayer-meeting of Christian Endeavor is a prayer-meeting of promise-pleading, too. They repeat the promises, and then they present the promises as arguments before the Throne.

GIVING HOLY SPEECH TO WOMEN.

Also, that old typical New Testament prayer-meeting was a prayer-meeting which gave holy speech to women. Look there! What is that? That shining, that mighty, celestial, that wavering, gleaming tongue of flame! Behold it! It is on the head of Peter. Yes. It is on the head of James. Yes. It is on the head of Matthew. Yes. It is on the head of the son of Alpheus. Yes. It is on the head of Mary. Yes. It is on the head of Salome. Yes. It is on the head of Mary Magdalene. Yes, yes. In all that company there is not a single head unmitered with the celestial flame, as much on women's heads as on the heads of men.

Unmitered in the prayer-meeting women prayed for the gift, or they would not have received the gift, and when the gift came, it came to woman just as much as to man, for the shining, wavering flame was on the heads of all of them.

Paul says, "Let the women keep silence in the churches." Yes; Paul does say that, and if I believed that Paul meant, when he said that, what is the common interpretation of his meaning, I would submit to the apostle ; I would not say that the world has outgrown the apostle. I believe in implicit and accurate and abundant submission to inspired authority; but because I am sure that the usual interpretation of that Scripture has been a huge misconception and blunder, I declare that the new prayer-meeting of Christian Endeavor is in close accord with the old typical prayer-meeting of the New Testament, because it gives to woman holy speech, for do you know what the meaning of the words "keep silence" is? Paul says, "Do not let the women lall, lall, lall." Don't you see what he means? That is the Greek word *lali*, which means to make a disturbance and a contention. Paul says never let women do that. The men had better take that to themselves as well. But Paul does distinctly say, "When a woman prayeth or prophesieth, let her do it with her head covered." That is, according to the custom of the times, in decent fashion. Why, a woman may pray in the church. Why, prophesying is simply foresaying your faith in Jesus and your love for Him, and exhorting others to come to Him, and Paul distinctly admits that women find tongue for praying and for prophesying in the meetings of the church.

THE HEART OF CHRISTIAN ENDEAVOR.

Therefore, I declare the new prayer-meeting of Christian Endeavor is in exact accord with the old typical prayer-meeting of the New Testament, because it does give to woman, and insists on giving to woman, and God grant it may forever and continually insist on giving to woman, holy speech. These miserable padlocks on the gracious lips of woman ought to be unlocked and broken off and flung away forever.

I had other points to speak on, but my time is up and I will stop. God bless you. Hold to the prayer-meeting. The hearth and heart of Christian Endeavor is the new old prayer-meeting.

NOTES AND SUGGESTIONS UPON THE PRAYER-MEETING.

BY REV. JAMES L. HILL.

The Book of Acts is the story of and argument for prayer-meetings. It was then the people's meeting and not the ministers'. The topic was probably specific and vital.

After the meeting has come up to a good standard of excellency do not experiment very much with it.

It is a good rule never, except as a measure to give notice of being about to conclude an animated meeting, to call upon persons to participate. The more this is done, the more it will be expected. This rule does not apply to first creating an atmosphere of prayer at the preparatory lecture or to the prayer-meeting in large cities, where pastors must do this at times to eliminate the religious vagrants.

In some vestries there are no back seats. The settees or chairs being portable, only such are left accessible, and those close about the leader, as will be required. This makes the room seem full. Persons on the wall seats are not likely to help a meeting. They do not feel themselves to be in the charmed circle. The sexton can in a moment add seats in an exigency.

If a meeting begins at a quarter before eight o'clock, it ought to conclude promply at a quarter before nine. Let it be understood that persons, after the formal meeting is dissolved, will not leave the vestry before nine, thus promoting acquaintance and making strangers feel that they certainly must attend again.

The successful pastors, like Drs. Withrow and Scudder, and like the lamented Beecher and Goodell, have all had animated prayer-meetings. We have not far to go to find why Methodist churches grow so rapidly. They bring the lay element into prominence. They utilize the Christian light deposited with the church.

We can do the people no good at a prayer-meeting unless they are present. Nothing draws them like a good meeting. Dr. Scudder, in order to build up his famous prayer-meeting, visited all accessible churches where good meetings were held and studied their methods.

In the matter of a Sabbath School prayer-meeting one must be willing to begin with a few. If you believe in such a service and would enjoy it, then find another who feels as you do and your meeting is begun. It will not do to pile on wood very much faster than it can be brought to a blaze.

Having such a subject as "What Have I to be Thankful for?" ask the participants to name not two things, but one thing. Thus will it seem easier to take part, and a certain definiteness will be secured that will impart vigor to the meeting.

An expedient which works admirably in the hands of Mr. Moody is to name a chapter or parable or miracle, and ask each person to name but one interesting thing about it. Persons thus fall easily to work before they know it. This, by the way, is a favorite method of teaching the Sabbath School lesson. Simply ask each member of a class to come prepared to make but one point. The points thus made, when aggregated, will be more than sufficient for the half-hour, and everybody will thus get involved in the work.

In certain notable prayer-meetings, beside the selection of a leader, there is the appointment by the prayer-meeting committee of a number of subordinate helpers, whose duty is to instantly follow the leader with remarks. These subordinate helpers come to each meeting with definite grounds of assurance that participation will not lag.

One duty of these helpers may well be to keep the names of all the different persons whose voices are ever heard in the prayer-meeting. Then by encouraging others to repeat a verse of Scripture or of sacred sentiment, additions can constantly be made to the catalogue of participants.

In glancing over the new list of topics, whatever is suggested ought at the time to be put down in pencil on the margin or elsewhere for a later reference. If not in the pocket, a good place for the topic card is in one's Bible or in the frame of the mirror in one's dressing case, where he will see it every morning.

There are few expedients that will so much improve a prayer-meeting as to increase the number of persons who start impromptu hymns. "The continuity of the meeting has been broken because," says the *Congregationalist*, "there was so much time spent in looking up hymns. (The hymn book is over-worked in many meetings.) How much more spirited, how much warmer the meeting if, at a pause, somebody who could do it (and so many can), would strike a familiar tune!" As a rule, during the last half-hour of the meeting such hymns are best as come up spontaneously.

When the interest will warrant it, immediately before the leader's opening remarks, a few moments of silent prayer, concluding audibly with the Lord's Prayer, will give good tone to the meeting.

It is found that the meetings are often best when, after the leader's opening remarks, a few minutes are devoted to a succession of short prayers. This encourages timid persons to participate early; moreover, it gives laymen an opportunity to change the elevation or key, if that with which the meeting was opened cannot be sustained.

In many cases, it may be permissible for a leader only to clear up the incidental truths in the moments allowed to him, and then, in some interrogative form, leave the main thought under the topic for the other participants. If he goes farther, the most acceptable service he can render is to show the cleavage in the subject. He is best fitted to do this.

In parlor companies, ladies are not silent. Why should they be dumb in the great social gathering of the church.

One pastor is known who says plainly to his people: "Now if you should think of anything lugubrious to say, don't say it." He makes it a rule to have nothing brought to the meeting that is not cheerful. He furthermore insists that this is a meeting of the church, and that members must give as well as get. He throws the entire burden on his helpers, and he has an increasing number, doing as little as possible himself, but being careful always to do his full share.

A very shrewd observer has recently said that he had noticed that those meetings called up participants most, where the leader purposely leaves certain loose ends for persons to seize.

Another successful pastor finds it best to state his theme always in an interrogative form. Nothing excites the mind like a question. Such as this would be an interrogative theme: "How shall we deal with those who criticise Christians and cavil at religion?" It is difficult, even now, in writing, to pass on without tarrying to give a word of answer and to state an incident or two that would throw a little light on the matter, as seen, at least, from one point of view.

After giving to the meeting, at the beginning, a good,

strong lift, the leader ought to be a good listener. The frequent complaint is made of persons presiding in denominational clubs and in public assemblies, that they talk too much. So, too, a superintendent of a Sunday School who talks much in the desk, throwing in his speeches at every interstice, soon grows weak in his influence over the scholars. Then when his time comes to speak, and when he has something really to say, he can scarcely get attention, because he has worn out the welcome of his speech. It is easy for a leader who spends all his time in a library of books and papers to follow each speaker with a word or two of additional comment, but it is unwise to do so. It is well for the company to come to know that the leader keeps back quite as much as he utters. There is much to be still said, and they must say it or it will go unuttered. It is not a lecture service, but a conference. No individual ought to undertake to exhaust the subject, lest he exhaust the attendants. The prayer-meeting is the people's opportunity.

It is found to be expedient to read, besides the verses containing the topic, a short, spirited selection of Scripture which will state the theme in another form or throw a sidelight upon it. Many men can catch at one feature of an incident, or can comment for a moment on one of the verses read, when they cannot make a straight-away or clear-swung speech upon "Contentment" or upon the "Immortality of Truth."

Themes that should always have precedence at an evening service of prayer:
1. Any reason for personal thanksgiving.
2. Any hindrances to the better life.
3. The religious bearings of any recent event.
4. Any interesting work of grace.
5. Any special answers to prayer.
6. Any illustration of the wisdom of God's Word.

7. Anything observed or experienced which honors Christ, fulfills a divine promise, or indicates the leading of Providence.

8. The religious point of the Sunday School lesson.

Let us bring our best life into the prayer-meeting, and make it the register of all the best thoughts and feelings and struggles and triumphs of each week.

PRECEPTS.

1. There should be a great deal of Bible in these meetings. Said a teacher to her scholars, "Let us each look up a verse on the subject and repeat it at the evening prayer-meeting." How it freshened up that meeting!

2. Talk about the prayer-meeting before it and after it and through the week.

3. Choose out some person and use all your ingenuity and tact to see if you cannot, sooner or later, bring him to the meeting.

4. "Double the number of persons present and you will more than double the interest and power." A young man recently said, "I will be one of a dozen to take part, but I cannot be one of a few."

5. In a meeting let us have now and then an expression from your real heart-life.

6. Let us have the last part of our meeting first. If participation ever seems hard, it is because we are waiting for others to give us an impulse, while all the time others, for the same reason, are waiting for us. On leaving a church, an admirable compliment was paid a young man in these words, "He would always take hold of the cold end of the meeting."

7. You will not get others to do their duty by not doing yours. If participation becomes prompt and brief and very general by the elders, younger persons can much more easily sandwich in their brief testimonies and prayers. In matters of benevolence "He gives twice who gives first;" so he speaks twice who speaks first, once in giving full

effect to his own remarks and again in those incited to speak after the atmosphere has been warmed for them.

Dr. Goodell said of his prayer-meeting, "It is a place for replenishing the daily losses of the soul." And Dr. Scudder, out of his own experience, wisely remarks : "Even those who were not church-members liked to come. It became a joy to me and a fountain of refreshment. Often I went in dejected and came out inspirited."

NONSENSE CONCERNING THE PRAYER-MEETING.

BY REV. SMITH BAKER.

In an article upon prayer-meetings, in a recent paper by a learned and most excellent minister, we find a few strange sentiments, which we had hoped were out of date, but which we fear are still the destruction of far too many social meetings, viz. "Many intelligent people are driven away from the prayer-meeting because they learn nothing there." Indeed! They may be intelligent, but not spiritual. If they were consecrated persons, they would seek to make the meeting more intelligent. The object of a prayer-meeting is not instruction, but sympathy and helpfulness. Where one person is driven away from a social meeting because he learns nothing, ten are driven away because it is all ideas and no emotion. Making them so much a place of instruction has been the death of one-half of our prayer-meetings. "Emotional people pour out their feelings in the vestry of the church with a saintliness becoming an archangel, and then the next day do deeds which ill become a common Christian." We are sorry the good man has had such an unfortunate experience. The statement in itself is an unintended, but certain misrepresentation of the truth. As a rule, the prayer-meeting talkers, whom the world has least confidence in, and who are the most inconsistent, are the long talkers who try to get off new ideas, and preach little sermons and appear instructive. When a man cannot come to prayer-meeting unless he is instructed, then all that such a man might say would be religious "cant."

"Christian experience, which is exalted so highly by some, is really worth but little in building up character." An amazing statement! When the truth is, there is no Christian character without an experience, and it is the need of an experience which makes our prayer-meetings so dull. The world does not want to hear a man talk never so learnedly unless he has an experience. It has been these dry, intellectual words, coming from the head and not from the heart, which have driven the people from our prayer-meetings, and destroyed their power. What many prayer-meetings need most is to choke off three or four long-winded men who try to be instructive, and give the time to half a dozen common souls whose hearts are full of love to God, and let them tell what Christ has done for their souls. Such sentiments as we hear quoted would discourage any young man from prayer-meeting work, and drive him out of the church prayer-meeting into the young people's meeting — one of the saddest mistakes ever made. No; if any young brother, no matter how ignorant, has a desire he wishes to express, or a testimony to give, let him do it, and so cultivate the gift God has given him; and if any of these people who are religious, but not spiritual — who have ideas, but not grace — stay away because they are not instructed, let them stay, and thank God for it. Any person who will stay away from a prayer-meeting because he is not instructed, is a wet blanket in the church and needs reconversion. As well try to kindle a fire with icicles as to quicken a church with intellectuality. The churches have lost power and souls long enough by this everlasting pious nonsense about instruction. Let the minister instruct the people from the pulpit, and then let the brethren witness to the truth he teaches; such is the only work of a prayer-meeting aside from the prayers.

THE PRAYER-MEETING THE TEST OF A GOOD SOCIETY.

A familiar letter from the President of the United Society.

My Dear Friends:

One of the very best papers that I have heard in frequent attendance upon Christian Endeavor Conventions, was by Mr. Jamison, of Urbana, Ohio, on "The Prayer-meeting Committee." One thought that he brought out I wish to emphasize, and that is, that the average weekly prayer-meeting is the test of the society. We are too apt to delude ourselves with the idea that if we have good consecration-meetings, that is proof positive of the flourishing state of the society, or if, in seasons of special interest, we put on a spurt and have a few extraordinary meetings, that is enough; but either of these ideas is as pernicious as it is false. The Christian Endeavor Society is not a "sprinter," that can make a hundred-yard dash and beat all competitors; it is a steady-going, summer-and-winter, day-in-and-day-out society. It was established for constant service, not for a spurt nor for a few extra galvanic twitches of life once in a while. The test of any society is not what it does once in a great while, but what it does fifty-two weeks of the year.

PYROTECHNIC SOCIETIES.

Some men, as Sam Jones would say, are "built" on the grand pyrotechnic plan. They make a most brilliant display on certain special occasions, but the rest of the time they are like the dead sticks and frames in which the rockets are fastened. These are far from being the most useful men, and though they may dazzle or startle the world, they leave little lasting impression when they go out of it. It is very much so with some societies. I have heard of those that have suddenly increased their membership to two or three hundred; everything was "booming" for a while; but the stick came down finally; not a third of the active members proved to be "active" active members, and outsiders have looked on and said, "I told you so; this Christian Endeavor movement is just like all other young people's societies. It sweeps clean while it is a new broom, but the broom part wears off after a little and leaves only the handle."

A FEW TEST QUESTIONS.

How is it with your society? Was it more flourishing at the beginning than it is now? If so, something must be wrong, for the genuine Christian Endeavor Society, as the experience of more than eight years has shown, grows stronger with every passing year. Is your consecration-meeting so much superior to the regular weekly meeting that there is a sensible "sagging" experienced at other times, and the wish expressed that you could have a consecration-meeting four times a month? Do you have a large attendance when the roll is called, and a light attendance at the other meetings? Then there is evidently some work for the lookout and the prayer-meeting committees to do in your society.

THE CONSECRATION-MEETING NOT THE TEST.

The consecration-meeting should be different in some respects from the other meetings, to be sure; but it should be a difference in kind of interest rather than in degree of interest. The ideal society will have just as large an attendance and just as helpful a meeting the other three weeks in the month, and the consecration service can only be what it ought to be, a re-dedication of everything to God, when the other meetings have indicated a continued and unswerving purpose to serve God always. We cannot renew our allegiance once a month and then take it back for the remaining days until the secretary calls the roll again. No matter how good the consecration-meeting is, do not think for a moment that that will make up for indifference to other meetings and other duties. The consecration-meeting is rather the place and time when the batteries of zeal, love and devotion are stored with energy for future service, but if this power expends itself at the storage-house, it is a very useless kind of electricity that is generated.

WHAT SHALL BE DONE?

Perhaps your regular weekly meetings are as helpful and profitable as any, and with certain slight and inevitable fluctuation you see little difference between the meetings. If so, this letter is not for you; but if there is a noticeable difference, do not rest satisfied until you have brought the average meeting up to the highest standard which has been set by the best meeting that your society ever held. There is no reason why a Christian Endeavor Society should ever have a poor meeting. Even if the meetings are "pretty good," do not let the good be the enemy of the best.

What shall you do? I would have a joint meeting of the lookout and prayer-meeting committees, talk the situation over, realize that there is no reason why you should not have the best always, and then set to work to get it.

Perhaps there are too many members in your society (there cannot be too many active members, if they are all faithful); but if any active members have lost their interest and are willful and persistent in their absence, it is easy to know what to do about them.

Perhaps many of the active members are only careless and thoughtless, members who neglect an occasional meeting simply because they cannot be made to realize that constant and regular attendance is required. Divide the names of such among the members of your committees, see each one quietly and in a kindly way; do not wait until they are on the ragged edge of dismission from the society, until they have missed two consecration-meetings, unexcused, but go to them at once and win them to a better and more whole-hearted service.

Possibly the unfaithful ones are the younger boys and

girls who come, but often forget their pledge to take part. Sit near such, get a verse of Scripture for them, or suggest some word that they can say, and give them to understand that active membership means something and that their pledged word is a very sacred thing.

DON'T APOLOGIZE.

Another helpful thought of Mr. Jamison's was that the committees have no reason to apologize for doing their duty. They should not go in an apologetic, least of all, in a cringing spirit, to delinquents. To have the best meeting possible is their duty ; they were chosen to remonstrate with unfaithful members, and they are simply fulfilling the trust to which they were elected when doing this duty. They will never forget, I am sure, that a loving and gentle attitude should be maintained toward even the most careless and obstinate, but no one ever need apologize for doing his duty. If your average meeting is not up pretty near to the standard of the best, will you not think of this? With God's help you can soon bring it up so that four times a month and fifty-two times a year you will go home at the close of the prayer-meeting, saying to each other, "I believe this is a little the best meeting that we have ever had."

Your friend,
FRANCIS E. CLARK.

A GOOD PRAYER-MEETING.

BY W. L. AMERMAN.

In considering the general public duties of the prayer-meeting committee, we naturally take up the preliminary work before the meeting. This includes every kind of invitation and announcement that can successfully be used. It is well to invite the presence of visitors at the meetings; if not always, at least, at frequent intervals, to give a better opportunity for demonstrating the helpfulness of the society and thus obtaining recruits, unless in the judgment of the committee the presence of outsiders is detrimental to the meeting; as, for instance, it may sometimes be at the outset of the society's existence. The best means of attracting these visitors, especially from among the new-comers to the church, should be carefully considered by the committee.

Another important matter is the selecting and announcing of a suitable topic for the meeting, which should be, like terms of tuition, "always quarterly in advance." No leader has any right to come to a meeting with his subject locked up in his bosom or other obscure location, and after briefly expounding it, expect his audience to take up the new theme and "occupy the time."

It is well, at the monthly consecration-meeting to furnish a general theme, or some personal question to be answered, which will be suggestive to all, and will tend both to unify the meeting and to prevent sameness in these services. For example: "How much owest thou unto thy Lord?" "What have I gained by Christian service?" "Is the Christian life worth its price?" etc.

The topic list published by the United Society of Christian Endeavor is excellent and always available. It is hardly necessary to remind the prayer-meeting committee that they are responsible for the convenient arrangement of the seats, leader's table, the supply of Bibles and hymn-books in every seat, and of good air all around.

THE CARE OF THE MUSIC.

If not in the hands of a special committee, this also devolves upon them. The opportunity of leading at the piano or organ should be given to different members of the society in turn, so that all who can play may have the benefit of the experience; serving, perhaps, two or three weeks consecutively.

Leaders for the meetings should be chosen by the committee well in advance, and often more with regard to the development of the individual than to his capability for conducting a meeting smoothly; but when, for this reason, inexperienced ones are put forward, the committee owe it to them and to the society to see that they receive necessary assistance and are properly prepared.

A RESERVE FORCE.

The members of the prayer-meeting committee should hold themselves as a reserve, ready to throw their weight where most needed in the service. Not always at its close, oftener at the very start, reinforcing a weaker leader by supplementing his words, and sending the meeting on with increasing momentum. When wanted, they should be on hand, filling the gap before it yawns; bringing out the important point that seems in danger of being overlooked; correcting wrong impressions; helping to get back to the subject if an erratic member has side-tracked the train; "backing up" the leader by observing and emphasizing his suggestions; remembering the neglected request for prayer, and fastening and deepening, by well-chosen words, the impression for good which has been produced.

WORK OF REPRESSION.

As the committee concentrate attention and thought on improving the meetings in every possible way, certain common but discourteous practices will engage all their patience and perseverance.

The habit of coming late is one; another is the thoughtless chatting just before the meeting, or sometimes even after it has begun, which so often effectually dispels serious thoughts. Trifling after the close of a solemn meeting is the worst possible offence, as it defeats, on the verge of attainment, the very purpose for which the society has been founded.

Hardly less objectionable than the familiar "sidewalk committee" is the group just inside the door, which often obstructs entrance till after the commencement of the service. The best rule for governing the number of ushers to be employed, the amount of welcoming to be done at the door, etc., is to allow just as little that may distract the attention of those present as can possibly be made to answer the purpose.

ENTERTAINING ANGELS.

The ideal prayer-meeting committee, if it has the co-operation of the ideal society, will doubtless arrange to entertain angels unawares in a more suitable manner than by forcing them to march through to the front of the room and take the seats which the regular attendants consider so undesirable. It is somewhat inconsistent to "earnestly invite" and "heartily urge" and "cordially welcome," as per printed and pulpit announcements, and then to receive them with the same uncivilized treatment which we accord to late comers and unaccompanied ladies! The wise committee will judge of all these things, not as great or small in themselves, but by their effect upon the meeting. Only those who are working hard and watching closely will appreciate the importance of these apparently trivial matters. It is sometimes possible, however, by the use of tact, to enlist the help of an old offender in removing the very practice in which he has been foremost. When once he begins to combat it, he will quickly appreciate its injurious tendency.

MONTHLY REPORTS.

In making their monthly report to the business-meeting, the committee should always have some definite suggestion to offer — the point connected with the prayer-meeting that most needs the society's attention — and should not allow the matter to rest there, but should bring it again to the notice of the members until the desired end is attained.

PRACTICAL SUGGESTIONS.

Let me make, in closing, a few brief suggestions.

Don't aim for a big meeting (you might as well aim to paint a big picture) aim for a good one.

Try to get the members to bring their own Bibles to the meeting, just as they take their own tennis rackets to the court.

Study variety in the service — rather than have two meetings just alike, face the chairs the other way.

Never let the same member fail to fulfill his pledge twice in succession; if this occurs, it is your responsibility as well as his. "Bad nursing kills many a patient."

Cultivate the personal element in testimony; better talk with the heart than with the head.

Never be satisfied till, in your meeting, souls are won to Christ; and don't be satisfied then!

And now let me add the thought that the prayer-meeting committee who are doing faithfully their duty toward others, will themselves be growing in spiritual power.

To whatever extent its members may help those about them, they will themselves be still more blessed of Him who says, "If any man serve me, him will my Father honor." And if we are not thus receiving the seal of His approval, let us look carefully within and see if any lack of full and hearty obedience is keeping back the success we seek. If from any hearts the cry now goes up, "Master, we have toiled — and taken nothing," may He give grace, as He summons them to a fresh attempt to new methods, bolder launching out and deep-sea fishing, for each to respond, despite weariness and discouragement, "Nevertheless, at Thy word, I will."

SOME LITTLE FOXES WHICH MAR THE PRAYER-MEETING VINE.

A familiar letter from the President of the United Society.

My Dear Friends:

It is an old proverb, but none the less true for being rather stale: "Trifles make perfection, and perfection is no trifle." So it is in our meetings for prayer. If the observance of these little matters of which I shall speak do not make perfect meetings, they at least go far toward preventing unnecessary failures. We will never forget, of course, that the presence of the Spirit of God insures the good meeting; and yet, just as the musician can make better music with a flawless instrument, so the Spirit can use us better the more nearly we attain to flawlessness of character.

SOME LITTLE FOXES.

Among some of the little foxes that spoil the young people's prayer-meeting we may mention the scattering of the attendants over a large room. A dozen people can have just as good a meeting as a hundred, but they will not be likely to have a good meeting if two sit in the northwest corner of the vestry and two in the southeast, and four more on the west side and four in the center. An empty chair is a lonesome-looking object, whether it is at the family table or in the prayer-meeting room. Do not oblige the pastor or the leader of the meeting to urge you every week to "come up and take a front seat." How often I have heard the pathetic appeal made (I will not tell you how often I have made it) to "please come up and take the front seats!" Then there is a pause as though the reluctant attendants would not even take that trouble to insure a better meeting; until, if the leader insists on it and waits long enough, at length a few move up toward the center, where they know they ought to have gone in the first place. What an exceedingly little matter this is! And yet it makes all the difference between a good meeting and an indifferent one.

If you were calling on me you would not be careful to seat yourself at the extreme opposite end of a long parlor and talk across forty feet of vacant space. Why should we talk at each other in that way in the family sitting-room of the church? This far-off-back-seat idea shows a radically wrong conception of the meeting. It is a survival of the pernicious notion that in the prayer-meeting the minister is going to talk at you, and it ignores the true idea that it is a place for brothers and sisters to talk with brothers and sisters about the common Elder Brother. When we thoroughly get this true idea of the prayer-meeting into our hearts the front seats will cease to be at a discount and will command a premium at once.

"LOUDER."

Another of the little things that spoil many a meeting is the low, mumbling tone in which certain prayer-meeting utterances are given. Scarcely anything is more trying than a number of testimonies or Scripture verses given in a voice utterly inaudible except to a person with an audiphone and an ear-trumpet. "How can they hear without a preacher?" says Paul. How can they hear, I would like to ask, if you mumble something under your breath, so that your next neighbor cannot catch it? You may have the wisdom of a sage, but it will do the meeting very little good. I frequently feel like crying out "louder, louder," when some of these brethren and sisters, with feeble lungs, begin to speak, and I think I should do so if it would not be considered an improper thing in a meeting.

LEADING IN PRAYER.

When leading in prayer there is an especial temptation to smother our voices by leaning forward on the back of the chair in front. Let us remember that expression, leading in prayer. While we pray to God we lead the petition of others, and this cannot be done intelligently unless they hear what we say and pray over with us the petition that we offer. The head should not be buried and the mouth covered up, but, whether we kneel, or stand, or simply bow our heads, let us pray so that we can be heard.

APPROPRIATE HYMNS.

In giving out a hymn that same difficulty is often found. "Mum-mum," remarks some one in the room. "What number?" says the leader. "Mum-mum," again comes the voice. "What hymn did you say?" asks the organist. This time, "number ninety-nine," comes the feeble response; but however appropriate the hymn, the good effect of it is half spoi'ed by this time. And this leads me to say, that if you give out hymns, give out those appropriate to the subject and to the tone of a meeting. Sometimes I hear hymns given out that are about as appropriate as the "Dead March in Saul" to a wedding, or a hallelujah chorus to a funeral. As I have said before, I think it is usually best for the leader to give out the hymns which are to be sung with the instrument, though, of course, not infrequently some one in the audience can make even a wiser selection. If so, let him do it, or better still (and this is very rarely inappropriate), let him start it without any announcement. These are little things, do you say? Yes; but they are not to be despised if their observance will make our meetings better.

Your friend,
FRANCIS E. CLARK.

SOME MORE "TRIFLES" THAT MAKE PERFECTION.

A familiar letter by the President of the United Society.

MY DEAR FRIENDS:

I am daily more and more convinced that the difference between success and failure in life depends upon a very narrow margin of excellence. In these days of sharp competition, it is the man with a little more pluck and perseverance, a little more brain and will-power, a little more judgment and foresight than his fellows, who wins the day.

MARGINS.

The same law holds good in religious life and in the work of our societies. The society that is more particular than others to look after the little things will be the successful one, and success means souls won for Christ, and the spiritual life of every member quickened and strengthened; not merely good prayer-meetings and active committees.

Most of our societies, in these days, are a good deal alike in their principles as they appear upon paper; they have accepted the prayer-meeting pledge as an essential feature; they have the consecration-meeting and the various lines of committee work; the difference between them in efficiency, sometimes so noticeable, depends upon a seemingly slight margin of faithfulness, earnestness and zeal. In this light, "little things" become great.

125 PER CENT. AVERAGE ATTENDANCE.

One noticeable difference between societies is found in the average attendance upon the meetings. If the average attendance is small, compared with the membership of the society, something is wrong and that something should be remedied. At a recent State convention I found in the question-box the question, "What would be considered a good average attendance at the weekly prayer-meeting — 75 per cent.?" I replied that 125 per cent. would be about right; for if the society numbered one hundred members, at least enough more ought to be attracted by the character and spirit of the meetings to make an average attendance of 125. Perhaps this is too high a standard for some places, but in many it can be realized, and a little increase of interest and personal solicitation will bring it about.

HOW DO YOUR MEMBERS TAKE PART?

The character of the participation also tells the story of the society. Is it almost wholly confined to Scripture verses, sometimes hastily found after reaching the meeting? Are there a certain number of active members whose voices are never heard and who are never disturbed in their unfaithfulness by the lookout committee? Then something is wrong about that society. It is the general disposition that I am writing about, rather than any particular kind of participation. To recite a verse of Scripture may be the most appropriate possible part for one to take, but if it is done as a makeshift, to cover up laziness and indifference, as a means of barely keeping in the society, it becomes a snare.

"PLEASE SING THE FIFTEENTH HYMN."

So with other things. By the breath of song our hearts may be lifted up to God, but if barely for the sake of fulfilling the letter of the pledge, a dozen different ones get off with the cheap participation, "Please sing such and such a hymn," the whole tone of the meeting is lowered. If one can best express his feelings by the verse of a hymn, he can give it out, to be sure, but, in every such case, it should be prefaced with a few words of remark, otherwise, the impression is given that it is just a makeshift and a "get-off." In other words, the whole matter is summed up when we say: "The true Christian Endeavorer does not see how little he can do and barely keep his pledge and stay in the society, but how much he can add to the power of the meeting and the efficiency of the society."

REVERENCE.

I think, too, that some societies may well give more attention to the deportment of the members. I am not speaking of laughing and whispering now — only the young hoodlum of either sex will disturb a religious meeting in any such way, but of less pronounced forms of irreverence. Do the members assume a reverent attitude in prayer. Are the heads all bowed, or the eyes all covered, or is there an unmannerly and unchristian staring about? To say the least, if such irreverence does not show a heart indifferent to the highest things, it shows a certain spiritual rudeness, if I may so term it, a callousness to sacred associations.

BETWEEN THE SERVICES.

A pastor in the West has written me, asking if I would not call attention to the behavior of our members between the services, when the Christian Endeavor meeting precedes the evening service. After the tension of the hour of prayer, there is a tendency to too great relaxation, perhaps even to boisterousness, on the part of some in the fifteen minutes of intermission. This matter certainly will not be overlooked in the model society. A few kindly words from the lookout committee, or the prayer-meeting committee, or, perhaps, the president will usually remedy the evil, which is almost always a matter of thoughtlessness.

Pardon me for writing of these little matters. My only excuse is the old adage, "Trifles make perfection, and perfection is no trifle." In our societies, on these "trifles" may hang the destiny of many souls. In view of this, nothing can be accounted small.

Your friend,
FRANCIS E. CLARK.

HOW SHALL WE TAKE PART IN THE CHRISTIAN ENDEAVOR MEETINGS?

BY JESSICA WOLCOTT ALLEN.

The same cause produces different effects among different people. Remarks that to some may appear open to criticism, to others may be inspiration. These thoughts come to me as a preface to what is said in this chapter.

The spirituality, intellectuality and requirements of societies vary considerably, yet it seems probable that some suggestions may be made which will be applicable to all.

STAND UP.

I believe the best way sometimes to address the multitude is through the second person directly. So let me ask you, first of all — How do you take part physically? Do you lean back in your seat and speak in a weak voice which cannot be heard beyond the seat in front of you? Or do you stand up and "speak a word for Jesus"?

It is frequently noticeable that those who have the courage to rise are usually the ones who speak loud enough to render it unnecessary, so far as hearing them is concerned. It is the weak-voiced, faint-hearted sit-downers who are too often one and the same. But even if your voice is strong and can be heard in the most remote corner, the effect is much better when you stand. If you cannot "muster" courage to do so at your next meeting, try it at the first consecration-meeting. When your name is called, stand up instantly; and, after once doing so, there will no longer come over you the terrible sensation we all know too well, of the drifting away of one's strength when it is most needed. If your voice is naturally weak, do not strain it, but make only a slight exertion in this direction, turning your attention principally toward distinct utterance and correct emphasis.

SEEK FOR VARIETY.

It appears easier for some people to offer prayer, while others more naturally make a few remarks. Still others have "a gift" for neither one, and do not feel like trusting themselves with anything but a prepared verse to recite or something written to read. Vary your participation from one time to another, as you are able to. It is not necessary to advocate the use of biblical quotations. Yet it must have been apparent to any member of a large society that these should be left for those younger ones who in a great measure depend upon them.

Whatever the subject of the meeting may be, there is always a certain number of especially appropriate quotations that can be made use of.

If one who is able to take a very broad view of the subject — one whose education and mind permit him to follow out many lines of thought — if he take the most familiar verse of the Bible which naturally suggests itself to any mind, in connection with the subject, does he not, by repeating it in the early part of the meeting, run the risk of bankrupting some less wealthy-minded neighbor? If a good thought comes to you, even though it be a little off the main line of the subject, you had best make use of it, as it will come out in the meeting as a sort of "relish."

BE YOURSELF.

Monotony is a prominent feature to be avoided. If one listens carefully at meetings, one will perceive the danger-signals in this and other directions. One signal is seen in the tendency at some meetings for each one, before speaking, to repeat the topic or the Scripture verse which is given with it. This is obviously unnecessary, as the subject will receive sufficient attention through the course of the meeting, and this repetition only wears it threadbare. One of the surest reliefs from monotony is the imposition of personality upon the meeting; that is, in this way: If you offer prayer, use your own natural language and tone of voice, never borrowing familiar phrases of others. Or, if you make a few remarks, when you have no original thought to offer, clothe the one which you borrow in the dress of your own expression, instead of reading it from book or paper, or writing it out to read. Some of the best effects of the best remarks are destroyed in every meeting by a lack of this personality that draws us into the closest contact with another's thoughts. You cannot make such an attempt on account of your frequent hesitations? Ah! dear, hesitating soul, it is just when those anxious seconds, which seem like hours, come, that the audience is yours. They have the same feeling under similar circumstances, and so give you their uttermost sympathy, and listen with an intensity of attention which no fluent speaker can command. One of the grand features of the Y. P. S. C. E. is that we can try to do the best thing in the best way, no matter how poor the result of the attempt may be, remembering we are endeavoring to attain our ideal. It is a grand Christian training school of the church.

BE BRIEF.

Now, if the society to which you belong is a small one, it may be your duty to make an exertion to take more time in the meeting than you usually do, but this fact may be readily discerned if you notice how the time is occupied. It is better to be brief, and then, if opportunity seems to require it, to take part a second time, than to appropriate more than your share of so valuable an hour by reading perhaps eight or ten verses of a poem, the whole thought in which might be expressed in two or three sentences.

A single thought clearly expressed is better than a series of complex ones. It will make a better impression in the meeting, by giving it a "crisp" character, and it will be more easily retained in the minds of the listeners.

There are many lines of thought in connection with this subject that have been ignored because of their prominence, but "of making" criticism and suggestions and of writing there is no end, unless we make one. As a parting word, I beseech you, in doing your share toward sustaining a meeting, strive to furnish some spiritual food to satisfy soul-hunger, to strengthen some weakness, to revive faintness, to soothe a great pain, or to illuminate a gathering or gathered darkness. Your words should not be boats upon which an audience may merely float away on a pleasant little intellectual voyage, but transports conveying some good thing to all those who hear.

TWO SUGGESTIONS FOR THE IDEAL PRAYER-MEETING.

BY REV. S. W. ADRIANCE.

PRAYER-MEETING VARIETY. It is wonderful what a vast number of changes may be introduced by merely a different arrangement of old factors. One of the best games I know of, is to take a word like "thanksgiving," and in a given time see how many words are wrapped up in it. This is done by simply re-arranging in many ways the letters which are discovered in it. This is just the kind of variety possible in our Christian Endeavor prayer-meeting. It is not alone by importing brand-new methods, but by re-arranging old ones. This ought to be the thought of the prayer-meeting committee. A new method, which at the start was full of freshness, may be used so often in exactly the same form that it loses its power.

CLOSE THE MEETING ON TIME. No truth is more evident than that a meeting may be ruined after it has succeeded. I have repeatedly known leaders to extend a meeting so long that it ended in a dreary, sorrowful failure. Sometimes this happens by neglect. Sometimes there has been such a delightful series of testimonies that the leader is unwilling to close at the end of the hour. Sometimes it is the fault of the meeting. The first half-hour has been dull, and then those present began to wake up. But nothing is an adequate reason for prolonging a meeting. Like a call, it would far better be short than long. One meeting extended beyond the time forms a precedent for others, and there is established a dangerous habit of waiting till the last fifteen minutes before taking part in earnest. All pastors who have made the prayer-meeting a success are very rigid in closing the meeting on time. If the testimonies have been brief, and all have participated, close then, in the midst of that genial interest. By all means, shorten the meeting five minutes, rather than lengthen it.

VARIOUS KINDS OF MEETINGS.

MEMORITER MEETINGS.

Many societies are finding memoriter meetings of great profit and interest. The general plan of the meeting is similar to the following, the details being varied according to the taste of each society. No Bibles, hymn-books or notes are used during the service. The leader repeats the Scripture lesson, or, if he chooses, asks the society to repeat it in unison. In the latter case, the lessons should be announced a week or more before the meeting, in order that all may have an opportunity to learn it thoroughly. The singing may be led by the organ or may be unaccompanied. In either case, as no books are used, it is of course necessary to sing familiar hymns, unless the leader has previously announced the hymns which he wishes sung. The corresponding secretary of the society in Princeville, Ill., writes that their last consecration service, conducted in this manner, was "one of the most earnest meetings of the year." We shall be glad to receive and publish further details, if desired.

A MOTTO MEETING.

Our motto is a plain and emphatic declaration of our principles, of the vital spark which has made Christian Endeavor the power it is in our land. "For Christ and the church" is the watchword of every true disciple of Christian Endeavor, and as long as we cling to that foundation of our faith we are sure to march onward in spiritual progress. I wish every society in our land could thoroughly realize this. There is occasionally a society which has not grasped the power which lies in the thorough inculcation of this motto. The true object and mission of the Endeavor movement is to occupy a position with the Sunday School as a training school of Christianity. In union there is strength. Churches all over our broad country pay tribute to the value of this branch of church work. Do not, then, let our motto become dimmed. Keep it ever before your local society; and once a quarter or once a year hold a "motto" meeting, where every one shall declare personally his allegiance to Christ's church. God has blessed us, and will do so, if we are true to our fundamental principles.   GEORGE A. RAND.

A PSALM SERVICE.

To have a knowledge of the Bible we must be acquainted with the Old Testament as well as the New, the Psalms as well as the Gospels. A psalm service on this plan would be interesting to many. After the reading of a psalm by the leader, at the close of the opening prayer, let the congregation repeat in concert the Fifty-first Psalm. The committees can each read: Prayer-meeting committee, One Hundred and Twenty-fifth Psalm; missionary committee, Seventy-second Psalm; social committee, Nineteenth Psalm; musical committee, Sixty-seventh. The members of the committees may read these in concert or one out of each committee can read them. For the benefit of some heavy-hearted one read the Twenty-third or Forty-sixth or One Hundred and Twenty-first Psalm.

Ask some of the younger or the associate members, who are afraid of the sound of their voices in prayer-meeting, to sit together and repeat in chorus the First Psalm or some familiar psalm. It will help the meeting to have eight or ten tell which is their favorite and why. Have two-minute papers read on the Historical Psalms, the Prophetic Psalms, the Authors of the Psalms, the Inspiration and Canonical Authority of the Psalms.

Our service will not be complete without the Eighth and Ninetieth Psalms. If possible, have these read by some one who loves them, and who, in the reading, can bring out their peculiar beauty.

With singing and prayers this may be made a helpful service, or it may be changed into a praise service by omitting the papers, and reading and repeating the Ninety-first to the One Hundredth, the One Hundred and Third, One Hundred and Seventeenth, One Hundred and Eighteenth, and the One Hundred and Forty-sixth to One Hundred Fiftieth Psalms.

Another advantage is, that those who prepare this service will learn a great deal about the Psalms in the week's preparation for this meeting.

BIBLE READINGS.

Another way in which to give variety to the meetings is to have occasional Bible readings. Each member is expected to bring his Bible, but it is well for the leader to have an extra supply for chance visitors and those who invariably forget their possessions. The Scripture lesson may be read responsively by the leader and the members, or may be divided and read by several members in turn. The leader should carefully prepare his Scripture references, to have them as varied and pertinent as possible. They may be previously given on slips of paper to different members, or, better still, in order to insure every attendant's having a part, may be given verbally during the meeting, the leader reading the name and number of book, chapter and verse, and each member responding by repeating the same after him. In this way, no confusion arises from two or more persons having the same verse. After the references have all been given, the reading should begin, the leader calling for the references. The meeting should be as informal as possible, and any member should feel free to introduce or follow the verse he reads with original remarks or appropriate quotations. The Trinity M. E. Society of Lock Haven, Penn., and the Kirk Street Congregational Society of Lowell, Mass., report successful meetings at which this plan was tried.

CORRESPONDENCE MEETING.

A small but active society in Deposit, N. Y., has written us of a plan which other societies, similarly situated, may like to adopt. This band of young people is too far from other societies to belong to local unions or to attend conventions. As a substitute, the prayer-meeting committee has arranged for a correspondence meeting, and has asked several societies to send letters giving encouraging news, suggestions for new work, and reports of progress. This will doubtless commend itself to other isolated societies which can thus gain some of the advantages to be derived from the conference of Christian Endeavor workers.

A QUAKER SERVICE.

We like the suggestions given below, by W. S. Creighton, for an occasional meeting, though it ought to be understood, always, that every active member should take some part. "To wait for the spirit to move" should not be used as an excuse for saying nothing. The Spirit is always urging every Christian to make some acknowledgment of Christ in such a meeting, if he will listen to the voice.

On a recent Sunday evening, the Christian Endeavor Society of Broadway M. E. Church, Louisville, Ky., held what was called a Quaker service. The prayer-meeting committee selected no leader or organist and made no suggestions in regard to the service, except to request each member beforehand to take such part as the influence of the Spirit moved him to take. At the hour of service a brother started a song without the organ; during the singing, a timid young lady voluntarily took the leader's chair, and, at the conclusion of the hymn, read the lesson announced for the evening and the verses she had selected, and then sat down. A young man gave out a hymn, and took his position at the organ and played it during the entire service. Then prayers, songs, talks and Scripture readings followed each other in rapid succession, calmly, quietly, and with an earnestness that was felt by every one present. The prayer of one young lady was so heartfelt, it seemed as if she brought her Saviour right down by her side and was communing with Him in our midst; oh, it was a grand prayer for the guidance of the Great Shepherd. The meeting was intensely interesting from first to last, and many of us were sorry to see the time for closing it come. With a heartfelt "Praise God from whom all blessings flow," we went up-stairs to the regular services of the church. We think the idea a good one, and write you about it so that other prayer-meeting committees may make use of it. As our pastor said at the conclusion of the service, "This has been almo t an ideal meeting." It was entirely voluntary, and each one took part as the Holy Spirit moved him.

A PRAYER-MEETING PROGRAMME.

We are constantly receiving programmes of Christian Endeavor services, and many of them are so well arranged and so suggestive that we are very glad to give them to others. Rather a model of its kind is this of what might be called an invitation-meeting:

You are requested to fill out blank spaces with texts, and bring this programme to the meeting with you.

Y. P. S. C. E.

FIRST PRESBYTERIAN CHURCH.

Sunday, May 19th, 7 P. M.

PROGRAMME.

Song.   No. 151.
                    Prayer.
             TOPIC: "*Come Unto Me.*"
Song.   "Come Unto Me."
                  Quartette.
WHY?
    a. Pardon.   . . . .
    b. Salvation.   . . . .
    c. Life Eternal.   . . . .
Song.   No. 199.
WHEN?
    a. To-day.   . . . .
    b. Now. Do not delay. . . . .
Solo.   "Why will you do without Him?"
HOW?

  a. Through Christ.
  b. Believing.
  c. Just as you are.
Song.   No. 211.

I COULDN'T THINK OF ANYTHING TO SAY.

Mrs. J. W. Talladay, in an excellent address given before the district convention at Seneca Falls, N. Y., punctured with a sharp pen the old, oft-repeated excuse for non-participation in the prayer-meetings — "I couldn't think of anything to say." "There are 77,743 verses" (said she in effect, if we remember the figures rightly) "in the Holy Scriptures which you can repeat; almost any one of them would be better than silence." Surely while there is a thesaurus so full of treasures to draw upon, there is no room for the weak excuse, "I couldn't think of anything to say."

WAYS, THEMES, SOURCES.

Rev. Albert D. Smith, of Bedford, N. H., sends us the following hints for the prayer-meeting:

WAYS OF TAKING PART.

1. Repeat a passage of Scripture.
2. Repeat (or read) an appropriate selection from other literature.
3. Ask a question, oral or written.
4. Say a word from your own thinking or experience.
5. Offer a short prayer.

"Freely ye have received, freely give."

SOURCES OF PREPARATION FOR TAKING PART.

1. Your private Christian life and experience.
2. Your encouragements and discouragements in Christian work.
3. Your conversations with fellow-Christians.
4. The sermon on Sunday.
5. Your Sunday School lesson.

6. Your private Bible reading.
7. Your religious reading.
8. Your general reading.
9. Your knowledge of Christian work anywhere.
10. Think much of the meeting.

"Whatsoever things are true, whatsoever things are honorable, whatsoever things are just, whatsoever things are pure, whatsoever things are lovely, whatsoever things are of good report, think on these things."

HINTS CONCERNING METHODS FOR THE PRAYER-MEETING.

HOW TO TAKE PART.

BY MILLIE E. BRANDELL.

Be yourself. Do not try to be anybody else. I heard of some girls who said they would not take part in meeting because they could not talk like a certain young lady who attended.

Suppose you are invited to take tea with a family consisting of a father, a mother, a young lady daughter, a boy twelve years old and a little girl four years old. You sit down to the table, and every one feels perfectly free. The father gives an item of news, perhaps about the President's trip. The mother tells something which she heard when calling the day before. The young lady describes an experiment tried at the high school. The boy repeats some verses which his teacher taught him. And by-and-by the little girl makes you all laugh by telling how the dog ran away with her doll. You think what a nice, pleasant family! How I am enjoying my visit!

On the other hand, suppose the little girl should say to herself, "Because I do not go to school, I am not going to say anything"; and the boy, "Because I am not in the high school, I am not going to say anything"; and the young lady, "Because I cannot talk like father and mother,

I am not going to say anything." So they keep still. What would you think? Something like this, I imagine— "I wish I was at home; what a stiff family!"

Sometimes, I am afraid, when strangers come into your prayer-meetings, they wish they were at home, and think you stiff because so many keep still. A prayer-meeting should be like a family circle, where every one, from the oldest to the youngest, feels perfectly free to speak of the things which are helping or hindering him in his spiritual life.

ONE-SENTENCE PRAYERS.

They are a feature of our societies. They have been of great value in connection with our work. As our prayer-meeting pledge binds us to participation, and as our numbers are so great, some measures have become necessary in which, so to speak, the multitudinous prayer may arise. One person must not continue the petition too long, or he becomes difficult to follow. Promptness and gravity are essential to its successful use. Here is what one writer, who is particularly well qualified to speak, is moved to say from his observation and experience:

"I also most heartily recommend the one-sentence prayer as being the best way for young persons, who have never prayed in public, to begin. This prayer should be held near the close of the meeting. All should bow their heads and each one offer a prayer of one sentence, such as — "O God, bless our meeting"; or "O Saviour, help us to live Christian lives"; and other short petitions. The most timid can do this, and then, getting used to their own voices in public, will be ready to offer longer prayers, thereby adding interest to the meetings and receiving a blessing to themselves. The good effects of such prayers ought not to stop with ourselves, but to reach out into the church prayer-meetings, where they will create new zeal, and assist and encourage the laborers in the church."

PRACTICAL QUESTIONS CONCERNING THE PRAYER-MEETING.

Question. Why do you advocate the use of the Uniform Prayer-meeting Topics?

Ans. Because they are selected with the greatest care by those peculiarly experienced in such work. Because they are practical topics and not too hard to talk about. Because they are better than the average prayer-meeting committee will choose. Because they are explained, every week in many periodicals.

Ques. We are young and inexperienced, and have joined the Y. P. S. C. E. for what help we can get in our Christian life, but we have one difficulty. When we come to the prayer-meetings we have considerable enthusiasm, but it is soon dampened by a middle-aged man who gets up at the first and makes a long, tedious speech, and often follows it by a long prayer. After that we do not feel much like speaking. We do not like to speak of it to any one for fear of giving offense, and he will not be short, even when the request is made. What shall we do about it?

Ans. The only advice we can give is to go to your pastor. Lay the case before him, not in a fault-finding but in a kindly way, and ask him to see that the brother is reminded to take less time. We think your pastor will help you out of the difficulty.

Ques. When members confine themselves simply to the reading of a Scripture passage in the prayer-meeting, is it well for the leader to try to draw them out by means of questions on it?

Ans. If this were done judiciously it might be a good plan, otherwise it might drive them away from the meeting. A better way still is to go to such members privately and show them that they are not living up to their full privilege and duty.

Ques. Do you think it advisable to publish the names of those who are to lead the meeting.

Ans. That is a matter for each society to decide. In most places there is no objection to this plan. In other places, if the young people came out much more largely when some of their companions lead the meeting than when others lead, it would be better not to publish names. Of course the *members* of our societies would go, anyway, whoever led.

Ques. Should every active member be expected to take his turn in leading the prayer-meeting or should only the more experienced and competent be asked?

Ans. Unless the society is very large we think all should usually take their turns in leading. It need not at first, however, be made a matter of conscience. The best meetings often are held where one of little experience is in the leader's chair, since all the others feel a peculiar responsibility to help.

PART V.

THE PRAYER-MEETING PLEDGE.

FOR WHAT DOES THE PLEDGE STAND.

A familiar letter from the President of the United Society.

Here is the revised pledge as recommended by the United Society:

"Trusting in the Lord Jesus Christ for strength, I promise Him that I will strive to do whatever He would like to have me do; that I will make it the rule of my life to pray and to read the Bible every day; that I will support my own church in every way, especially by attending all her regular Sunday and mid-week services, unless prevented by some reason which I can conscientiously give to my Saviour, and that, just so far as I know how, throughout my whole life, I will endeavor to lead a Christian life.

"As an active member, I promise to be true to all my duties, to be present at, and to take some part, aside from singing, in every Christian Endeavor prayer-meeting, unless hindered by some reason which I can conscientiously give to my Lord and Master. If obliged to be absent from the monthly consecration-meeting of the society I will, if possible, send at least a verse of Scripture to be read in response to my name at the roll-call."

Let me say emphatically that there is no disposition on the part of any one to force any form of words upon any society. This is not only a free country, but the Society of Christian Endeavor is a peculiarly free and flexible institution. Every society is at liberty to frame a better pledge than this, if it can; but we hope that no society calling itself Christian Endeavor will ever think of leaving out the ideas of pledged and definite service. You may be assured, too, that this form was not thrown together hastily; every word was weighed, and there is some reason for its being where it is. Moreover, nothing really new is imported into the pledge; but simply one or two matters are defined and made clearer.

"THE RULE OF MY LIFE."

Some tender consciences have been troubled at the idea of promising to read the Bible and pray every day, and have been debarred from signing the pledge on that account, saying that in sickness, or certain conceivable circumstances, they could not read the Bible. Of course, the idea has always been simply that this was to be their regular, customary habit of life. Thus it is here expressed, "I will make it the rule of my life to pray and to read the Bible every day." This has always been the intent and purpose of the pledge, as I understand it, and by this phrase the intent is made plain.

CHURCH ATTENDANCE.

Then comes that clause about supporting one's own church, especially by attendance at all the regular Sunday and midweek services of the church. This, too, has always been a Christian Endeavor principle. The church has always been made supreme. It is simply putting into words the principle that has been insisted on at every convention, and adopted a score of times at State and national meetings, that the church and her services are supreme. Besides, there is no unreasonable burden put upon any soul. We promise to fulfill this duty of attendance upon the services of the church, unless prevented by some reason which we can conscientiously give to the Saviour. This is the Christian Endeavorer's only excuse, because it is the Christian's only valid excuse for the omission of any regular duty. Any Christian ought to be ashamed to offer to himself, or any one else, any other excuse than one which will satisfy his own conscience; and this reason is especially provided for in this pledge. The burden, too, is left just where it ought to be left, on the individual conscience.

TWO ESSENTIAL IDEAS.

Now this first and general part of the pledge stands for two essential things in the religious life — private devotion, and loyalty to our own church; private devotion as exemplified by prayer and Bible reading, loyalty to the church as expressed by regular and constant attendance upon her public services.

If there are any more important features for us to emphasize, I confess I do not know them. Some may object that it is loading down the pledge too heavily. I think not. It is simply making definite an idea for which the society has always stood. There is no other way in which a Christian can better show his devotion than by attendance, even at personal inconvenience, on the services of the church. I should not be in favor of putting every Christian virtue into the pledge; in fact, I can think of no other element that ought to enter in. Some people are very unreasonable about this. They want to ride every hobby right into the middle of the pledge. One gentleman recently wrote me in a humorous vein, desiring to have the subject of good ventilation for vestries put into the pledge. If he had not been facetious this request would have indicated a very low sense of the solemnity and importance of this obligation. At any rate, there is no wish or intention to make the pledge a dumping-ground for every notion, but to make it stand for certain all-important requisites in the Christian life. Taking the first part of that pledge is often the turning-point with the young soul. It is a test of fitness for active membership. If one is willing honestly to promise these things, he is fit to be an active member. But it may be said, "This is more than many of the fathers and older Christians themselves are willing to promise." That, however, is no objection. It is a heroic generation of young Christians which is growing up; and if the sadly decadent habit of church attendance is to be improved, it must be by the young Christian.

VERY LITTLE TO ASK.

And, after all, it is very little to ask of

> "A soldier of the cross,
> A follower of the Lamb,"

to attend the regular Sunday and weekday services of the church "when not prevented by an excuse which he can conscientiously give to the Saviour." Will any true young Christian refuse this? I cannot believe it.

REMEMBERING THE CONSECRATION-MEETING.

These duties relate to the Christian life in general, whether one is a member of the society or not. The only other slight change in wording relates to the distinctively Christian Endeavor part of the pledge; namely, the sending of an excuse for absence from the consecration-meeting. Many have interpreted that word "excuse," as a detailed reason for absence which they were unwilling always to give, considering their excuse a private matter. The intention is simply to obtain some expression from the absent one at the roll-call meeting to show that it was not forgotten. This result is better attained, it seems to me, by sending some message, at least a verse of Scripture, to be read at the meeting when the name of the absent one is called. Very seldom is this impossible, and the rare occasions when one cannot thus show his interest in the meeting is provided for by the words "if possible."

NO GRIEVOUS BURDEN.

To sum up, then, I do not think there is any grievous burden imposed on any tender conscience, nothing that is not fully within the power of any true young Christian always to fulfill. I do not think that there is anything new added, simply that the Christian Endeavor principle is made more plain. As was said before, this form is offered in the way of a suggestion — a suggestion, however, which I hope will be adopted by new societies and by old societies when they have occasion to revise their constitutions. At any rate, let this stand for the principle and declaration of our societies on these important matters.

Your friend,
FRANCIS E. CLARK.

SOMETHING MORE CONCERNING THE PLEDGE.

A familiar letter from the President of the United Society.

I wish to write again upon an old subject, but one that is as important as it is old — the prayer-meeting pledge.

The last word has not yet been said upon this theme, and will not be until it is accepted beyond a cavil as a fundamental principle of Christian Endeavor societies. I hear once in a while of a society that is thinking of giving up the pledge. To be sure, I hear, within the same length of time, of a hundred others that unfortunately started without it, and have wisely remodelled their constitution and reorganized their society, adopting it in all its binding force; but, though the cases are few, I am always especially sorry to hear of a society that takes any backward steps in this direction, for I am confident it means disaster and a short life to the society.

WHY NOT LEARN SOMETHING FROM EXPERIENCE.

Why not learn some things, let me say to any societies that are thinking of weakening their obligation, from the experience of others? Surely, it can hardly be supposed that your society is wiser than all the other eleven thousand societies. No one is arrogant enough to believe this, I hope, and if experience has placed any one thing beyond question, it is that to continued life and a steady, healthy growth, the prayer-meeting pledge is indispensable.

The failure of every society that has failed, so far as I know (with the exception of one or two that have been crushed out by prejudiced pastors or churches), can be traced directly to a lack of the prayer-meeting pledge. Is not that significant?

WHY EXPERIMENT?

There is no reason to suppose that your experience will be different from that of every other society that has made this unfortunate experiment. If only one society or two could testify concerning the value of the prayer-meeting pledge, you might well say, "This matter has not been proved. The efficacy of this idea has not been tested. Other societies can try their plans and we will try ours." But this is no longer a matter of experiment. One thing has been proved, and that is, that only those Societies of Christian Endeavor that live up to the pledge have prospered for any great length of time.

THE DISTINGUISHING MARK.

Without the pledge, a Society of Christian Endeavor has very little advantage over any other young people's society.

The idea of young people's organizations in the church is nothing new. They have existed for many years. They have done some good, but in most churches they have attained very little permanent success. Why? Because some important element was lacking. But here is an organization called Christian Endeavor, which has brought in a new and quickening element into young people's societies. Why leave out the distinctive element, and still call it a Society of Christian Endeavor? It does not make a woodsaw cut any better to call it a razor, and, besides, it confuses ideas and mixes up implements which ought to be known by different names.

If any one wishes to have an old-fashioned young people's society or a new-fashioned young people's society, he is perfectly at liberty to have one, and, if it is better than the Christian Endeavor society, we will all thank God and adopt it; but it is manifestly unfair to adopt the name and leave out the most essential principle which has made the society successful.

WHAT IS THE PLEDGE?

Many people object to the pledge simply because they have not read it or do not know what it means. So far as it particularly relates to the Christian Endeavor Society, it is a promise to be present and to participate, in some way aside from singing, in every prayer-meeting, "unless prevented by a reason which can conscientiously be given to the Master, Jesus Christ." The argument which supports this pledge is very simple and very logical.

1. Young people's prayer-meetings are necessary to the best life of a church and of the young Christians.

2. If so, it is the duty of the young Christians to attend and sustain them.

3. The only excuse which avails for the non-performance of any duty is one that can conscientiously be given to the Master, Jesus Christ.

4. Such an excuse is accepted, and such an excuse only ought to be accepted, by the Society of Christian Endeavor.

Therefore, the pledge is not only necessary, as experience has proved, but is an entirely reasonable promise for any young Christian to take.

A VOLUNTARY OBLIGATION.

It should never be forgotten that this obligation is a voluntary one. No one ought to be compelled or overpersuaded to join the society. Whenever one wishes no longer to remain, he can go out. He ought not to be forced to remain. It is not a life-long pledge, but, while one is an active member, it ought to be a sacred pledge. If there are only six out of a hundred young people who are willing to take it, let these six form the active membership of the society.

OBJECTIONS.

"This duty is involved in church-membership."

Certainly, but is the duty performed? This pledge makes the duty definite and forcible. No new obligation is assumed, but it is worth quite as much to renew and make vital an old pledge as to form a new one.

"It may be impossible to fulfill my pledge sometimes."

Then you have an excuse which the Master will accept.

"It will serve to make the members hypocritical."

Experience proves the reverse.

"Our pastor and church do not believe in such pledges and are not willing that we should take them."

Then do not have a Society of Christian Endeavor until they are willing.

"I have known of a society that has got along pretty well without it."

I have known of a hundred that have not got along at all well without it, and I have known of many thousands that confess that this is absolutely essential.

NO BACKWARD STEP.

I have the greatest sympathy for all societies that started in the wrong way or find it difficult to live up to the pledge. It often takes months to reorganize wisely and on the right basis, and to bring all the members up to the standard. With failures and mistakes, when a society is struggling to raise its standard, we may all well have sympathy; but I have no sympathy with a society, which, in the light of these eight years of experience, deliberately lowers its standard and weakens its pledge. That any such society will pretty surely fail, as it deserves to fail, is the opinion of

Your friend,

F. E. CLARK.

MAGNETIZING THE IRON-CLAD PLEDGE.

One of our valued correspondents, whose happy thoughts the readers of *The Golden Rule* have frequently shared, reminds us that while the "iron-clad" pledge is proving to be more and more necessary to our societies, it should always be made of "magnetized iron," to attract and draw within its reach all the young people of the community. There could not be a better suggestion. The cheery words of faith, hope and charity, the cordial grasp of the hand, the welcoming smile, will magnetize the iron-clad prayer-meeting pledge, and none will desire to escape its influence.

INVERTEBRATE SOCIETIES.

BY REV. NORMAN PLASS.

Of all the names by which the pledge of our Christian Endeavor Societies may be designated, I prefer to call it the "backbone" of the society.

Let me tell you why.

When in college, among the Berkshire hills of Massachusetts, I used to see come riding down from the mountains, a man whom a casual observer would deem intoxicated. Such, however, was not the case. The poor fellow, it was said, had came into the world with a scant supply of bones, and the most conspicuous of all for its absence was his backbone. As a consequence of this alleged defect, he could not easily assume or maintain an erect position, and every jolt of the wagon caused him to perform various antics of a painfully amusing nature. It was hard to tell whether he was trying to maintain his equilibrium, or to describe a curvilinear periphery.

Without stopping to pass judgment upon the physiological possibility or impossibility of the case, but assuming the explanation to be a true one, you will at once discover why the word "backbone" is truly descriptive of the importance of our pledge. How like to this man are those societies that come into existence without the pledge. Claiming to be Christian Endeavor, but lacking this most important part of their anatomical structure, they are simply invertebrate — a mere promiscuous conglomeration of adipose and skinny tissue, without sinew, muscle, or nerve, without structure or strength. Every jolt of the wagon in which they ride causes them to sway from side to side; every obstruction with which they meet makes us shudder lest they be pitched precipitately from their seats; and they need constant strapping at the back, and bolstering at the sides, and bracing at the dashboard, in order that they may continue upon their journey at all. It would seem to have been better for them never to have been born than to come into life without the spinal column.

Let us never lose sight of the importance of the pledge. Occasionally we see a society which came into existence with the vertebral column in perfect condition — not a vertebra wanting, each perfectly articulating upon the other — which for a time grew and developed, but suddenly is afflicted with a terrible attack of curvature of the spine. Its backbone seems to be twisting and turning as though trying to squirm its way out, and all concerned seem to be anxious to have it get out.

Now we want no such disloyalty to our backbone as that. We must be in love with it. We must cling to it for our lives. It is the token of the highest type of life, and our highest usefulness depends upon the persistency with which we cling to it.

Let us briefly mention a few of the heresies that are the progenitors of these invertebrate societies:

One is an under-estimation of the importance of the pledge. Many of these invertebrate societies were born before the pledge had been so well tested and its importance proved. Now the necessity of the spinal column is being more abundantly shown. Many of these invertebrate societies, convinced of their mistake, have submitted to a surgical operation by which a backbone has been inserted within their structure, and they stand in our midst to-day erect and firm, endowed with newness of strength. Every year fewer societies in proportion to the whole number are being born of this progenitor.

Another heresy, procreator of invertebrates, is the fear of the pledge. It is an innovation, and as such many upon whom the societies will count for help will oppose it. Some declare that they will not sign it; others threaten to leave the society if the pledge is adopted. Hence many societies fear its adoption and remain invertebrate. But if convinced that the pledge is a good thing, we should go straight ahead and adopt it. Let those who do not care to sign it stay out. All that are worth having will come in. What if some do turn aside? Better ten earnest members who are loyal to their pledge than a hundred half-hearted ones. Yet it is the exception where the introduction of the pledge lessens the number of members. Oftener is it the touchstone that reveals the true metal where before we never imagined it to exist. I have read this testimony from one of our observant pastors: "Strangely enough, the stricter the pledge the greater the vigor, and the larger the number of active workers." Some may turn away from the society because of the pledge, and become dead to it, but, as is said of mosquitoes, seven others will come to every funeral, and come to stay.

Still another heresy, fruitful of invertebrates, is the idea that the society had better start without the pledge and gradually grow into it. As a matter of fact, this evolution from the pledgeless to the pledged condition is much like that which would develop the monkey into the man. You can't begin with a duck's egg, and develop from it that other aquatic animal, the hippopotamus. If your first growth isn't a genuine cub, your final development cannot be an old bear. Science has found no secret and invisible line of transition from the invertebrate to the vertebrate state. The society that wants the pledge must incorporate it, and not seek to absorb it. There are animals that absorb their food, but they are mostly parasites. A man would not expect to get outside of a turkey by sitting down at the table and holding the bird under his arm. Swallow the pledge at once, and you will find it sweet to the taste, pleasant to digest, easily converted into muscle, and a constant and unending source of growth and strength.

May the time soon come when the name invertebrate, as applied to societies that profess to be Christian Endeavor, shall be no more, for the reason that societies that are now invertebrate shall have been transformed, and others of their kind shall have ceased to be born into the world.

THE INTERPRETATION OF THE PLEDGE.

A Familiar letter from the President of the United Society.

Curious letters sometimes come to my desk, asking something like this : " How is the prayer-meeting pledge to be interpreted?" or, "What is the responsibility of active members as to the prayer-meeting obligation?" I frequently feel like answering — " Why, what do the words mean? Consult a dictionary; that will tell you what 'absolute necessity' means, and what 'attendance' and 'participation' signify."

Really, these words have no mysterious and occult meaning in the constitution of the Society of Christian Endeavor. These words are good English, and good American as well.

But, not to treat the subject flippantly, I suppose such questions mean : How strictly shall the obligation be interpreted? How rigidly shall the vow be adhered to? And to this there is only one answer : " Just as rigidly as any vow." Just as sacredly must this promise be kept as any promise. There are no grades, so far as I know, in the binding nature of promises. One pledge is just as sacred as another, if both are reasonable, and made with serious intent.

ONE REASON FOR THESE QUESTIONS.

It is not altogether creditable to our religious earnestness that we should even ask these questions, and yet it is not unnatural, since too many Christians have, all their lives, been practically considering their church vows as the lightest of all. They have promised "to support the worship and ordinances of the church," but, except in seasons of special revival, they are never seen near the prayer-meeting. They have promised "to give as the Lord hath prospered them," and out of an income of forty dollars a week they give five cents. They promise "to pray for the peace of Zion," and in the first church quarrel they take a vehement partisan position.

I am not saying these things to find fault with the church, or to criticise Christians (to constitute one's self general religious censor is a poor business), but I mention these plain facts to show how the idea of the insignificance of church vows has become ingrained in the Christian world. It is not strange, then, that young Christians should be slow to realize how binding and solemn are their religious obligations. I have seen middle-aged Christians, very good people in their way, too, who have joined our society as active members, and have not attended one meeting a month, and apparently they have had no compunction of conscience. They have been doing immense harm all the time, and yet have gone on serenely and smilingly, as though every duty was conscientiously performed. They, apparently, did not know any better.

Let the young friends, whose religious habits are not yet fixed, start out better, understanding the sacredness of our vows, and living up to them.

DEFINITE VOWS.

One good thing about our promises in the society is, that they are definite. We promise not only to be good, but to be good for something; not only to do right, but to do right in some definite direction.

It is very easy to make an indefinite, general, hazy promise to be better, and then it is very easy to break that promise. Our pledges in the society are definite, particular, comprehensible — let us live up to them honestly. There is a captious, disputatious spirit, of course, to be avoided, the spirit which strains at a gnat and swallows a camel, a spirit which refuses to make any promises, and gives the poor excuse of possible non-fulfillment. Said a young lady the other day, in a very pert and uppish way, which was meant to be very bright and captivating:

"Oh, I'll never join that society. I may some time want to go away from home for a summer vacation, and if I promise to attend every meeting I can't get out of town for a single week." Of course she knew better, and was only talking for effect; but just such silly objections are being constantly raised by those who ought to be ashamed to raise them.

SANCTIFIED COMMON-SENSE.

In all these duties there is an excellent opportunity for the exercise of sanctified common-sense. Each one of us must decide what is a good and sufficient reason for him, for absence from the weekly prayer-meeting; but he must decide with a tender and sensitive conscience. A social engagement, the call of a friend, the last interesting novel or magazine, a threatening sky or a little rain, for persons in health, are not sufficient reasons. But, as to my telling you what is or is not a good excuse for you, or as to your giving me the same advice, that is quite impossible. God gave us both consciences, and a fair share of common-sense, I hope; and He meant we should use them in deciding all these duties. Any reason which you can give on your knees to the Lord Jesus Christ, with a good conscience, for non-attendance or non-participation, is a good excuse, and no other is worth the giving.

I do not think our pledge can well be put in a more reasonable or sensible way than it is in our model constitution.

Please study it once more, and I do not think you will have any real difficulty in interpreting these promises.

FRANCIS E. CLARK.

PRACTICAL QUESTIONS CONCERNING THE PLEDGE.

Question. Is it not a little unreasonable to demand that every active member shall take the prayer-meeting pledge.

Ans. That question is answered by the pledge itself, which is in substance: "I promise that I will be present at and take some part aside from singing in every weekly prayer-meeting of the society, unless prevented by some reason which I can conscientiously give to my Lord and Master, Jesus Christ." Is it a Christian's duty to attend and sustain a weekly prayer-meeting? If so, then he can only be absolved from this duty by an excuse which he can conscientiously give to Christ. There is the whole thing in a nutshell. No other good excuse is conceivable, and this excuse and this only may be given by an active member of the Y. P. S. C. E. If he keep his conscience tender, he will make no mistake in this matter. The pledge is not only essential to a true Christian Endeavor Society, but it is as reasonable as it is necessary.

Ques. Is it necessary to sign both constitution and pledge, or is signing the pledge sufficient?

Ans. Every member should sign and keep the printed pledge, to serve as a reminder to himself. He should also sign the secretary's book as a member of the society. This book should contain the constitution.

Ques. Does not the prayer-meeting pledge develop a wordy, insincere type of piety?

Ans. By no means. It is the great foe of speech-making in the prayer-meeting. It compels brevity, and encourages sincerity and earnestness.

Ques. Have there not been many instances of societies that have flourished without the prayer-meeting pledge?

Ans. No; we have never known of any that flourished for any length of time without the pledge. There may have been such societies, but we have not known of them. To be sure, while everything is new and the enthusiasm fresh, a society may prosper, but the pledge gives it staying qualities. Many do not seem to know what a flourishing society or a meeting of real power is. By their standard a society and a meeting which are very far from the best are considered good. Let no Christian Endeavorer be satisfied with anything less than the best.

Ques. If the excuse or reason is a valid one and the absentee knows it, and if he does not wish to tell it, as it is strictly private between him and God, how can he fulfill that clause? By sending a testimony?

Ans. The constitution is satisfied if the absentee sends word that he could not be at the meeting. It is not expected that one will go into particulars as to the nature of the excuse. It is much better, however, not only to send word that one is not able to be present, but also to send a written testimony or verse of Scripture. We hope all societies will adopt this plan of requiring from absentees at least a verse of Scripture, to be read as a token that they have not forgotten the meeting or their vows.

Ques. Does the following quotation from the pledge, "unless hindered by some reason which I can conscientiously give to my Lord and Master Jesus Christ," apply to reading the Bible every day, as well as to attendance and participation in each meeting?

Ans. Yes.

Ques. What would you consider a valid excuse for not reading the Bible every day?

Ans. Serious illness, attended by unconsciousness or delirium, or shipwreck without a Bible on a desert island.

Ques. Would it be wise for a society, having recently reorganized, to weaken the pledge by striking out the clause regarding the Bible reading.

Ans. No. To answer these questions very seriously, sanctified common-sense must be used in connection with all religious work. Every Christian knows what will constitute a valid excuse for himself, and the tender conscience will make no mistake. There are no ordinary circumstances in which the Christian cannot find a few minutes' daily in which to read at least one verse out of God's word. This is not distinctively a Christian Endeavor feature, as is the pledge to attend and participate in the weekly meeting, but we cannot see why any young Christian should refuse to pledge himself to make it "the rule of his life" to read the Bible daily, or should have any difficulty in living up to such a pledge. If he cannot read a chapter he can read half a chapter, or if not half a chapter a paragraph, or if not a paragraph a verse.

Ques. Should a pledge against the use of liquor and tobacco be made a part of the regular Christian Endeavor prayer-meeting pledge?

Ans. We think not. Circulate another pledge for those worthy objects, and get as many signatures as possible. It is very poor policy to load the prayer-meeting pledge down. There is enough in it already.

PART VI.

THE CONSECRATION-MEETING.

CONCERNING THE CONSECRATION-MEETING.

A Familiar letter from the President of the United Society.

I have had more than one letter asking for suggestions for the Consecration-Meeting. Occasionally I hear of a society that tries to get along without one, but such news almost always comes with the additional information that the society is living at "a poor dying rate," and that it wishes to re-organize and re-form. So I have come to the conclusion that a monthly consecration-meeting is not only a benefit, but a necessity to the most efficient type of Christian Endeavor Society. Like all the other features of the society, the consecration-meeting has proved its right to be by the blessings it has conferred, and the society that refuses to have such a meeting is exceedingly unwise, since it is rejecting not a theory but a proved blessing. I have two or three suggestions to make:

THREE SUGGESTIONS.

First, Make it a very solemn and serious hour. There are no such sixty minutes in the all four weeks of the Christian Endeavor month as that hour of consecration. No hour that may be so filled with blessing, no hour that may be looked back upon with such delightful memories. A spirit of quiet, reverent solemnity should pervade it. It should be surrounded with the atmosphere of the communion table, for, like the communion season, it is an hour for the renewal of allegiance. A brief, earnest prayer should always be offered before the roll is called, asking that every one whose name is called may in spirit and in truth re-consecrate himself to God.

Second, Let there be as much variety as possible. There will necessarily be some sameness, for all the names must be called every month; but you do not need to begin with just the same name always. Begin at different ends of the alphabet, or in the middle sometimes. Above all things do not have the names called in a bungling, "slouchy" way. The secretary or whoever calls the roll, should be familiar with every name, and know just how to pronounce it in a quiet but distinct tone. To boggle and blunder through the names very soon destroys all the seriousness of the meeting.

LOOK AFTER ABSENTEES.

Third, Let no unexcused absence go unnoticed. The sentiment of a society should be such that any such absence would be considered a very abnormal and exceptional thing, something for the lookout committee at once to inquire into; not something that shall slide along unnoticed until the unfaithful member is on the edge of expulsion. The conscience of the society, if I may so speak, as well as of the individual members, should be very sensitive on this score. Let every case of unexcused absence be at once followed up. Cultivate such a spirit of loyalty that an absent member would no more think of being away without sending a note, or at least a verse to be read at the consecration-meeting, than a loving child would think of being away from home without occasionally writing to the home friends. For the sake of suggesting a pleasant variety in our consecration-meetings, I am glad to give you the letter which Rev. S. W. Adriance recently wrote to a young man who asked advice concerning a praise and consecration-meeting combined. He allows me to copy his letter for the benefit of all. Certainly praise and consecration lie not far apart, and such a combination as Mr. Adriance describes would often be helpful. Of course this suggestion is only for an *occasional* meeting, and it would not answer in a very large society where all the time is occupied in calling the roll. Here is his letter:

My Dear Brother:

It seems to me a delightful union, that of a consecration and praise-meeting for an occasional service. I would not try to keep the two ideas apart. In Romans xii: 1, the apostle, you remember, stirs them up to praise by the mercies of God, and then upon that urges them to consecrate themselves out of gladness. It is easier to consecrate ourselves when we are full of praise than at any other time. As to practical methods:

First, I would at the start read one selection of three or four verses on consecration, with one verse of a hymn between; then three or four on praise.

Second, I would sing two verses of a hymn of praise, such as Coronation, and then say, "Such a Saviour is worthy of consecration," and sing two verses of "Draw me Nearer," or some such hymn.

Third, Lead the rest in repeating all together the twenty-third Psalm, which, in the last two or three verses, is full of grateful praise.

Fourth, Go personally to ten or fifteen before meeting and ask part of them to give a reason for praise, and part to be ready with a personal word of consecration.

Fifth, Make a little order of the meeting. I suppose you call tne roll of active members. Arrange it something like this: Singing—"We praise thee, O God, for the 'Son of thy love'"; Calling roll—Mary Barnes, William Adams, James Wilson, Helen Clark, Stephen Potter, Ernest Everett. Singing—"Thine, Jesus, Thine." Elizabeth Evans, Susie Robie, Will Stimson, Robert Gates, Hamden Greenleaf. Ask two or three to offer prayer for the associate members, and sing, "I am praying for you." And so on through the list.

Sixth, In preparation for this I would look on the list and discover who do not usually take part except with a verse, and go to them personally, urging them to give an additional word of consecration or praise when their names are called. If any of your members are sick, get some one to procure a little note from them, or a word of greeting.

Seventh, Ask them to follow one another with brief prayers, each to express some thought of praise and not to contain any petition. We ask most often in our prayers; in a praise-meeting we ought to return thanks.

Eighth, At the close, after a moment's silent prayer with bowed heads, all rise and sing the consecration hymn, "Must Jesus Bear the Cross Alone?"

The prayerful ingenuity of every prayer-meeting committee will no doubt suggest many other helpful methods of conducting the consecration-meeting.

Let us put so much earnest thought and effort into it that this meeting shall prove the gem and pearl of all the month.

Your friend,

FRANCIS E. CLARK.

CALLING THE ROLL.

BY REV. F. E. CLARK.

The most important thing about the consecration-meeting is the calling of the roll. This should be a most solemn service. It should be preceded by earnest prayer, and the names should be called, as has been said, in a quiet, serious way by some one who is familiar with them and will not stumble over them. How suggestive is this roll-call! "Your name is on the active list," this roll-call says to every young Christian, "because you are supposed to be an active Christian. Does your life bear out that supposition?

"If you are not present your name will be called just the same, and if you have no excuse your unfaithfulness will appear to all.

"Your name is called because you have confessed yourself to be a Christian. Have you been living as a Christian the past month? Do you resolve so to live next month?

"Your name is called because it is written among the Christians on earth; is it written in heaven?"

These questions and a hundred others are forced upon our souls with every consecration roll-call. Let us never omit it as the months recur. There is very much in the constant, regular recurrence of such a meeting. Dr. Bushnell has a sermon on "The Disciplinary Effects of Routine Duties." That is a wonderfully suggestive phrase.

A consecration-meeting once a year or at occasional, irregular intervals would not accomplish much, but the very fact that it recurs as often as the months recur is of itself an education. I hope no society will think lightly of this "means of grace."

A SUCCESSFUL CONSECRATION-MEETING.

Some societies find it difficult to have a successful consecration-meeting. Some fail to respond. Others do so simply with a text of Scripture that has no special adaptiveness as a testimony. Many of the readers of *Ways and Means* will be interested in a brief account of a consecration-meeting held recently by the Y. P. S. C. E. of the First Presbyterian Church of Marshalltown, Ia.

We use the national topics, and, therefore, our subject was "Coming to Christ." The leader opened the meeting and then called for brief prayers, to which about six responded. Then he suggested to them that, in harmony with the subject and as this was a consecration-meeting, it would be interesting and profitable if each would describe briefly what was the special cause of his coming to Christ. Twenty-three responded in about fifteen minutes, a stanza of a hymn coming between the testimonies at intervals.

Here are briefly the responses: "My sense of gratitude to God who had loved me so." "A personal invitation from the pastor led me to think of the matter." "In a heavy thunder-storm a sense of danger led me to serious thought." "After reading Bancroft's 'Footprints of Time' I became convinced that Christianity had done more for the world than anything else, and could do more for me." "A note written me by a friend during some revival meetings." "A personal appeal by a lady." "Revival-meetings a few years ago." "A narrow escape in a railroad accident where some were killed and many wounded." "I was brought up in a Christian home, but felt a lack of something which others enjoyed, and which I wanted." "During a severe storm I took refuge in a cellar, and there began the serious thoughts which decided me to be a Christian." "I heard a man speak in a meeting, and he seemed so full of the love of Christ that I wanted to enjoy it too." "Thoughts during a severe sickness." "Sunday School teacher's instruction." "Prayers that I heard in a prayer-meeting." "My father and mother." "My Christian parents' instruction." "The thought that Christ died for me." "The influence of the Y. M. C. A. here." "These Y. P. S. C. E. meetings." "Some of my young companions who had found Christ." Several said that they could not tell just how or when, but they knew that they loved Christ and wanted to serve Him. Many spoke of impressions deepened in these Y. P. S. C. E. meetings.

After this the roll was called, and then a collection taken up for religious work. Then a report from each of the committees.

These exercises were interspersed with appropriate hymns, some with and some without being announced.

An hour was all too short for this meeting.

It was led by the pastor, who takes it in turn as one of the active members.

DOES AN EARNEST CHRISTIAN NEED THE CONSECRATION-MEETING

"I have consecrated myself once, why should I do it over and over again, at every monthly consecration-meeting?" some have reasoned. "It seems like weakening a vow to repeat it every month. Since I have given myself once completely I have nothing left to give." But we think this is mistaken reasoning, arising from a misapprehension of the spirit of the service. The consecration-meeting does not imply that one has never yielded himself to God, but rather the contrary. It is a service especially for Christians, for those who have consecrated themselves before. It is a renewal of vows before made. Just as an affectionate child might say twenty times a week, "I love you, mother; I want to obey you better and help you more." So the disciple that lives nearest to his lord is most often impelled to cry,

> "Take my life and let it be
> Consecrated, Lord, to Thee."

Surely, none of our readers have reached that plane where they think that they no longer need to renew their vows of allegiance and loyalty. If so, they have got beyond David and John and Peter and Paul. In fact, they have reached the point where a prayerful consideration of 1 Cor. x:12 seems especially needed.

THE PERSONAL ELEMENT IN THE CONSECRATION-MEETING.

BY MRS. W. W. DUMM.

Nature revels in diversity and this gives her delightful mystery. Everything has a character of its own. This same principle of diversity is shown on a nobler scale in man. "It takes all sorts of people to make a world," is a saying as true as trite. Christ recognized this law of personality in His dealings with men. He taught all His disciples to follow Him; that was the grand aim, yet taught in such a way that the personality of each was developed. Divine appreciation and sympathy helped each to become his best possible self.

"But" says one, "what is the difference between a

consecration-meeting and the regular one? Is not consecration implied in all prayer-meeting effort?" In a sense, yes. You gain wisdom from the thought and spirit of a regular meeting, but you do not get the inspiration which comes from seeing into somebody's heart. Oliver Wendell Holmes says that the human heart has two doors — a front door and a side door. The front door is on the street. The side door opens at once into the sacred chamber, life's temple and shrine. The regular meeting is the front door, where all are welcome. The consecration-meeting is the side door, which leads into the audience-chamber of the King Himself.

How does personality show itself in the consecration-meeting?

First, by testimony of experience. All religious experience which amounts to anything means more than an isolated hour of exalted feeling now and then. It goes deep down and takes hold of life, and is woven into its warp and woof. Testimony is worth what the person back of it is worth, and we instinctively recognize it as he speaks. His personality flashes across to us, and the vital touch stirs our footsteps to a livelier gait Zionward. It is not "wit, wisdom, words, worth or eloquence of speech," that makes a bit of your heart-life helpful; it is the sincerity of the heart itself, which can never fail to touch others, however faultily expressed. The varied experiences are a guide, a warning and an inspiration for the coming month.

Secondly, it is consecration. Some young Christians give themselves to God at conversion; it is a real giving, but settled, signed and ended there. Afterward they develop; perhaps it is the gift of music, or the advantages of wider reading, or growing public ability. Every month marks an advance in their developed power, but the consecration remains at a standstill. Enoch walked with God; he did not start and stop, becoming a spiritual obelisk. No, he walked with God, with the light step of youth, with the strong step of manhood, with the step of age, until "he was not, for God took him."

Could better epitaph be written?

> Our Friend, our Brother, and our Lord,
> What may thy service be?
> Nor name, nor form, nor ritual word,
> But simply following Thee.

THE CONSECRATION-MEETING.

BY PROF. AMOS R. WELLS.

The goal of all right striving in this world, the goal on the way to which all other good goals lie, is consecration to God's service. Therefore the consecration-meeting is the strictest measure of the success of our societies. I want to point out the way toward a successful consecration-meeting. It is often as important to know what roads will not lead to a place as to know the right road. There are

THREE ALLURING BLIND ALLEYS

which promise success in this matter, yet bring a society flatly up against blank failure.

One is reliance upon numbers. Numbers are often a calamity. The larger your attendance, so much the worse for the meeting, if the enthusiasm will not go around. I have seen what promised to be good meetings smothered under numbers, like a bonfire under too liberal additions of fuel. Let us pray for our societies that they grow in numbers no faster than they grow in grace. In our Endeavor work numbers follow success; they never precede it.

A second blind alley is undue reliance upon methods. All ways are fair which are thoroughfares to the goal; no method is a means.

The third blind alley is reliance upon eloquence and readiness of speech. Have any of us ever congratulated ourselves on a good consecration-meeting, wherein only the tongue was consecrated? Success will not come to our consecration-meetings because invited by an eloquent orator, who presents a petition of sixty names, and spreads a velvet carpet along the way.

Why, what does consecration mean? It is devoting from a common to a sacred use. All the body and all its work transformed into something buoyant and strong, all the commonplaces of this common earth made sacred and touched with divinity — that is consecration. And do you wonder that I hold the one success of a consecration-meeting to be in this spread of a spirit of consecration through it? Once this spirit is abroad in men's hearts, it finds its own methods, it brings its own great eloquence, it gathers its multitudes.

If a consecration-meeting is to promote consecration, the work of the members in regard to it must be in three directions —

EXAMINATION, APPLICATION AND SUPPLICATION.

Examination must show us what parts of our being are still put to common uses. Few matters of our living are studied so poorly as the living itself. This should be our preparation for the consecration-meeting — the discovery, in some one particular direction, of the need of consecration. And the second point is application to our need of all the words and influences of the hour. If we grieved over each meeting as a personal failure, unless it showed us some one lack of ours, and helped us in some definite way in regard to that lack, few such nights would fail to leave a blessing with us. But there is also no consecration without supplication — without the upward look to the Consecrated One, the Christ. Consecration to God means consecration to all the universe, and one of its very first and most logical evidences is thought for another's welfare. So that all this that we should do for ourselves in our consecration-meeting must be done at the same time for some one else.

How shall we know when honest, humble self-examination and faithful reception of all help that comes, and earnest prayer are doing their work, are lifting us into the higher life? Well, consecration is a process of crystallization. The common carbon, graphite, is dingy, soft, incoherent; but the crystal, the diamond, has marvellously won hardness, firmness and brilliancy. And so we Endeavorers may glory in the achievement of consecration, in proportion as our incoherent infirmities of will have crystallized into the regular facets of a God-directed purpose; in proportion as our soft and crumbling fear has grown firm with a divine confidence; in proportion as our dullness and dingy gloom has become radiant with heaven's own happiness. Now man has made the diamond; but the man-made diamond is a puny affair, and so is a merely human consecration. We may try to crystallize it from the clearest mental solution; we may lay our shrewd plots to intercept the swift crystal in its chemical interchanges; we may try to form the precious gem by force of fire and pressure; our consecration-crystallizing comes not by brain or craft or energy. God has a laboratory above our own; there comes no spiritual power but from without, above. And, therefore, only as we earnestly strive after the power and presence of the Consecrated One, the Christ, will our meetings become consecration-meetings indeed.

HELPFUL HINTS FOR THE CONSECRATION SERVICE.

BY REV. H. W. POPE.

It is a good plan to open it, occasionally, with a moment of silent prayer, to be followed by the leader; and, by the way, it always seems more impressive if the leader kneels.

We are not likely to over-do the matter of reverence, and perhaps it is just as well to make this service a little different from the ordinary meeting. Let careful preparation be made for this service, and special prayer be offered for the weaker members, that they may be led to take an advance step. Then let the stronger members be on hand early, and take the more timid ones up into the "area of higher pressure," and sit by their side. Seated there, where the spiritual currents are strong, and the atmosphere surcharged with the spirit of devotion, many a timid brother or sister will gain courage to pray or say a word for the Master.

"These are little things," you say. Yes, but souls are lost and won by little things, and let us never forget that great spiritual battles are being fought in all these meetings. "And all this takes time?" Yes, but what is time for if not to help one another? "Bear ye one another's burdens, and so fulfill the law of Christ."

After letters are read from absent members, call upon some one to pray for them. At the close of the service let the leader inquire, "Does any one know of a brother that is sick? Does any one know of a member that is in trouble, or in want, or out of employment!" Strengthen the bond of union in every possible way.

MEMORIZING SCRIPTURE.

One society that I know of learns a short psalm each month, repeating it in concert at each meeting until it is well committed, and then taking up another. The recitation of such choice passages is very impressive, and the habit of committing Scripture is an invaluable one.

THINK ON THESE THINGS.

Mr. C. H. Yatman, the well-known Y. M. C. A. worker, has compiled the following list of subjects for active and associate members to think about.

FOR ACTIVE MEMBERS.

1. What are you a member of the society for?
2. What responsibilities are on you as a member?
3. What have you done to meet these responsibilities?
4. What moral and spiritual disaster your neglect entails.
5. What account will you give of your stewardship?
6. What does the Master think of your work in His vineyard?
7. What will be the final result at the judgment?

FOR ASSOCIATE MEMBERS.

1. How quickly our years are slipping by.
2. How long ago you might have become a Christian.
3. How these years have been worse than wasted.
4. How that for lost opportunities you will be judged.
5. How great is God's mercy to you now.
6. How soon justice will take mercy's seat.
7. How awful it is to be forever lost.

A TESTIMONY RECEIPT.

BY C. D. S.

I am one of the Christian Endeavor girls, and having just recovered from a severe attack of a disease known to Y. P. S. C. E. members, and fearing that some one might be coming down with it, I would like to suggest a simple remedy which I hope will check it in its first stages.

There are those who are really conscientious in regard to speaking in the prayer-meetings; they fully intend to avail themselves of every opportunity for publicly confessing Christ, yet are kept back by their pride. How surprising it is that we should ever imagine a company of people making it their business to notice all our little mistakes! As if they would treasure up in their minds a slight tremor of the voice, a hesitancy in manner or an error in grammar made by one timid disciple, when forty or fifty testimonies were given during the same evening!

I saw a definition of bashfulness the other day, stating it as "panic-stricken vanity." There may be more truth in that than we think. Before going to our Y. P. S. C. E. prayer-meetings, I used to say to myself, "Now, this evening, I am going to be the first one to speak, and then I shall be ready to enjoy the rest of the service."

When the time for testimony came, Satan, with all his forces, strove to prevent me from taking part. You know how I felt, the quick beating of my heart and the imaginary tremble in my voice seemed insurmountable obstacles in my way.

Finally, I would decide that after the one sitting next to me, or a friend in the same row, or Miss ——, on the back seat, had spoken, then I would speak.

But affairs did not always turn out as I expected, and I kept growing more and more uncomfortable every minute. At last the leader of the meeting would say, "We have just one minute left for testimonies," then, sometimes, but not always, I would jump up suddenly, and say what I had not the moral courage or humility to express early in the evening.

I soon found that I was losing all the pleasure and profit the meetings afforded, because each moment I kept thinking of my present duty, and realized that I was delaying its performance.

Finally I confided my trouble to a dear Christian lady, asking her if it was necessary for me to always go through this same struggle at every meeting.

After kindly pointing out to me my mistake, she said, "Just say to yourself, 'That point, with God's help, is settled, now and forever, that whenever an opportunity offers, I will testify for my Master.' Then, leave yourself in the hands of the Divine Leader, without worrying or fearing a failure, and when the time comes, do not stop to debate the question a moment, but go forward in the strength of the Lord, and Satan will find he has lost your case. Are you willing to make the effort?"

Now, my dear classmates in Christian Endeavor, let us lay aside all these weights, not allowing the enemy a chance to defeat us, for the strong hand of our Heavenly Conqueror is very near us; we may clasp it if we will, and, cheered on by the voice of the Captain "who never lost a battle," we can take our orders from Him, and obey promptly, cheerfully, and for Jesus' sake.

PART VII.

FOR LEADERS OF PRAYER-MEETINGS.

HINTS TO LEADERS OF PRAYER-MEETINGS.

A familiar letter from the President of the United Society.

I want to say a few words in this letter to the leaders of the prayer-meetings, and as I hope all the members of our societies take their turns, when their turn comes, if they are asked, this letter applies to all our active members.

THE FIRST TIME.

It seems like a good deal of an undertaking, I know, when, for the first time, you are called to sit in the leader's chair. As you think of it beforehand, you feel that you are going to be very conspicuous; your heart nearly fails you (I have in mind the younger and more inexperienced now), and you almost resolve that you will go to the prayer-meeting committee and beg off. I am quite sure you would do this were you thinking only of your own pleasure, but then, you remember that your own pleasure is, comparatively, a very small consideration in this matter; that it is for Christ's sake, and "in His name," that you make this attempt. At once the matter assumes a new aspect, and you have no further hesitation.

GETTING READY.

Then, as the time for "your meeting" draws nigh, you begin to think of the subject, and read the Scripture lessons that bear on it, and, if you have the uniform topics, you carefully read the published notes, and are surprised, perhaps, to find that you really have a good deal to say. At length that special evening to which you have been looking forward so many weeks **comes, and from** your knees, with a heart full of desire for God's blessing, you go to the prayer-room. But, somehow, the good things you thought of saying have vanished, your voice almost fails, you say scarcely anything you meant to say, and a good many things you never meant to utter, and, on the whole, you feel, perhaps, that your part was a miserable failure.

NOT A FAILURE, AFTER ALL.

I have no idea that it was a failure, however, by any means, and have very little doubt that the meeting was a much better one than it would have been if you had been thoroughly self-possessed and glib, and had gotten off the long and elaborate speech that you had thought out. It is especially true of a good prayer-meeting that it is not by might nor by power (not by eloquence nor loquacity nor oratory), but by my spirit, saith the Lord. Just now it seems to be the fashion to give advice by means of the familiar "don't," so let me suggest

A FEW PRAYER-MEETING "DON'TS"

that it would be well for a leader to regard:

1. Don't read too long a passage of Scripture or too many passages. A very few verses are quite enough. If you search the concordance through, and read every passage that bears on the subject, what will those poor boys and girls do who have learned the very same verses? To be sure, they can repeat them after you, but it is much better to give them the first chance. I heard of one society, recently, where the leader usually read all the daily readings which the papers give us. That, of itself, good as the selections are, would be about enough to kill the meeting. If the passage on the topic card is a long one, read only a part of it, and rely for further Scripture recitations upon the members.

2. Don't take too much time with your opening remarks. Remember that in a Christian Endeavor meeting the leader is only one of many who are under the same obliga-

tion as he is to take part. The leader who takes fifteen or twenty minutes for his opening remarks is surely robbing some one else of his time. Ten minutes are usually enough for the leader to occupy with hymns, Scripture reading, remarks and all the opening exercises.

3. Don't lose control of the meeting or let it run itself. Have an appropriate hymn ready for any emergency; introduce some exercise in which all can take part if there is any pause, as the repetition of the Lord's Prayer or the Twenty-third Psalm.

4. Don't let the meeting drag tiresomely along after the proper time to close has come. It is sure, in such a case, to get "frayed out at the ends," as some one has said.

POSITIVE SUGGESTIONS.

But a few positive suggestions are worth more than a whole column of "don'ts," and I cannot do better than to give you the following excellent suggestions to leaders, which have been prepared by Rev. E. A. Robinson. These have been printed upon a slip, so that they may be handed to each leader in that society a day or two before the date of his meeting:

1. Be prompt in opening and closing the meeting.
2. Try to speak so that all may hear.
3. Stand, rather than sit, while reading the Scripture and offering prayer.
4. If possible, select hymns that bear on the subject of the meeting.
5. Use only a short Scripture selection (four to six verses).
6. Always announce the subject of the meeting.
7. Try to add a word of your own to the Scripture reading.
8. Be brief in opening, and when necessary remind others that they should be brief also
9. Always repeat the number of any hymn that is called for.

10. Pray for the meeting before you come, and remember it in prayer after it is over, that the Lord will bless it to His glory, and the good of all present.

It is not ye that speak, but the Spirit of your Father which speaketh in you. — *Matt.* x : 20.

My word shall not return unto me void, but it shall accomplish that which I please, and it shall prosper in the thing whereto I sent it. — *Is.* lv : 11.

The leader who follows these suggestions cannot fail to do his part well. They are well worth preserving for frequent reference.

Your friend,

FRANCIS E. CLARK.

HELPFUL HINTS ABOUT LEADING A MEETING.

We know by experience the "chills and fever" feeling which steals over many a young disciple, as he wakes in the morning and reluctantly confesses to himself, "To-night I must lead the meeting." We know how the Bible is thumbed for an appropriate passage to read, how the papers, editorials, news columns, advertisements and all are scanned and squeezed for a unique thought, how books of meditation and devotion are searched for poetry, and how, as the hour of meeting draws near, the leader grows anxious, because he knows not what to do, and nervous because he has nothing to say. He dreads — oh, how he dreads that meeting! He will rejoice — oh, how he will rejoice when it is over! Accordingly, with nerves unstrung, forebodings strange, apprehensions gloomy, he takes his place, and many a time the meeting responds to his temper — "it is twitchy, jerky, intermittent."

We have found our way out of such fretful experience, and three things have helped us. May we hand them over to you in the garb of exhortation?

First, then, be natural. If you will notice religious leaders, you will find that those having the greatest power over the audience are the men who in every way seek to make the distance between themselves and their audience as infinitesimal as possible. They remove the pulpit; they cut down the platform; they sit in a common chair; they speak a familiar language, rather than a precise one; they are dignified, but theirs is the dignity of friendship, and has nothing of the refrigerator chill about it; they believe God is honored by distinct utterance, and so they always speak to the person in the back seat; if they announce a hymn, they indicate so that he can hear whether two or four verses are to be sung. Believe me, the neglect of a leader to tell not only what to sing, but how much to sing, is many a time to the prayer-meeting what the fly is to the ointment, the dust to the machinery, or the little foxes to the vines. Be natural, then, in manner, in action, in speech, for it is thus and not otherwise that the audience is put at ease, which is an important requisite to the successful conduct of a meeting.

But, secondly, do not lead the meeting to death, lead it to life. The leader is neither an absolute monarch, nor a petty tyrant. It is his mission neither to appropriate the meeting nor so to chaperon it that constraint will settle, cloud-like, over the assembly, striking the timid dumb, and making the ready hesitate. Having put the audience at ease by being yourself natural, the next thing is to put the audience at work, to help everybody to feel not alone a pressing responsibility, but also a gracious privilege. Call for hymns and passages of Scripture from the floor; break up monotony by the use of a simple illustration; encourage the worshipers to a free expression of prayer, of exhortation. Do not be afraid of bad grammar; it is better, far better, than no grammar, and not seldom is it the coarse home-spun of some glittering gospel truth. After opening the meeting, the leader should be like a life-preserver — to be used only in an emergency. So far as possible, let the meeting lead itself, for this is the way of life.

But, third, select a simple subject, and say a few simple things about it. Take your subject from your experience, speak from your experience. He does not most edify and help his fellow-Christians who indulges in word-pictures, and splits hairs, and chops logic. Nay, nay. It is he whose simple recital of a personal experience of joy or sorrow, of temptation or victory, quivers with heart-throbs, and reveals a heart humbly devoted to Christ, and a desire honestly felt for his fellowmen — it is he who speaks to edification. The old, old story is, after all, the sweetest, freshest, gladdest which ever has been, which ever can be made subject of a prayer-meeting. Tell it simply, sincerely, succinctly; people are longing to hear it, and go away from the meeting you lead disappointed if you do not tell it to them. Do not shun it because it is simple. It is sacred, it is sublime, it is soul-saving.

PROMPTNESS.

BY REV. DWIGHT M. PRATT.

Promptness should be catalogued as one of the Christian graces. It is essential to successful Christian life and service. It is indispensable in a prayer-meeting.

1. PROMPTNESS IN ATTENDANCE. We read that Gen. Washington never delayed meals for tardy guests, but, on their arrival, greeted them without apology, saying, "Gentlemen, we are punctual here." No better words for a motto for the place of prayer than these, "We are punctual here." Rarely can a meeting recover from the depressing effect of five or ten minutes of interruption by squeaking shoes and slamming doors. To proceed under such circumstances is time often worse than wasted, for it dampens ardor and checks the glow of heart essential to spiritual fervor. To find a room packed at the appointed

moment with eager, earnest people ready to do their part in song or prayer or testimony, or at least in respectful listening, is inspiring. The importance of prompt attendance cannot be overstated.

2. PROMPTNESS IN BEGINNING. The Apostle Paul termed the Christian a soldier. The soldier on duty is a model of prompt, energetic action. No delay is pardoned. Every man must be in his place on the instant. The precision of a company on drill, the obedience, the self-discipline required, the ardor, awaken in the beholder a kindred enthusiasm. He would like to be a soldier himself, and share in the energy of such an heroic life. A similar discipline is necessary to the soldier of the cross. He has made a long stride in Christian attainment when he has learned to be on time at every call of duty. In one sense the prayer-meeting is the place of drill. It is at least a place for spiritual exercise. Here the Christian uses and develops his spiritual powers to the glory of God. The service should consequently begin with a promptness and vigor indicative of consecration and readiness for service. To a looker-on such punctuality and ardor prove that the disciples of Christ love and rejoice in the place of prayer.

3. PROMPTNESS IN TAKING PART. The room may be filled at the appointed hour, the leader in his place and ready to begin at the last stroke of the bell, the opening services may be all that could be desired; yet all this is of little avail in a social meeting without the prompt co-operation of those present. In a company of mature saints pauses might be spiritually refreshing, but taking human nature as it runs in an average prayer-meeting, delay in prayer or testimony argues spiritual coldness. Waiting for others has killed many a prayer-meeting, and quenched the first spark of life in many a trembling, hoping, aspiring soul. True consecration includes a sense of personal responsibility and a spirit of independence. Should each

Christian bear the social meeting on his heart, plan for its efficiency, and come prepared to lead off in prayer, testimony or song, it would revolutionize the average prayer service. The impression would be made that Christians were so fervent, so alive they could not refrain from utterance. Such a spirit is contagious. It quickens cold-hearted disciples. It wins unbelievers. It honors the Master. We are speaking of soul enthusiasm, not of surface activity. Christ will impart to the eager disciple His own zeal. His word, as in the case of Jeremiah, will be like a burning fire in his bones, so that he cannot forbear. Love for the Lord Jesus Christ begets independence, manliness and strength. Waiting for others to first act results often from a feeling of inferiority, or, at least, of inability. We argue that they are more qualified for utterance or service. This is a snare of the devil. Such reflections have no place in a consecrated Christian. All God asks of us is prompt fidelity. He is no respecter of persons. He only requires the service for which He has endowed us. But He does require this. It should be rendered joyfully and promptly by every Christian. What is true of the prayer-meeting is true of every department of life. Promptness renders service acceptable. As the parent chides the tardy and unwilling child, so God cannot delight in us, unless our obedience is hearty, joyful, immediate.

Promptness, let us repeat again, is one of the eminent Christian graces. To secure it would remedy nearly all the evils that confront us in our efforts to serve and honor Christ our redeemer.

PART VIII.

OFFICERS AND COMMITTEES.

THE DUTIES OF OFFICERS.

A familiar letter by the President of the United Society.

I have long wished to write to the officers of our societies, for I believe that great possibilities of usefulness lie in every one of these offices. Much depends upon the spirit with which their duties are undertaken. It goes without saying that there are no offices in our societies to be striven for or desired for any honor that attaches to them, but yet every one, however humble, should be considered a position of trust and responsibility which cannot be declined except for the most weighty reasons. If President Harrison, and the Earl of Shaftsbury and Senator Frelinghuysen considered it an honor and a privilege to be Sunday School teachers, surely there is no office or committee in our societies which we may not aspire to honorably fill if it comes to us unsought.

I am glad to say that I have heard of no trouble in our societies arising from the distribution of the offices, but it may not be out of place to read before each semi-annual election of officers, as some societies do, the clause which is found in many constitutions, and which seems to me to place this matter in its true light. It reads as follows :

"While membership on the Board of Officers or Committees of this Society should be distributed as evenly as the best good of the Society will warrant, among the different members, the offices should not be considered places of honor to be striven for, but simply opportunities for increased usefulness, and any ill-feeling or jealousy springing from this cause shall be deemed unworthy a member of the Society of Christian Endeavor. When, however, a member has been fairly elected, it is expected that he will consider his office a sacred trust, to be conscientiously accepted, and never to be declined except for most urgent and valid reasons."

THE PRESIDENT.

But I will suppose that the officers have been elected. In many societies a new set has just been chosen. The first one whom we naturally think of is the President. Some of his duties are very plain; to preside at the monthly business-meeting and to see that necessary business is transacted, is obviously his duty, but there are other matters equally important which come within his province. A general insight and supervision of the society falls to his share. Are there as many committees at work in the society as there ought to be? Are they doing their work conscientiously? Do they make monthly reports concerning what they have done? Perhaps there is some committee that for months has done little or nothing. That should be looked into and remedied. Do unruly boys disturb the back seats? Have the members an unfortunate practice of being habitually behind time? Is there unbecoming, boisterous conduct after or before the meeting? For all these things the president should be on the watch.

OTHER DUTIES.

Perhaps he sees that some members are withdrawing into the background, losing their interest or giving place too much to those of more energetic, active temperaments. There is a chance for him to exert all his tact and skill, and, either personally or through some one else, win them back to more earnest endeavor. He should call an occasional meeting of all the committees, and at least a monthly meeting of his cabinet, the executive committee. He should be a man of power, but not a one-man power.

He should remember that it is far better to get ten men to do ten men's work than to do ten men's work himself. Of course, when I use the masculine pronoun it is understood that it is only for convenience. The young lady president may be just as effective. I am not presumptuous enough to offer this advice to the pastors when they chance to be presidents; they will doubtless know what is best to be done, and I think that usually, after the society is fairly started, they will put the labor and responsibility of the presidency upon one of the young men or young women of the church.

THE VICE-PRESIDENT.

The vice-president has been sometimes thought to be a supernumerary, a kind of fifth wheel, but I think this office should be regarded in anything but this light. In the first place, it is very necessary to have some one to take the president's place in case he should be necessarily absent; and in the second place, if all the duties which I have indicated belong to the chief executive, there is abundant labor for two earnest workers. Let the president and vice-president frequently consult together; let them divide the duties of supervision, always, of course, under the direction of the president, for some one must be at the head, and, if the work is faithfully done, the vice-president will find no lack of opportunities.

THE RECORDING SECRETARY.

The ordinary duties of keeping correct minutes and accurate lists of the active and associate members, with additions, absentees, etc., are readily understood; but to do this in the best way requires some little conscientious effort. One duty of the recording secretary is usually to call the roll at the consecration-meeting. This should be done quietly, distinctly and accurately. Do not boggle over the names and raise a titter of laughter by any absurd mistake. Let it be a solemn and most earnest service, always preceded by earnest prayer.

THE CORRESPONDING SECRETARY.

The corresponding secretary should be a PERMANENT officer. Please notice the emphatic small caps. We do not indulge very much in italics or capitals for emphasis in *Ways and Means*, but I should like to put the above word in still larger capitals. Do not change the corresponding secretary every six months or every year. Instead of "life or good behavior," according to civil service principles, I would say let the corresponding secretary remain in office as long as connected with the society—the good behavior is taken for granted. His duties are to receive and respond to legitimate communications which come to the society. He is under no obligation to respond to the scores of people who may wish to use the societies for advertising purposes or to sell their wares, and I would advise him to disregard all appeals, chain-letters, etc., from irresponsible parties who wish to raise money. Money should be given only through accredited channels, which are known to be reliable, like the great missionary societies of the denomination with which each church is connected. However, frequent letters of invitation are received, letters of inquiry, too, as to methods, etc., which may well receive his courteous attention.

IMPORTANT DUTIES.

An important part of his work is to fill out the yearly statistical blanks for which the United Society asks in preparation for the annual convention, as well as a similar request from the State officers, though I hope these requests will not be multiplied. To fill out this annual blank will take but a few minutes, but it should be done promptly and accurately. The corresponding secretary, in responding to all legitimate calls upon his time, should remember that he is the only link that connects the societies to each other, and through which the methods of work found useful in one society can be made known to another.

THE TREASURER.

This letter is already too long, but I must say a word about the treasurer. His duties, of course, are to receive, keep safely and disburse, as the society may direct, the funds which come into his hands. I think he may wisely exercise his ingenuity in devising the best way for his society to raise funds for missionary work. A very few dollars are needed by any society for itself, but much can often be done for the cause of Christ at large. I would earnestly recommend the weekly or monthly envelope pledge plan as incomparably the best method of raising money for all purposes.

Your friend,

FRANCIS E. CLARK.

A TALK WITH SOME OF THE COMMITTEES.

BY REV. JAMES L. HILL.

So definite is my wish to make these few remarks personal and informal, that I will imagine, not a difficult or unpleasant thing to do, that we are gathered together, officers and committees only, at the parsonage; that we have partaken, in goodly fellowship, of our simple refreshment; that presently the prayer-meeting committee is to hold a conference by itself in the parlor, the lookout committee in the sitting-room, the social committee in the dining-room, and the fruit and flower committee in the study. Respecting the whole society, let us first see distinctly that it will not do to stop growing. When we cease to make new wood, decay and disintegration begin. So enormous is our outgo of young people to attend school and enter business that we must look right after our income. Let us grasp the idea that the first condition of growth and revival is a spirit of expectation. Anticipations, like prophecies, always tend to fulfill themselves. When hope dies we are twice dead; when a society expects little it will not be called to enjoy much. Before Christ comes, as was true historically, there is wide-spread eagerness; "for we are saved by hope." A society that is not looking for improvement in numbers and condition grievously needs mental and spiritual quickening. Let us, too, keep in vivid remembrance the fact that the moments immediately succeeding the meeting are priceless. Resolve, in advance, just how you will use them. Let the president run and speak to this young man. Be near the associate member who is signing himself as active. If you can honestly do so, speak of your pleasure in hearing those who were courageous in doing their duty. When societies meet Sunday night, let us also see that in meeting our friends we are so subdued in tone of voice as not to be observed by the congregation that is gathering for the second service. But chiefly let us regard this: It is possible to name a theme for a meeting and to have the meeting proceed almost automatically, when there is a large active membership that keeps the pledge. At times we need to break right through and over all routine and come close to God. We will then, perhaps, divide the time, as some societies do, giving the first half to earnest, continuous, brief supplications for a deeper consecration. The equipoise between testimony and prayer cannot be disturbed with impunity. This matter affects the subsequent portion of the service. Scripture verses, and contributions of sacred sentiment begin to carry a greater amount of spirituality.

Now, before we separate into these several rooms already designated, where the pastor and the president of the society will call you, let me say specifically to the

PRAYER-MEETING COMMITTEE

that you will find nothing else so fruitful as personal work. Arrange our membership in divisions. Each of you in a quiet way shepherd one division. If any one is growing cold-hearted and disposed to shirk his duty, give the matter serious thought as to what shall be done. Have you not noticed that our meetings are a little uneven? Is there not all the while a steady factor? When some of our young friends are leading, let us call our reserves right out. And we are not without them. Of each of you divine glory can "make a pillar in the temple of God."

Now, let me turn and say to the

SOCIAL COMMITTEE,

that I appreciate your difficulties. People are sated with entertainments. It is harder to provide for social life now than it was when Dr. Holland and Wendell Phillips began to lecture, and all these bureaus of entertainment to send forth singers in troops. Social conditions have been revolutionized within a generation. Notwithstanding your difficulties, you have your duty. We must connect the social life of the young with the church. Blessed are those young disciples that dwell in God's house. We must be able to say that they saw God and ate and drank. We must impart a sacredness to the whole life. I would fish in deeper water. I would give over the spirit of competition. This year I hasten to recommend that you entertain at a festival all the officers and committees of the various auxiliaries of our church. Have five-minute addresses from those chosen to speak; for the ladies, for the congregation, for the Sunday School and for the local union. Sit at the tables while these addresses are being made. It will blend the society and church; and each will better understand the other.

TO THE LOOKOUT COMMITTEE

I want to express my pleasure in their frequent meetings. If the society is prosperous, they have much to do; and if it is not, they have more. It is a pretty good rule for this committee to discard any method of work if it is easy. Another principle of human nature than that of thrift probably suggests it. In bringing new members into the society, it is a good rule to call upon them in their homes respecting the matter. This locates them and recognizes them, and begins official acquaintance. Here is the standard for the lookout committee: Can we sincerely say of our society that all we ask for it is more of the soul? If not, awake, lookout committee, awake, awake.

Finally, I wish it could be made as plain to the

FLOWER COMMITTEE

as it is to me, that much of their efficiency consists in promptness. A remembrance sent from church to persons detained by accident or otherwise from Sunday worship gains power if it is sent at once. If it is delayed until one has dragged through an illness and is on the point of returning to church, it is mockery. If some of the committee are about the vestry before all services to hear of cases of trouble and affliction, and if the congregation is publicly invited to communicate names to the committee, it will be well. This committee ought to act as intermediary between the sick and larger sources of supply than the vases at the pulpit on the Sabbath day. Such sources exist in most congregations. If in doing their work promptly bouquets should be sent, by mistake, to those detained not only on beds of sickness, but on lounging-chairs of wellness, the committee's work would be suggestive — you thought they were sick. They acted as if they were.

Service upon committees is not drudgery; it is opportunity. It would be no kindness to do the work for you. Field is needed for your ingenuity, tact and personality. No matter how ingenious and capable any individual member may be, it is good both for him and for the others, that he should act largely in conjunction with the other members of the committee.

PRACTICAL QUESTIONS CONCERNING THE COMMITTEES.

Question. When I ask for a report from lookout or prayer-meeting committee, the answer generally is, "What can we report?" Ours is a small society in a small place, and so the names of leaders, etc., are usually remembered. I thought I would ask if you would print a report of a lookout and prayer-meeting committee that has actually been used. Perhaps it may suggest a new line of work for us.

Ans. The mistake is often made, and perhaps our correspondent who asks the above question shares it, of expecting a novel and unusual report each month from the committees, and when this cannot be given, as from the very nature of things it often cannot, the committees feel absolved from making any report. This is an entirely false conception. The object of the report is to show that the committee have done what they could; that they have not been idle. Such a report is always a stimulus to those who hear it and to the committee that make it. If they have done very little, let them report that little. If they have done absolutely nothing, let them report that with contrition, and resolve to do better; but on no account let the written report, which is to be filed by the secretary and kept, be omitted. Very often this report gives the various committees opportunity to offer a needed exhortation to greater faithfulness. We hope that every society that has not adopted this system of monthly written reports will do so at once. In accordance with the suggestion of our correspondent, we shall be glad to publish one or two actual reports that have been given, as a help to others.

Ques. What is your opinion as regards the propriety and advisability of holding Y. P. S. C. E. committee meetings on Sunday afternoon?

Ans. It depends altogether upon the object of the committee meeting. If it is simply to consult concerning some phase of the spiritual interests of the society, we see no objection.

Ques. Is it best to re-elect a president for two or three

successive terms, and is it advisable to re-appoint committees instead of appointing new ones to serve on the committees?

Ans. Only in exceptional cases, when it is manifestly for the advantage of the society to continue the same officers, is it best to re-elect them. Always choose some new members on the committees.

Ques. Should the substance of the reports of committees be placed on record in the secretary's book, that is, as a part of the regular proceedings?

Ans. The reports need not be copied in the secretary's book, but should be placed on file.

Ques. Should the lookout committee interview all absentees from regular meetings or simply from the consecration meetings? In a reorganized society, will it be wiser for the lookout committee to interview all who are silent at the regular meetings, or simply at the consecration meetings?

Ans. These two questions are essentially one. Wisdom and common-sense as well as faithfulness should be exercised, of course, in regard to all such matters, and the interview of the lookout committee should take place whenever it will do the most good. The consecration and roll-call meeting gives the best opportunity to show who is absent without excuse, but if an active member is habitually absent from or silent in the regular meetings he should be reminded of his duty. While the lookout committee should avoid anything that looks like officiousness, its great danger is that it will not be sufficiently prompt and faithful. Anything that begins to look like habitual or wilful absence or silence should be looked after. The committee is elected by the society for this purpose, and surely cannot be blamed for simply doing its duty.

Ques. Should the president of a society be present at the meetings of the different committees?

Ans. It would be a good plan for him to be present if possible.

Ques. Do you consider it necessary or expedient to require that the president of a Young People's Christian Endeavor Society shall be a member of the church?

Ans. By all means, the president of the society should be a member of the church. There may be good reasons why one of the younger members cannot be a member of the church *for a time*, but the president of the society, being a prominent and conspicuous member, and usually one of the older ones, should set to all the good example of church-membership.

PART IX.

THE LOOKOUT COMMITTEE.

THE LOOKOUT COMMITTEE AND ITS WORK.

A Familiar letter from the President of the United Society.

TO THE LOOKOUT COMMITTEE.

It is about time, I think, that some of the accumulated good things which I have been treasuring up for a long time should be handed over to you. In this part of the book you will find some of them, though the work of the lookout committee is such a prolific subject that I shall not be able to crowd into one issue half the matter that is waiting its turn.

I am often asked which is the most important committee connected with our society. Comparisons are said to be odious, and where each committee is of vital importance in its own sphere, there is no need of instituting comparisons, but I think if I must give up any committee, the last one I would want to part with would be the lookout committee. It is more unique and peculiar to the Christian Endeavor Society than any other. It affords an unrivalled opportunity to do good, and that is the standard value in all the committees.

There is a chance if you are on this committee to exercise all your zeal and wisdom and piety and sanctified sense. Faithful and efficient as are many of our Lookout Committees, we have not begun to exhaust the possibilities which they contain for helping the society and aiding the pastor and blessing the church. Let me divide what I have to say under four short heads. What you can do for the church, for the society as a whole, for the active members, for the associate members. A minister always feels more comfortable, you know, when he gets his sermon well divided up into firstly, secondly, thirdly, fourthly. First,

FOR THE CHURCH.

I will leave this part of your work for you to settle with your own pastor. He is the best adviser. But be sure and lay the matter before him and ask him what he wishes you to do for the church. The very asking of this question and offering of this service in themselves are acts of no small consequence. At the beginning of my pastorate, I remember that two or three young ladies came to me at the close of one of the first prayer-meetings (it was before a Christian Endeavor Society had been established) and said, "What can we do to help you, Mr. Clark? Please let us know, and remember that we are always ready to do what we can for the church and its pastor." That simple assurance gave me new courage for months to come. I may safely leave this division of this little sermon for you and your pastor to subdivide and illustrate, and to add the improvements. If I know anything about your pastor he will give you plenty to do if you cordially offer your services.

FOR THE SOCIETY.

To the Society, as a whole, the lookout committee holds a very important relation. What the "standing committee" is to the church, what the governor's council is to the State, what the president's cabinet is to the nation, such, to some extent, is the lookout committee to the society. This committee is the door through which the new members enter in. What the society shall be, whether careless and inefficient, or faithful, earnest and zealous, will depend largely upon this committee. If the door is opened too wide, so that all who wish come in to the active membership, whether they are earnest Christians or not, the society degenerates swiftly and surely. If, in your term of office, you admit some unfaithful members, you will do the society an injury which half a score of future committees may not be able to remedy. Of course you cannot ensure complete faithfulness, and the highest style of Christian character on the part of every one who joins the society, but it is your duty to make sure that every applicant knows what he is doing, that he has seen the constitution, that he understands the pledge, and that you have his promise, with the help of God, to live up to it.

TO THE ACTIVE MEMBERS.

Here your work intermingles with the labors of some other committees, like the prayer-meeting, the calling committee, etc., and yet it is quite distinct. You should know who among the active members are habitually absent from the meetings; you should find out who, if any, are negligent to their vows; you should take the names of those who do not respond to the roll at the consecration-meeting, and look them up at once. Do not wait until they have forfeited their membership before calling on them, but after the first unexcused absence from a consecration-meeting call on them, and you may be able to save them to the society. Your committee should sit in different parts of the room, if the meeting is a large one, so as to have some oversight of all, in a quiet way. A record book, which you carry in your pocket, and which will show at a glance who are present and who have taken part in each meeting, is a valuable help and easily kept, after you once get accustomed to it. "But," you say, "I do not like to act the part of spy." No one asks you to do this. You are simply asked to do the very duties for which you were chosen when you were elected upon the lookout committee. No one can complain of you for doing your duty. If any active members are willfully unfaithful and obdurate, then let the society drop them after three consecutive unexcused absences from the consecration-meeting. You do not drop them, they drop themselves by their own unfaithfulness. The rule is not a hard one. It is a mistaken kindness to the active member to keep him after he has violated the pledge; it is disastrous to the society to do this.

TO THE ASSOCIATE MEMBERS.

Your relations to the associate members may be exceedingly helpful, if you will but make them so. Remember that every one of them, and, for that matter, every young person in the church and Sunday School is a candidate for active membership in the society, and in the church, and do not be satisfied until you have done all you can to bring this about. Do not be in too much of a hurry to bring them into the society as active members until they give some good evidence of being active Christians, but, on the other hand, do not delay a single week in bringing them in after they are willing to say that they will live for Christ, and do their duty as active members. To sum it all up in a word, your duty is to do all that you can to keep the Society active, earnest, efficient, spiritually-minded. No slight task, is it? But you can do it "through Him who strengtheneth you."

ANOTHER WAY OF HELPING THE SOCIETY.

Bringing just as many of your members as possible under the stimulating influence of Christian Endeavor conventions, conferences, union meetings, etc. These meetings will often do you more good than you imagine, by awakening an interest in the whole society, and by stimulating all to renewed earnestness. A single delegate has often brought back enough inspiration from one of our great conventions to kindle the enthusiasm of a whole society.

Your committee is such an interesting one and the subjects it opens are so prolific that the only trouble is to know where to stop, but I will let others give you their idea of what the lookout committee should be and do. I will only add that observation and correspondence lead me to believe that the great majority of our lookout committees are exceedingly earnest and faithful, and to them is due no small share of the success of our societies. That this may be true of every one is the wish and prayer of your friend.

EYES WIDE OPEN.

BY REV. W. H. G. TEMPLE.

Was there ever so perfect an organization as the Y. P. S. C. E.? It is no inanimate piece of machinery. It thinks, speaks and acts. It watches and works. It is human to the core, and there it is divine. The executive committee is its brains; the musical committee, its voice; the prayer-meeting committee, its heart; the social committee, its hand-grasp; the flower committee, its æsthetic faculty; the missionary committee, its pocket; and the lookout committee, its eyes. There you have it — a man, redeemed, intelligent, cordial, artistic, generous, wide-awake! And as all the other faculties and organs of a man lose some of their value when the eyes are dimmed by blindness or closed in sleep, so the lookout committee stands first on the list. "The light of the body is the eye." The life of our society is its watch-tower force. It is a

LOOK-OUT COMMITTEE.

It casts its eye over the parish, takes in its boundaries, sees "who is who," makes distinctions, searches out those who have escaped attention, discovers real merit in young manhood and womanhood, and resolves to utilize it. It uses pencil and paper freely, makes lists, classifies the persons tabulated as probably active or associate, thoroughly inspects every nook and corner of the special territory under its care, and then, proceeding to definite action, becomes a

LOOK-UP COMMITTEE.

It follows up every advantage, button-holes people, makes personal appeals, extends invitations to each one to become a member, tries for a direct committal to Christianity first, and then accepts the associate position as a temporary compromise; explains all the glowing features of the society, drives home argument with illustration, means business in every interview, never gives up, continues zealous till its time of service expires, and then hands over its unpersuaded list to the succeeding committee.

It is also a

LOOK-IN COMMITTEE.

There are present members in the prayer-meeting to greet, there are absent ones to record. After securing new members it is just as necessary to follow up their attendance. An intermittent society will pulsate a feeble life. Punctuality and persistency go hand in hand. Here is an opportunity for faithful routine work. But suppose members are frequently absent? Then they fall into the grip of this universal guardian of the society's interests, this time under the name of the

LOOK-AFTER COMMITTEE.

In this garb it hunts up the delinquents, goes at them like a sunbeam, not like a thunder-cloud; smiles but does not scold; leads them into friendly conversation, puts on no airs, seeks the reasons for irregularity, draws out carefully and ingeniously the excuses, and then becomes a

LOOK-INTO COMMITTEE

at once. Advises, helps, encourages, restores. But let us return to the prayer-meeting, for this ubiquitous posse of workers has assumed the role of a

LOOK-AROUND COMMITTEE.

Some have dropped in from curiosity; they must be greeted and invited to come again. Some have come according to promise; they must be interviewed and their opinion secured. Some are strangers in the town; they must be made to feel at home. Some have gone through great sorrow, their attire betokens it, their sad faces proclaim it; they must have a hand-grasp and a word of sympathy. In all these duties the eye must never rest. Constantly looking, discriminating, selecting, recognizing. And then, after all this, what? Time is passing. Is there any progress? Have there been any mistakes? Have the past months brought any new feature, any encouraging fact. Is the church feeling the effect of the new spiritual life? Are the objections of the croakers being practically answered? Here is the whole field. Is it being uniformly cultivated? Has each member of this pioneer company been earnest and intelligent in the discharge of his or her various duties? A glance back, a glance forward. So it becomes a

LOOK-OVER COMMITTEE!

Eyes wide open early and late and all the time, this band of servants of the Master is truly a Look-out, Look-up, Look-in, Look-after, Look-into, Look-around, Look-over, but never an Over-look, Committee.

HINTS FOR THE LOOKOUT COMMITTEE.

BY REV. J. C. JACKSON.

1. Hold frequent meetings — certainly not less than once a month, when the monthly report is to be made up, and just before it is presented. Let the entire situation be canvassed at these meetings, and ways and means devised for its betterment.

2. Be all the time on the lookout for new members. Explain to young people what the society is and does. Get from the church books a complete list of the young people of the congregation and Sunday School for material upon which to work, and add to it from the outside. Use this list at every committee-meeting.

3. Be careful that everybody who comes into the soci-

ety fully understands what he undertakes and promises, especially regarding the prayer-meeting pledge. Keep all supplied with constitutions, and use them.

4. Adopt a systematic marking plan for all the meetings of the society. If not for all, then for the consecration-meeting. Divide the names of the society among the committee; let each member enter his names in a small pass-book, and be responsible for their oversight. Mark those absent from the meeting with a small "a", those present with a cross, and when a member takes part, draw a circle around his name. This marking need not necessarily be done openly in the meeting; this would, perhaps, look rather too much like compulsion, but let each committeeman carry his names in his head during the meeting, mark afterward, and deal accordingly. It will do no harm if it is generally known that this marking system is carried on. Then these books, beside affording data for making visits, etc., will be useful in writing up the monthly report.

5. Kindly look at the work of the other committees, if occasion demands, and assist them in it. Let it be understood that the lookout committee is not meddling when it attends to whatever concerns the welfare of the society, but only minding its own proper constitutional business.

6. Do not make associate members of church-members who are not willing to become active members. Hold a prayer-meeting with them instead. Something is the matter with them.

7. Do not make your associate members' list a black-list of dead-heads and dead-beats. Everybody on it must face inward toward the church. If they insist on facing out, walk them out.

8. Raise money by the envelope system. Do not levy a tax, but let all contributions be voluntary.

9. No age limit can be fixed for membership. "It's a

matter of good health. A person with yellow jaundice is too old at thirteen."

10. The lookout committee has been very properly called "The Pastor's Cabinet." By meeting with it frequently, a live pastor can obtain invaluable information, not to be had elsewhere, regarding the spiritual standing of any one of the young people of his church. By utilizing this committee, he can bring forward many a young person into a decided Christian life or establish him when wandering therein. Let pastors not hesitate to use this committee, and let the lookout committee always hold itself at the service of the pastor.

SOMETHING FOR EACH OF US NOW TO DO.

A HINT FOR THE LOOKOUT AND PRAYER-MEETING COMMITTEES.

The Y. P. S. C. E. of the "Beth-Eden" Baptist Church, Philadelphia, Pa., has recently adopted a method of keeping its members "up to duty," or, at least, up to the requirements of the "pledge" taken. The method is found to be very practicable, in this society at least. On a special evening of each month the members of the prayer-meeting and lookout committees and the chairman of the executive committee meet for the purpose of "looking in" among its own members, some of whom, at times, may be growing delinquent, and are thus failing to let their light shine. After a brief review of the past month regarding the benevolent and social work undertaken and accomplished, at which point obstacles that may have hindered are removed and new work is planned, the actual benefit of the weekly prayer-meeting is discussed. Each member of the prayer-meeting and lookout committees receives at the outset a list of five or six names from the roll of members, whom they pledge themselves to look after, and the attendance of every active member at the last consecration-meeting and any part taken therein by them is reported from these lists and thus satisfactorily checked up on the schedule. This scrutiny includes, of course, the committees whose names head the list, for they believe in the maxim, "Physician, Heal Thyself." In this growing society, this method is already bringing about satisfactory results, and while no idea of compulsion is conveyed or felt, each conscientious member believes it to be "a good plan."

SUGGESTION FOR LOOKOUT COMMITTEES.

Rev. H. W. Pope, of Palmer, Mass., sends us this admirable card for use after consecration-meetings:

DEAR FRIEND: We noticed with regret your absence from our last consecration-meeting, especially as no response was given, nor reason for absence rendered.

If, at any time in the future you are obliged to be absent from the consecration-meeting, we trust that you will send us a word of greeting, at least, which is always gladly received, and is also in accordance with the rules of our society.

Fraternally yours,
THE LOOKOUT COMMITTEE.

In many societies the chairman of the lookout committee makes a record of the absentees from each meeting and sends to the members of his committee a slip of paper, with the following printed at the top:

TO THE LOOKOUT COMMITTEE:

The following members of our society were absent from the last meeting. Will you please ascertain the reasons for their absence? Note them upon the back of this slip and return it to me as soon as possible.

This seems an excellent method, ensuring careful and unofficious attention to each delinquent member, and enabling the chairman to see that the right person is sent at the right time to perform this difficult task.

COVENANT REMINDERS.

Rev. A. B. Christy, pastor of the College Hill Church, of Hudson, O., has prepared for the lookout committee of his Y. P. S. C. E. three forms of calling attention to absence from the consecration-meeting. All bear the clause of the constitution referring to absence from the monthly meeting, and all are signed by the chairman of the lookout committee. The first bears this message:

"It is our duty to ask why you were absent unexcused from our last consecration-meeting."

The second reads:

"It is our duty to ask why you were absent unexcused from our last consecration-meeting. This is your second consecutive absence."

The third is as follows:

"We regret that you have been absent from three consecutive consecration-meetings unexcused. We trust that you do not wish to leave the society, but have a good excuse."

These reminders pave the way for the personal interviews with the delinquent members.

PART X.

PRAYER-MEETING COMMITTEE.

HINTS FOR THE PRAYER-MEETING COMMITTEE.

SIX SUGGESTIONS BY REV. J. C. JACKSON.

1. Let each member of this committee be ready to speak or pray when a pause occurs — to fill any gap.

2. Pick out texts to read, or appropriate verses of poetry, and assign them in advance of the meeting to timid members, so that these timid members may have something to do.

3. Privately ask certain ones before the meeting to be ready to take part during any pause, or whenever a chance is given. Make preparation in advance to keep things moving.

4. Appoint two ushers, or more, to seat strangers and new-comers — a sort of "smile-'em-up" committee — to show people to the front seats.

5. Let the leader, or committee, put the subject and texts upon a blackboard, so that all can see them at once upon entering.

6. Let the Leader see to it that he is on hand promptly to open the meeting at the last stroke of the bell.

A SUGGESTION BY E. D. WHEELOCK.

From E. D. Wheelock, of Elkhart, Ind., we have received the following suggestion, which we are glad to publish for the benefit of those committees to which the plan may not already have occurred:

"You find it difficult to get some of the members of your Society to lead a meeting. They are too diffident and have never done such a thing. Suppose you appoint two leaders for each meeting, and let them arrange the meeting and the part they are each to take in leading it. Put a weak member and one of more strength and confidence together. The stronger will bear the chief burden, and the weaker will not hesitate to read the Scripture or to conduct the song service, and the very fact of having once been in the leader's chair will make him more ready to lead alone when necessary. At least one society has tried this plan, and with excellent effect both on the meetings and the timid members who took the part of assistant leaders."

"GENERAL UTILITY MEN."

The expression applies most admirably to the members of the prayer-meeting committee of a Y. P. S. C. E. in Ashaway, R. I. A correspondent has informed us of some of the duties devolving on this committee. Each member takes his turn in bearing the responsibility of the meetings. He sends the notice of the meeting and the subject to the pulpit, selects the leader and stands ready to take charge of the meeting if the appointed leader fails to appear. The members also endeavor to suppress the levity of the "gigglers," by sitting among them, on the back seats and in the far-away corners, and by showing themselves examples of devout and reverent demeanor. Moreover, some of the committee each week act as ushers, welcome strangers, etc. And finally, they make the meetings the subject of private prayer during the week, and consider it their duty to fill awkward pauses in the services. Our correspondent concludes her report with these words: "Need I say that the bi-monthly reports of the committee show a more prayerful spirit in the meetings, a greater consecration among the members and a deeper conscientiousness in keeping the pledge?" Truly, such results as these are eloquent tributes to the faithfulness of any committee, and some of these methods might well be adopted by prayer-meeting committees who find it hard to report any kind of progress.

THE WORK OF THE PRAYER-MEETING COMMITTEE.

A PAPER READ AT THE CHICAGO CONVENTION, BY M. A. HUDSON, OF SYRACUSE, N. Y.

The "Gospel of Work," or "Good Tidings of Work," has come to the young people, and they have come to love their prayer-meeting as one of the places in which to do their work. This love of the prayer-meeting has largely come about by the faithful work of the prayer-meeting committee.

It has justly been said that "the prayer-meeting committee is the captain of our companies of Christian Endeavor." No campaign can be successful unless there be not only the wise and able commander-in-chief, but skillful and loyal captains.

"This committee shall have charge of the weekly prayer meeting, see that a leader and topic are provided for each meeting, and shall do what it can to secure faithfulness to the prayer-meeting pledge."

The important work of choosing leaders and topics should be the first duty of this committee after it has organized, held a short prayer-meeting, and elected a secretary. Quite frequently, in choosing leaders, those who have never led before should be selected. A committee should then visit them, and gain their consent. To do this will require tact, but very little difficulty will be found, if this committee will assure them of hearty support at the meeting they are to lead. Their preference as to the date and the topic should be consulted. As for topics, there are none better than those issued by She United Society, although local needs may occasionally require one of a different character. For instance, to have the meetings varied, the music, temperance, or missionary committee should be invited to take charge of a meeting, and may have a special topic. In some societies, the Bible trainers' classes take one evening for a Bible reading.

After the leaders and topics are arranged, have topic cards printed in a neat and attractive manner.

The topic cards should be placed within easy reach of every member of the society, at least one week before the first meeting.

A good plan by which to help and encourage the leader, and also to notify him that his time to lead has arrived, is to have the chairman of the committee write him a letter a week before his meeting, assuring him of the committee's prayers and support. Scripture helps upon the topic and hymns bearing upon the subject may be given him. He should be assured of the prayers and support of the other committees. The social committee should be seen and asked to provide an usher and singing-books for the strangers and new members. The music committee should be invited to gather promptly around the organ with their leader. A series of short sentence-prayers can be arranged for the leader, and several who always wait until the last to testify can be invited to be first.

A list of the active members placed upon two small pocket memorandum-books, and left with two members of the prayer-meeting committee, is of great service in helping this committee to "do what it can to secure faithfulness to the prayer-meeting pledge." These books can be quietly marked during the meeting, *e. g.*, A for absence, No. 1 for present, and 2 for took part. In this manner a record of the faithfulness of each member is placed on file.

At the close of the month, when the chairman presents his written report, he can take the names of those who do not attend, and give them to the lookout committee, "that they may again interest them in the work."

A list of those who have not been faithful to their pledge ("to take some part") should be made, and after much prayer, and with the pastor's advice, they should be visited, with a view to their future faithfulness. If you are successful, encourage them with your sympathy and thanks for their faithfulness.

The leader, after each meeting, should be encouraged by some kindly mention of the meeting he has just led.

The duties of this committee should not end with the Endeavor prayer-meeting; for the regular services of the church claim our support. So let us try to induce more and more of our society members to attend the church prayer-meetings, and let their voices be heard there. Several committees have provided subjects for prayer for every day in the week; others have provided daily Bible readings and Bible trainers' classes. We have come to love our prayer-meetings; let us learn to love our Bibles. The class of which I have been a member two and a half years has been a source of strength to all the members. Children's and cottage prayer-meetings have been held by this committee, and have been the means of great good. With all our plans, let us not forget the source of all our help, and in closing I would urge upon this committee in the words of another — "Pray for the meeting. Pray for the pastor. Pray for the active and associate members. Pray, pray, keep on praying, and God will bless you and your meetings."

MORE HINTS FOR THE PRAYER-MEETING COMMITTEE.

BY MISS C. A. BARTLETT.

Preparation for the prayer-meeting is, in part, the duty of the leader, but it is, also, the special province of the prayer-meeting committee, for so the constitution provides:

"This committee shall have in charge the prayer-meeting, and shall see that a topic is assigned and a leader appointed for every meeting, and shall do what it can to secure faithfulness to the prayer-meeting pledge."

We are here told first that the committee shall have in charge the prayer-meeting. This includes not only preparation for, but assistance in, the meeting. There should be frequent committee-meetings, and that meeting will be found most helpful which is preceded by a devotional exercise. Thus encouraged and strengthened, bring into the work of planning for the meetings the united inventive genius of the whole committee. In so doing let each individual member be impressed with a sense of personal responsibility for the success of every meeting, from which they are not released until its close.

THE TOPIC.

Our next duty is to assign a topic. This requires rare wisdom and experience, and will often be a hard task to new and inexperienced committees. For this reason we heartily commend the use of the uniform topics. Nothing could be more admirable than these topics and their arrangement for the past year.

THE LEADER.

The next thing on our list of duties is the appointment of a leader. To do this we should aim to have the largest possible number of leaders, and to include in this the weak and timid as well as the strong and courageous. One of the best meetings our society ever held was led by a young girl of fifteen, who, on account of great timidity, had long refused to take the meeting. In selecting leaders from among the active members give an opportunity to all, but do not over-urge any. Leading a meeting should not be obligatory upon the active members, yet it is a privilege which few will refuse. In some societies the leaders are called upon in alphabetical order. This method has the advantage of giving all a share in sustaining the meetings at equal intervals of time. Now that we have provided topics and leaders, I fear that too often we feel that the obligations of the prayer-meeting committee are discharged. Our duties are only begun, and we have entered upon the hardest part of committee work, for it is a delicate and difficult task to fulfill the obligations embodied in the last clause of the article — "And shall do what it can to secure faithfulness to the prayer-meeting pledge." Too much emphasis cannot be placed upon this duty of the committee. It is an essential part that is too often overlooked or passed by as unimportant.

THE SHY AND THE CARELESS.

For many reasons there are often some in our meetings who fail to keep their prayer-meeting pledge. There are the diffident members, the uninterested members, the careless members, and finally there are the members who are satisfied to do a very little if they but keep the letter of their pledge. Upon the prayer-meeting committee devolves the task of reaching these members in some way and encouraging them to better service. There is but one sure and effective way of doing this, and that by individual effort; intelligent, systematic, but unobtrusive personal effort on the part of the committee.

In a large society the needed individual work may be simplified by giving to each member of the committee a portion of the names of the active members. Their individual characteristics may then be studied, and the plans adapted to suit them. This work must be carefully and prayerfully done, that it may be just the right thing needed, and give no offence. Of course, mistakes will occur, but these should only stimulate us to greater activity.

SOME GOOD METHODS.

Sometimes a happily-expressed wish, or a bit of personal experience, casually given, will bring about the desired result. Stanzas of some beautiful hymn or poem, given to a few of the diffident members, and read at the meeting, often add much to the interest. Let us also try to have more prayers in our meetings. They are needful to make the meetings spiritually helpful. As it is hard for many to respond to an unexpected call for prayers, we have found it helpful to previously ask a few members to respond to the appeal of the leader, or voluntarily offer prayer at some definite time. A series of one-sentence prayers brings forth wonderful results, both in raising the tone of the meeting, and in giving courage to the most timid. Do not let the prayers be long, or the sentences so involved as to be difficult to follow. Earnestness, brevity and alacrity are three essentials to the success of this plan.

To secure freshness and interest in the meetings variety of programme is needed. For this the temperance and missionary meetings offer a wide range.

Our last consecration meeting is worthy of mention. Letters were addressed to all of the absent active members, stating the subject of the meeting, and requesting them to send some expression of their feelings, to be read at roll-call. Letters were also addressed to all of the resident active members explaining the object of the meeting, and requesting their co-operation in making the meeting a success. Every answer at roll-call was read (as had been requested), thus securing brevity and directness of thought and expression.

These are only a few of the methods that may be employed by the prayer-meeting committee, but we know them to be practicable. Yet so varied are the needs of different societies, that they may not be of practical value to all. It is best decided by a careful study of your particular society, and wisdom will be given you to plan wisely for it.

A PRAYER-MEETING LETTER.

The following letter we consider a model of its kind. We therefore publish it, that committees desiring to send a similar communication may gain some suggestions from it:

DEAR FRIEND:
While as a society we must all feel that we have gained in prompt service in our meetings, and that, while we have had no great spiritual awakening, we have gained spiritual good to our own souls, let us not shrink from acknowledging the great work still undone. We still are not, at all times, ready enough to speak for Jesus. We do not pray enough. We ask from you a sense of greater personal responsibility. We ask you to feel that the success of each meeting depends largely on the part you take. If we love Jesus we shall feel this responsibility. If we do not, something is the trouble and we had better look into our own hearts. We ask a great deal. Christ demands much. He gives infinitely more than He demands.

Yours for more active service,
PRAYER-MEETING COMMITTEE.

SOME NEW YEAR LETTERS.

It is a custom, growing in favor at the beginning of the year, for prayer-meeting committees to send to the various members of their Christian endeavor societies letters containing reminders of the necessity of reconsecrated effort during the coming year. We give below a few such letters, which seem to us excellent in style and contents. The first is from the Presbyterian Y. P. S. C. E. of Cedar Falls, Ia.:

DEAR FRIENDS:
We are now entering upon another period of service for the Master. Will it be a "labor of love" with you? Are you ready with a firm endeavor to do active work for Him in our society and community this winter? We have plenty of work to do, let us join heart and hand and "do with our might what our hands find to do." When a call is made, will you be ready to respond with a hearty "Here, Lord, send me"? Will you endeavor to attend each meeting and come from your closet with His Spirit in your heart and His words on your lips, and earnestly endeavor to fulfill all your pledges to your Master? Please lend us your help.

The next is from one of the societies of Evanston, Ill.:

Our Society of Christian Endeavor has just entered upon a new year's work. We are sure that you feel a deep interest in the society and are ready to do your part toward making our prayer-meetings more interesting and helpful. This can be accomplished by all members doing the most and best they can, which means preparing for the meetings, attending regularly and taking part. If you have been in the habit of reading a verse of Scripture only, it would help both yourself and the meeting if you would, standing, either read a sentence or two bearing on the subject or give some personal testimony. We know that if we all do our part, the meetings will not fail to be helpful to all who may attend. Will you not invite your friends to meet with us, if they do not attend a similar meeting elsewhere, and pray that all of our society may be greatly blessed this winter?

Finally, is one signed by all the members of the prayer-meeting committee of the society in Concord, Mass.:

On Sunday evening, Jan. 6th, occurs the regular quarterly roll-call and consecration-meeting. Beginning, as it does, a new year, we feel that every member should make an effort to be present, and answer to his or her name. It is proposed, that upon that evening we repeat in concert our prayer-meeting pledge, as one of the exercises. The committee would also suggest that any member, active or associate, unable to be present, shall write a verse of appropriate Scripture, signing their name and sending to the prayer-meeting committee before the meeting. Let us all remember our motto, "For Christ and the Church."

MINUTE MEN.

One of the societies in Philadelphia has the following good plan: The prayer-meeting committee has appointed twelve "minute men," whose duty it is to see that there is no pause at the opening of the meeting. Their special work is at the very beginning, as soon as the leader has concluded. They are to take hold of the "cold end" of the meeting.

CAREFUL PREPARATION.

The prayer-meeting committee of the Clinton Avenue Congregational Y. P. S C. E., of Brooklyn, evidently offers no idleness to its members. The members have decided that their work is not accomplished when the topics and leaders are selected; they go to the prayer-meeting, feeling that their chief duty awaits them. Each member of the committee promises to take part in every meeting by prayer or remarks, to help diffident and neglectful members of the society, and to keep the society in mind daily, at the hour of prayer, beseeching God's blessing on its work and workers. It is not strange that the meetings, for which such careful preparation is made, are filled with spiritual power.

SUGGESTIONS FOR THE CHRISTIAN ENDEAVOR PRAYER-MEETING.

BY REV. EDWARD A. ROBINSON.

1. Let every member feel a responsibility for every meeting.
2. Be punctual and sit as far forward as possible.
3. Take part early in the meeting, the earlier the better.
4. Speak so that all may hear. "Whatsoever ye do, . . . do it heartily as unto the Lord."
5. Vary the part that you take in the meeting.

(*a*) Please sing hymn No. —. Is this really taking part?

(*b*) Verse of Scripture.

(*c*) Verse of Scripture with a testimony added.

(*d*) Short quotation of prose or poetry.

(*e*) A word of your own on the subject for the evening.

(*f*) A sentence prayer.

(*g*) A brief prayer, but longer than (*f*).

6. Commit to memory Psalms 1, 23, 24, 91 and 103, in order to be able to repeat them in unison, as may be desired, in opening a meeting.

7. Help the leader, or any speaker; especially if a young Christian has helped you, tell him of it.

8. Be on the watch for helpful suggestions and try to secure their adoption.

9. Greet any new-comer or stranger present at the meeting.

10. Think of the meetings; talk of them, pray for them, work for them, and God will surely bless them.

PART XI.

THE SOCIAL COMMITTEE.

SUGGESTIONS FOR THE SOCIAL COMMITTEE.

A Familiar Letter from the President of the United Society.

Fault has sometimes been found with the Christian Endeavor Society for not making the social element prominent enough. Sometimes it is said with a sneer, "Oh, that is nothing but a prayer-meeting society." I think the society can stand a good many such sneers, and the fact that there is any ground for them is one of the best proofs that it is true to its real purpose.

SOME THINGS TAKE CARE OF THEMSELVES.

There are parts of our nature that need very little stimulus, and the social part is one of these with most young people. It is hardly necessary to urge most of you to be socially inclined, jovial and full of fun. These things are all important, and when I see young people growing long-faced and lugubrious and melancholy, I will write a special letter on the importance of joviality. I don't expect to find it necessary this year, however.

Still, the Society of Christian Endeavor is something more than a prayer-meeting, and one of the departments of life which it need not stimulate, but should direct into the best channels. is the social department.

THE SOCIAL COMMITTEE.

For this reason, the social committee is very important. It requires as much sanctified common-sense among its members as any other on the whole list. It is not true that it can be made up of any members who are good nowhere else. The ideal social committee will be composed of earnest, consecrated young Christians, with much life and vigor and ingenuity, with a warm hand-grasp for strangers as well as for friends, and plenty of common-sense to give the needed balance. It will not allow anything at the social gatherings which will offend the moral sense of the church, and yet it will use so much wit and care in preparing for each occasion of the sort, that the old phrase "dull as a social," will never apply to the Christian Endeavor gatherings.

THE SCOPE OF THEIR EFFORTS.

The members of the social committee will not feel that they have by any means accomplished their work when they have provided the monthly or semi-monthly social, but will feel that in a certain sense all the social interests of the young people are under their care. We cannot do each other much good unless we know each other, and the work of the social committee is all summed up in a sentence when we say that it exists to make people acquainted with one another. It is helped by, and in its turn helps, the lookout, calling, relief and Sunday School committees, and, in fact, almost every committee, and yet it has a distinct work of its own to do, in making people feel at home in the church.

SPECIFIC WAYS.

It will let no stranger come into the prayer-meeting room without giving him a hearty hand-shake and welcome, and will not let him out again without introducing him to half a dozen members of the society. Some of its members will stand in the vestibule of the church on Sunday morning and Sunday evening, if the church approves, to give an equally hearty welcome to new-comers, especially if they are young people. It will not allow a new family to remain very long in the community without quietly finding out something about its religious proclivities, and giving its members an invitation to church and Sunday

School and Christian endeavor meeting. It will occasionally, perhaps, under the guidance of the church and pastor, and in connection with some of the other committees, make a canvass of the neighborhood with special invitations. Possibly a careful and systematic religious census can be undertaken. It will, of course, be very sure to have the best possible social gathering with no wall-flowers, no cliques and no unseemly boisterousness. The proprieties of the place will be remembered, but the "proprieties" will not prevent an out and out good time of the right sort.

A REAL DIFFICULTY.

A real difficulty arises from the great diversity of ages in many societies. What the children enjoy the older young people do not particularly enjoy, and what the older ones like is voted "stupid" by the children. Sometimes this trouble can be overcome by having two socials at about the same time for different ages, in one of which certain games for children can be introduced. In other places it will be better to devote part of the evening to the entertainment of the younger ones, and another part to exercises that the older ones more enjoy.

A VEXED QUESTION.

The question of what kinds of entertainment are proper, or whether it is ever best to raise money by entertainments or suppers, is perplexing some. I have little counsel to offer, but hope each society will consult its own pastor and church officers on the subject. Personally, while I think the systematic plan of giving is by far the best, and one which I hope will be universally adopted by all our societies, I see no harm in having a social once a year where some money will be raised for a good object in some appropriate way that the church approves.

THE GREAT SAFEGUARD.

After all, the great safeguard in these matters is to keep the social element and the entertainment idea in the right place. If it is understood that these things are only tributary to spiritual development and to the highest religious life, no harm but only good can result from them. Every social may be as much blessed as a prayer-meeting, and even an entertainment may be a means of grace, if it is constantly borne in mind that the object of every department of our work is, as our constitution says, "to make us more useful in the service of God." If that is kept steadily in mind, the social element cannot usurp or supplant the devotional, but the two will work together to make the devotional more social and the social more devotional, and both elements will bring us nearer to Him who was no ascetic recluse, but who went about doing good.

Your friend,
FRANCIS E. CLARK.

PLANS FOR SOCIALS.

THE NAME SOCIABLE.

Into this office, and into the hands of persons who go out to speak at anniversaries and conventions of societies of endeavor, the inquiries, like flakes of snow, come floating along — "What kind of an entertainment can you suggest to us? We have tried almost everything." To this oft-recurring interrogatory it is easy to state in the case of newly-organized societies what their first form of entertainment should be. It ought to be a name sociable. A gentleman or lady who writes a plain, open hand sits at a table near the door of entrance. As each guest makes his entrance he is asked his name by the social committee, and a lable is attached to him indicating to the company, wherever he goes, just who he is. While a person is being catechized as to his name, and is being supplied with a lable, which is pinned on by still others of the social committee, if tact is used, a stranger in the society begins to feel that a very pleasant acquaintance is begun.

Formalism has been broken down, and that at the start. Although it may never have been confessed, it is something deplorable to find how many strangers there are to each other in any large society. When these badges are placed upon persons, they are construed as the equivalent of an introduction, between those who meet, by the social committee. Whenever any one is to be announced to sing or play, his badge is taken off and held up and read, and then replaced. He goes by his ticket. The introductions must be in this form: A. B. and C. D. being brought together, the label on each is read to the other. Now to keep up the interest, let there be a platterful of pasteboard letters placed in an accessible position in the largest room of the house. One picks out the letters that compose the word Constantinople, or the word echo, and hands them to a friend to find out what word can be spelled with those letters. This game of anagrams has this desirable feature, it enables one to approach the timid members of the party. When the beginnings of acquaintance are made, the responsibilities of a social committee are over. One having guessed the word himself can turn over the letters to some person who has been receiving little attention, and thus have the wall-flowers brought up into the pretty group that surrounds the centre-table.

METHODS FOR SOCIAL ENTERTAINMENT.

BY MISS H. E. COLBURN.

You will pardon me, I trust, if, before giving the methods for social entertainment, I speak of the object of social entertainments.

Its chief object is the object of all the Christian Endeavor work, the bringing together of young lives for mutual helpfulness in serving Christ.

Youth has a right to be joyful, and usually seeks merriment of a pure, invigorating nature when it can be obtained; but when the best is not at hand, it too often partakes of the perverted and harmful.

In this busy life of ours we must have some recreation. "All work and no play makes Jack a dull boy," is always correct. The show boards, lecture courses, and social announcements reveal the demand for entertainments of all kinds and degrees.

Our young men and young women will have social enjoyment, and if the Christian Endeavor Society does not make its socials attractive, those for whom we should be most earnestly working and who most need Christian influence leave us and go elsewhere. In the larger cities especially, when these young people leave us, we know not whither they are led nor in what wicked diversion they may ultimately participate.

WHOLESOME SOCIALS.

We must make the Christian Endeavor Society enter into the lives of our young people in every way we can. There has been more than one young life brought into the Christian Endeavor Society, and then into the church, through the attraction of the socials. Our object, then, must be to have entertainments that will help our young people to the highest living, at the same time encourage and cultivate a desire for a good, wholesome, helpful, happy time.

The duties of the social committee as given in the constitution are well known. However, the welcoming of strangers, and the kind, sympathetic word to the diffident, should not be left entirely to the social committee, but should be the beautiful privilege of every member of the society. It is through these social chats that we come to know of the every-day life; of the burdens that some are carrying, and thus we may help them bear their load and tell them of the Great Comforter who will aid us in all sorrows if we but ask Him.

In choosing the committee for work at the socials, there should be at least five or six members, and the work be divided, one-half having charge of refreshments, if any, the other providing the literary or other entertainment.

The time for refreshments seems best at the beginning, both for those who serve and those who participate, and should be followed by the literary or musical programme. If there is any one who thinks refreshments unnecessary, let me tell him that in the reports I have received from different societies nearly every one suggests refreshments as a part of the entertainment, at least occasionally.

ENTERTAINMENTS SUGGESTED.

Any society can choose its own methods, these being merely hints, and not in any sense official programmes. They are appropriate and simple. They will not offend the taste of the most fastidious, and, while taking little time to prepare, will be sufficiently novel to interest those who come, and to warrant charging a small admission fee. Do not forget to tell something about the aims and growth and needs of the Christian endeavor movement if opportunity serves.

A COLONIAL SUPPER.

A very simple entertainment would be to provide an old-fashioned supper, in which the dishes our forefathers indulged in may be provided. The waiters may be dressed, if thought best, in colonial style.

A POP-CORN SOCIABLE. — BY MITCHELLA.

Having never heard of this idea being used anywhere but by our own young people, I give it to you, thinking it may at least be a suggestion to some social committee.

In giving the notice, ask each member to bring some article made from pop-corn that his neighbor may carry away as a souvenir. Let the committee receive and place these, unwrapped, upon a screened table. At **a signal,** form the company into marching order, take away the screen, and, having marched around the table once, that all may see the articles, distribute at the second passing around this table. We had some very pretty articles, a tiny chaise, made by stringing the corn on fine wire, with a little driver sitting up very straight on a burnt-corn seat, holding reins made of pop-corn fragments glued on to baby ribbon; shields, stars, fans, pictures and frames, made by rolling and sometimes coloring the corn; a number of dolls, tissue paper helping the wardrobe, and a sweet rooster which was good enough to eat, all but the feathers, for it was a massive corn-ball moulded into shape.

Have ready tissue paper bags — they are pretty made of different colors — filled with corn popped, and number them for one-half the number present, duplicate these numbers, and ask the company to whom you give the bags to find the person with the corresponding number, so that they may eat the corn together. This will promote sociability. We had a barrel of good apples rolled in — you may hide the rough exterior by colored shelf-paper, put on like ruffles, with tacks, the upper edge covered by pasting a piece of bordering around it — and allowed the company to help themselves.

Into the bags of corn may be put quotations of familiar prose and poetry, which are to be read by the holders, and see who can tell the greatest number of authors quoted.

A FLOWER SOCIAL.

The following suggestion, although it involves more intellectual effort than some may desire, is a good one, and is worthy of trial by the social committee.

Have a large bouquet composed of as many different flowers as possible. Then let the main feature of the evening be to see how great a variety of good English words can be formed from first the initial and then the final letters of the names of the flowers. To increase the sociability of the evening, let there be a number of button-hole bouquets made, equal to number of guests expected, one-half of which must be duplicates of the other half. These are placed in two baskets, from one of which each gentleman, from the other each lady as she enters, is given a bouquet. Those who possess duplicates are supposed to entertain each other for the evening.

A TAG SOCIAL.

To combine instruction, sociability and amusement in an evening's entertainment is not always an easy task. The following form of entertainment has been tried, and, as it proved a success, we give it to our readers for what it is worth. We called it a "Tag Social." To start with, a little calculation will be necessary. Estimate the number of guests expected to attend. This will guide you in the number of tags to prepare.

For example, if two hundred persons are expected, purchase two hundred medium size manilla tags. One hundred must be numbered from one to one hundred. Make the second hundred duplicates of the first. The committee will then carefully prepare one hundred questions, historical, scientific, religious, practical and humorous; the questions should be written on one set of the tags, and the answer to each one on the tag bearing the duplicate number, in legible hand. On the evening of the entertainment the reception committee should stand at the door, and as the guests arrive, give out the tags promiscuously, with the simple injunction, "Find your duplicate." In a very brief time, every one in the room will be eagerly seeking his duplicate, which has either the question or answer. Formality disappears. Introductions are not considered necessary. Sometimes two ladies hold duplicates, sometimes two gentlemen. There is no attempt at "pairing off" the company, nor is either party expected to devote himself to the entertainment of the other during

the evening. Having found their duplicate, enjoyed a
laugh over the conundrum, or expressed pleasure at the
sentiment of the poetical quotation, they pass on to see
what their neighbor has, or to exchange tags with some
one else. By this time the company are pretty well
acquainted, and thoroughly alive to the scheme. The
chairman of the evening steps to the platform, touches a
bell, which is a signal for silence. The chatter ceases;
some find seats, some stand. A musical number or recitation is announced, after which the master of ceremonies,
who has prepared a complete list of the questions and
answers according to the number, proceeds to call the
question numbers from his list, and the holder of the
duplicate number answers him as he proceeds. Answers
come from all parts of the room, so that all have the benefit of the fun, sentiment and wisdom of the whole series of
questions given out. After calling eight or ten numbers
there is another pause, and music, vocal or instrumental,
is introduced; then follows the calling of more numbers,
with music at intervals, until the list is exhausted. A fit-
ting supplement to this "feast of reason and flow of soul,"
as a closing feature of the programme, is the serving of
lemonade and cake.

EVENINGS WITH AMERICAN AUTHORS.

From Malden, Mass., we have received the following
scheme for an entertainment, which seems to us unusually
good. We have no doubt that it will favorably impress
many social committees, who are now racking their brains
for "just the right thing." F. D. G. thus describes the
plan:

Twelve of the leading authors will be sufficient for one
evening. Let us take poets: Longfellow, Whittier, Bryant,
and Lowell; novelists: Cooper and Hawthorne; preach-
ers: Jonathan Edwards, William Channing; essayists: Irving and Emerson; orators: Webster and Choate. Assign
each author to one person and get him to look up an

extract from some of the author's writings to recite, and also something interesting to relate about the author's life or work. We found it best to allow eight or ten minutes to each speaker, and to give out the parts a month before, so as to have time enough to study up. Get the music committee to furnish a little music for the evening. When the time comes to "open the meeting," it is best to have the president or chairman of the social committee explain the scheme, viz.: each speaker will first give his selection, then the chairman will give opportunity to the audience to guess the author, and, last, the speaker will relate the biography. Not more than one minute should be spent guessing. If they can't guess correctly just go on, and tell them without waiting. In this way, a pleasant and profitable evening may be passed. Of course it is not necessary to take American authors, for the English poets or the English novelists may be studied on the same plan.

CONVERSATION TOPIC CARD.

Our request for suggestions for social gatherings has been most kindly replied to by various societies. From the Park Street Y. P. S. C. E. of Boston, and from Oxford, Penn., come accounts of a novel method of inducing sociability, which may be described as follows: Cards with ten or fifteen topics of conversation and blank spaces for names are distributed early in the evening, and the gentlemen are given time to fill out the blanks. When the bell sounds, the gentleman finds the lady whose name is opposite topic number one, and converses with her on that subject until the bell sounds again, when he finds lady number two, and so on throughout the entire list. From two to five minutes are given to each subject, according to the number of topics. The society in Oxford made a slight modification of this plan, which is especially desirable where the feeling of sociability is not general and where there are more ladies than gentlemen. Instead of allowing each gentleman to choose the ladies with whom he talks, the cards are filled beforehand by the social committee, thus providing that no one is left alone at any time.

From many societies that have tried this plan, we have received enthusiastic reports of its success. See if it doesn't work well in your society.

TETE-A-TETE SOCIALS.

As a further explanation of the plan for tête-à-tête socials, given in the Exchange of November 22, we publish a portion of a letter received from the Christian Endeavor Society in Bath, N. Y., where the plan has been successfully carried out :

"At eight o'clock about eighty had assembled, when the pastor announced that it was time to fill the programmes for the conversations. All formalities were laid aside, young ladies asking the young gentlemen for conversations, as well as the young men asking the ladies. The gentleman wrote his name on the card belonging to the young lady, and she wrote her name on his card, opposite the subject they were to converse upon. The members of the social committee were careful to see that all were supplied with partners during each conversation; and, if they found any one who was seemingly neglected, it was but a moment before they and their partners were conversing with that one. With such a spirit, the committee carried our social through to a grand success, so much so that it will be repeated soon. The conversations were each of five minutes' length."

The subjects, neatly printed on white cards, were :

1st, The Weather. 2nd, Parades. 3rd, Our Society. 4th, Favorite Books. 5th, Music. 6th, What's the News? 7th, Traveling. 8th, Our Neighbors.

CIRCULATING LIBRARY SOCIAL.

A young people's society in Bennington, Vt., has recently given a successful "Circulating Library Social." Mrs. C. R. Seymour kindly furnishes the details of this somewhat unique entertainment.

"Members of the company are dressed to represent some book or character of a book. A band is pinned across the back, between the shoulders, lettered with the title or name of the character assumed. A belt around the waist has on it the name of the author. The 'books' march around the room to music, then to the platform, where they are arranged in tiers (by means of boxes of different heights) with backs to the audience. The large lettering in rows makes a fine show of volumes.

"A librarian who is well read addresses the audience, describing the books in the order in which they are shelved. The success of the entertainment depends largely upon the wit of the librarian. As the title of each book is named, it faces the company. Sometimes as in the case of Topsy, in 'Uncle Tom's Cabin,' the character sings or recites. After all are described the public are invited to subscribe to the Circulating Library, and each person is allowed to take a book home."

AN "S" SOCIAL.

The following programme of an "S" social, held in connection with a missionary society at Chicago, may be suggestive to some social committee·

SMALL SPE**S**CIE SOCIAL.

Second Sun after Sunday.

SEVEN SIXTY SHARP.

Section 1.

Selected Music, ... Sonatrice.
Some Missionary Statements.
Selection from Shakespeare, . . . Somebody.
Securing Society Shekels.

Section 2.

"Speech is Silvern."

Strange Customs, ...

Side Show, ...

Systematic Study,

. . . .

Sympathy,

. . . .

Scenes in a City,

. . . .

Selected,

. . . .

TETE-A-TETE AGAIN.

The tête-à-tête social has evidently been a favorite this winter, but sometimes the social committee, having made their general plans, are troubled to find fresh and interesting subjects for conversation. From a conversation order used by the Y. P. S. C. E. of the Second Congregational Church of Attleboro, at a recent social, we have taken the following subjects. These conversations were interspersed with music, and several subjects were appointed for each conversation, so that each couple of conversationalists could find something to their choice: "How to Make a Sociable Social," "Our Favorite Book," "Is Conversation a Lost Art?" "Jewelry," "One-cent Postage," "The Inauguration," "Admission of the Chinese into Our Country," "Wheat Crops," and, just before supper, "Will You have Some Refreshments?"

CHINESE FAN AND LANTERN FESTIVAL.

Since in so many of our cities our young people are interested in Chinese Sunday Schools, and are learning how grateful these Orientals are, and how generously they evince their appreciation at times, we feel that the following ingenious entertainment might be available in other places than in the Congregational Church of South Norwalk, Conn., where it was so successfully tried. We give the account in the words of Mr. John Francis, president of the society:

"A Chinese Fan and Lantern Festival was recently held in the chapel, which was beautifully decorated with fans, lanterns, Chinese curios, etc. A band of Chinese scholars and visitors was present, some of whom rendered selections on the 'yee-gin,' 'juk-come,' and other instruments. This, with singing, reading and recitations in Chinese, made a very interesting programme. A large and beautiful selection of fans was secured, and the purchase of a fan was the price of admission. Mr. Lee Hong, of Sacramento, Cal., placed his autograph on many fans, and greatly aided the committee in making the festival a success."

VARIOUS SUGGESTIONS.

Some of the socials centre around this feature of enjoyment: "The Rainbow Party," "Japanese Tea," "Box Supper," "The Crazy Tea," "The Gentlemen's Turn," are very attractive. The candy pull, sugar party, harvest supper, strawberry festival, the lawn party, the picnic, so well known to all the young people of New England, with their games and merry-making, may well have their place in social enjoyment. At these gatherings, games always come in for consideration.

Games are desired that do not cause too much commotion, and are at the same time interesting and not in the least questionable as to their propriety. "Geography," "Twenty Questions," "School," "Admiration," in fact, hundreds of games can be played that are bright and helpful.

The most beneficial programme consists first of the usual light refreshments, and then literary exercises. There are always musicians in every society, and usually some one who will read or recite. In music and literature there are almost limitless resources. An evening with an author is both instructive and enjoyable.

A LONGFELLOW EVENING.

Take for illustration a Longfellow evening: Readings and recitations from his poems are always agreeable. His lyrics furnish us with some of the most beautiful songs in our language. "The Arrow and Song," "The Bridge,"

"The Day is Done," "The Rainy Day," and others of his songs are always welcome and loved by all. A sketch of the author's life should be a part of the programme.

A musicale devoted to one composer is very beneficial. A Mendelssohn evening was greatly enjoyed by one of the societies. Mendelssohn, Mozart, Rubinstein, Schubert, Schumann, and many other composers have written both songs and instrumental compositions, and with a sketch of the musician's life the variety is sufficient to prevent monotony.

For a miscellaneous programme, "The Songs of Seven," by Jean Ingelow, read and illustrated by tableaux, is known to most of you. Parts of the "Courtship of Miles Standish," can be given effectively in the same way. A little thought will suggest other poems that can be successfully represented.

A few general suggestions may be of use. In the first place, have method in the preparation and the conducting of the entertainment.

Call upon different ones to assist, and try to make each one feel there is something he can do.

Variety of entertainment will help to keep alive an interest in the socials, and bring in the different ones to assist.

Consider carefully the demands and the conveniences of the society, and begin with that which is sure to succeed, and later the way may be clearly seen for something more elaborate. Above all, ever keep in mind the motive, which is to bring the members together in Christian sympathy and to make the Endeavor Society the happiest, most helpful and most blessed of all places for the coming together of young lives

So let us work and never be weary in well-doing, for we are His children in whom we should live, move, and have our being, serving "Christ and the church."

A BASKET SOCIAL.

A member of the Methodist Y. P. S. C. E. of Bethlehem, Penn., has sent us an account of an enjoyable entertainment, known as a "Basket Social." The ladies of the society brought dainty baskets, in each of which was neatly packed supper for two people and the card of the bringer. These baskets were then sold at auction to the gentlemen, who, on receiving the baskets, shared the contents with the ladies whose cards were found therein. By this means, the society easily raised $28.50. Our correspondent sends the advice that the baskets be numbered and sold by their numbers, rather than offered in open market, as thus no buyer can have the advantage of knowing whose basket he is securing.

AN AUTHOR'S BANQUET.

We do not propose to eat any authors, even those guilty of perpetrating spring poems; this is merely a name given to a popular social. As patriotic feelings ought to be stirred whenever it may be possible, we will confine our attention to American authors. We will first have an old-fashioned supper, consisting of beans, brown bread, Indian pudding, "mush" and milk, pumpkin-pie, hogshead cheese and any other colonial delicacies that can be easily furnished. To this and the subsequent entertainment, we will charge an admission fee of ten, fifteen or twenty-five cents. The supper is to be served at several tables, presided over by young men and women in costume, representing characters from the writings of various authors. Of course the number of tables and waiters is dependent on the size of the company. Some or all of these characters may be present. At the Irving table, Ichabod Crane and Katrina Van Tassell; at the Longfellow table, John Alden and Priscilla, Evangeline and Gabriel; at the Lowell table, 'Zekiel and Huldy; at the Mark Twain table, the Prince and the pauper; and at the Holley table, Josiah Allen and Josiah Allen's wife, Betsey Bobbitt and Thomas Jefferson (Allen). For the entertainment, many things will suggest themselves to the different societies. A rough plan would include — recitation of some portions of "Sleepy Hollow," by Ichabod Crane; reading of the scene between Priscilla and John Alden, by Priscilla; singing of "The Arrow and the Song," by Evangeline, or "The Bridge," by Gabriel; reading of "The Courtin'," by 'Zekiel; and dialogue between Josiah Allen's wife and Betsey Bobbitt or between Josiah Allen and Samanthy, taken from any of Miss Holley's books. This general scheme is capable of various development and will be found a source of great pleasure and entertainment.

MISSIONARY ENTERTAINMENTS.

If the meeting is held on Sunday evening, the exercises, for a part of the evening, can be a missionary concert. After fifteen or twenty minutes spent on the regular topic of the evening, the missionary exercises may begin. For these, much information may be secured from the various denominational papers and magazines, which every month are filled with most interesting accounts of the mission work in all parts of the world. The denominational boards of publication also issue leaflets giving many inspiring items of news. Readings from these, accounts of missionaries in whom the church is particularly interested, earnest prayers for God's blessing on the various fields, and singing of missionary hymns will make an interesting meeting, followed by a generous offering for the advancement of the work. For a meeting to be held on a week-day evening, many programmes suggest themselves. The publication societies of the various denominations issue leaflets giving suggestions for entertainments; collections of recitations, readings and dialogues suitable for such occasions are also easily procured. The Presbyterian Board of Publication, 1334 Chestnut Street, Philadelphia, publishes two pamphlets, under the name of "Missionary Exercises (Nos. 1 and 2) for the use of Sunday Schools and Mission Bands, consisting of responsive readings, dialogues, selections in prose and poetry, etc."

A publication of the same nature is "The Mission-Band Portfolio, a collection of dialogues, recitations and hymns," arranged by the Women's Baptist Foreign Missionary Societies, Tremont Temple, Boston. In these pamphlets may be found exercises for many ages and many numbers of participants. A dialogue recommended by the Women's Board of Missions (Congregational), 1 Somerset Street, Boston, is "Sowing Light," arranged for eleven girls and nine children, in the costumes of various nations. Other and less ambitious dialogues published by the same board are, "What's the Use?" "Another Missionary Meeting," for young ladies, and "Little Light-Bearers," for children. The Women's Foreign Missionary Society of the Methodist Episcopal Church, 36 Bromfield Street, Boston, have recently published "Bright Bits for Readings in Missionary Societies," with selections suitable for all occasions. They issue, also, several dialogues arranged for four, five or eight girls and young ladies.

GAMES FOR SOCIAL GATHERINGS.

[We must not forget the younger ones in our societies, and for them certain appropriate and rational games often afford healthful amusement. Especially if these social gatherings are held at a private house, or in connection with picnics, as they often are, are these games appropriate. We are uncompromisingly opposed to "kissing" games, and we publish these hints, kindly furnished us by Miss Colburn, though they relate to well-known games, with the hope that where any entertainment of this sort is best, they may take the place of the objectionable. — ED.]

CAMPS.

The company is divided into two equal parties or "Camps." A member from each camp goes from the room and together they decide upon some object for the others to guess. On returning, the delegate from Camp A goes to Camp B, and B's delegate goes to A. The members of the Camp then try to find out the object the delegate has in mind by means of questions so framed as to admit only of the answer "Yes" or "No." The camp which in this way first guesses the object has the privilege of claiming both their own delegate and the delegate from the opposing camp. Two other delegates are then sent out, who come back with a new object, and the game goes on until one camp has, by successful questioning, drawn all the members from the other camp. Some object about the room, like a door-hinge, makes a good beginning, but the questioners will soon enjoy tussling with something more difficult, like "The atmosphere of the planet Mars," or "The tree from which the handle of Washington's hatchet was made."

PROVERBS.

One of the company goes out of the room, while the remainder select a proverb which is given out word by word to the players, so that each has a word. If the proverb is short, it must be repeated until each one is supplied with his word. When the absentee is called back, he asks a question of some one, which must be answered in such a way as to bring in the word assigned to the person answering. The interlocutor may ask each one three questions. By learning, in this way, here and there a word, he is able to guess the proverb. The player from whom the interlocutor obtains the first clue takes his place.

SHOUTING PROVERBS.

The company is seated in a ring, and one member goes out of the room. The words of the proverb are distributed as in the previous game. When the one outside is called back, at a given signal each one in the circle shouts his word at the same time. This is repeated until in the medley the guesser can distinguish enough words to make a guess at the proverb.

DUMB CRAMBO.

The company is divided into two equal parties. Party No. 1 goes into another room while No. 2 selects a word having two or more meanings; for instance, "fair" (substantive), "fair" (adjective), "fare" (food), "fare" (price), fixing on one special signification. No. 2 then tell No. 1 that they have chosen a word rhyming with "rare." No. 1 proceed to act, in pantomime, all the rhymes for that word they can think of, trying to do it in such a way as to puzzle No. 2, who have to guess what word they act. When they reach the particular signification chosen, the parties change places, No. 1 choosing a new word and No. 2 acting the rhymes.

GEOGRAPHY.

First, a judge and two leaders are appointed by nomination. Then the two leaders choose their sides as in a spelling-match. The judge begins with "A" and points to one of the leaders, who is to give a geographical name before the judge counts twenty; then the judge points to the other and counts, and thus goes on from side to side, until one of the leaders fails to give a name before the judge counts twenty, then the other leader chooses one from the failing side. Then the judge begins with "B," asking first the leader who looses. When one side fails to give a name beginning with "B," one is chosen from his side, and then names beginning with "C" are given. The game goes on until all are chosen by one side or until the entire alphabet is exhausted. The leaders only are to give the names, but it is the part of each one to give the leader of his side every name of which he can think, beginning with the letter that is then used. The names are to be whispered to the leader. No name is to be given twice. All must abide by the decision of the judge.

A GOOD TEST.

How can we decide what entertainments to provide for our social gatherings is often a question which gives practical concern to our societies, and especially to the social committees. We recently heard a very simple but very effective test. Said a pastor of a large and flourishing society — "We have capital socials where all get acquainted and all have a right good time, yet I believe we could stop in the middle of any one, and without any shock or sense of incongruity, enjoy a prayer-meeting." There could hardly be a better touchstone for a social gathering of young people. No matter how gay and light-hearted and full of fun the young people may be, if they could go from that gathering into a meeting for prayer, and be at once in the spirit of prayer, there would be little danger of going astray on the social side. In other words, the social gathering where the disciple can commune with the Lord without any sense of incongruity, is the only proper place for the Christian, young or old. And this will make no one dull, or long-faced, or straight-laced. Was not our Lord at the marriage-feast at Cana? Did His presence interfere with the joyousness of that occasion? Rather, He added to its good cheer, as He will add to the joy of every festive occasion to-day where His people meet in His spirit.

PRACTICAL QUESTIONS CONCERNING SOCIALS.

Question. Should Christian Endeavor socials be solely for social enjoyment and cultivation of our social natures, or should they be partly for the purpose of raising money?

Answer. The primary object of a Christian Endeavor social, like every other department of Endeavor work, as said on another page, is to "increase our mutual acquaintance, and to make us more useful in the service of God." This it attempts to do by making the active and associate members better acquainted one with another. If this is remembered by all, we see no serious objection to using an occasional social for raising money needed for a good object. Such a social should be the exception, however; most of them should be attended by no expense.

Ques. Are there any conditions or circumstances which will permit a true Christian to participate in public dancing?

Ans. If by "permit" is meant, "make it best or expedient," we cannot conceive of such circumstances

Ques. Can one safely trust his own conscience to decide questions like the above?

Ans. Certainly. There is nothing else to trust but an enlightened and tender conscience; though every young person may wisely seek the guidance of those more experienced

Ques. What is the attitude of the Christian Endeavor Society toward the doubtful amusements — dancing, card-playing, etc.?

Ans. The attitude of the society is one of uncompromising hostility to every amusement that lowers the tone of Christian living, and interferes with Christian activity, and this, we believe, is true of the dance, the card-table and the theatre, as at present conducted. We would repeat the advice of Bishop Vincent on this subject — "Better not." This is in answer to many inquirers.

We have various questions about active members attending the theatre, opera, dances, etc., and one even that asks us if active members should go skating Sunday afternoons. We have answered these questions so often that we should enjoy a rest from them. Of course, Sabbath-breaking is removed from the category of doubtful amusements, and any young man who goes skating on Sunday is guilty of breaking the law of God. As to these doubtful amusements, we will say once more and emphatically they should be and will be avoided by earnest young Christians because, one and all, they lead the soul away from the highest spiritual activities. No Christian should allow himself to engage in any amusement concerning which he has the slightest doubt and upon which, on his knees, he cannot ask God's blessing.

PART XII.

MUSIC, TEMPERANCE, MISSIONARY AND SUNDAY SCHOOL COMMITTEES.

MUSIC.

MUSIC AND MUSIC COMMITTEE

A Familiar Letter from the President of the United Society.

CONCERNING OUR MUSIC.

I suppose that I am about the last person who should have anything to say on the music question, since a civil service examination for musical director of the smallest Christian endeavor society in America, I fear, would find me sadly wanting.

However, I do know a little more about the matter than a friend of mine, who shamelessly boasts that he cannot tell "Yankee Doodle" from "Old Hundred." Besides, it does not take a musical critic to say some things which are worth saying about the music in our societies.

TOO MUCH OF IT

In the first place, I think many of our societies have too much singing. Sometimes the impression is given that the gospel hymns are resorted to to fill up the time, and that is always a very unfortunate impression for any meeting to make. To say "Number 136," is such an easy get-off that I am always sorry to hear any one who takes no other part thus try to ease his conscience and fulfill his pledge. I would almost rather he kept still altogether. It is a very different thing when one says: "The one hundred and thirty-sixth hymn expresses my feelings to-night. I wish we might sing the first verse." But even then it is usually better for him to read the first verse. On the whole, I think it is, as a rule, wise for the leader to give out all the hymns that are sung from the book. He can suggest them at the appropriate times; they will be more likely to be in accord with the spirit of the meeting, and there will not be too many of them.

IMPROMPTU SINGING.

What I have been saying does not apply to the impromptu singing of which I wish we might have much more. There can hardly be too much of this. No time is wasted in fumbling over hymn-books and finding the place and playing over an old tune that every one knows as well as his mother's lullaby. There is nothing more spiritually stimulating than such singing, and it is a wonder to me that we do not have vastly more of it in all our meetings. In every society there are some who have this gift of starting a hymn without an instrument, and they ought to cultivate it.

WHAT CAN THE MUSIC COMMITTEE DO?

This question is often asked. To answer it comprehensively, I might say it ought to see that the society meetings have the very best music possible. It can often form a choir from the society which will be very helpful. This choir can, at least, sit together and lead the singing with a strong volume of sound. For special occasions like anniversaries, etc., they can prepare anthems and special music. In many ways, too, this committee can help the music of the church. Ask the pastor if he would like some assistance from the young people in the singing of the weekly prayer-meeting or in the evening service, or see if the superintendent of the Sunday School cannot use to advantage the musical talent of the society. I think that many such "Openings" will be found.

CHRISTIAN ENDEAVOR HYMNS.

Many societies, I think, can use to advantage some of our new Christian endeavor hymns. Of course they will not "sing themselves." No new tune will. But to learn such new pieces and to teach them to the society is just what this committee is for, and to introduce them occasionally is to introduce a pleasing and helpful variety.

I suppose that Mr. Adriance, the compiler, would be as far as any one else from claiming that "Hymns of Christion Endeavor" is a perfect book, and the design is to improve it just as rapidly as our Christian endeavor hymnology grows in volume and in value, but there are some admirable new Christian endeavor pieces in this book, besides many of the old standard favorites, as well as such universal favorites of later days as Dr. Rankin's "God Be With You," and "At the Cross." Moreover, it is so cheap that it can be used side by side with other books to supplement, as it was designed to do, rather than to supplant them.

IN GENERAL.

To speak in a general way, I do not think our singing is fast enough or strong enough to be the power it ought to be. It often gives the impression of being rather weak and languishing, with too much organ and too little voice.

If I am wrong on this point, my musical friends can charge it to my ignorance, and since I do not pretend to be any sort of an authority, I will hide behind one who can speak with more power, and whose words, I hope, will be considered by all our societies. Rev. Dr. E. P. Parker, of Hartford, wrote thus to *The Congregationalist:*

"How often, in our churches and chapels, we are compelled to wait for some brother or sister to grind out 'Boylston' from beginning to end, before we tackle it! That dreary, superfluous performance operates in the way of serious discouragement. We are disgusted, to begin with. Then the wretched interlude between verses is a relic of barbarism. It takes time and dreadfully abuses it, too. But, in particular, congregational singing in our churches moves in too slow a measure to be successful.

"Everywhere in the English churches I found that the tunes were sung much faster than with us. They sing five verses of an ordinary hymn while we sing two. There is life and spirit in the faster movement. You get through in due time. Convinced that they are right, I tried the same movements in my own church, and very soon found our congregational singing rapidly improving in all respects. With a note or two of organ preparation, let the singing begin. Abolish all interludes, and go on as quickly as may be, to the end of the hymn. 'As quickly as may be,' I say, because I know that there is little or no likelihood of moving too swiftly. The tendencies are all to dragging and dullness.

"Try the experiment with 'Old Hundred,' which is dismally dull as commonly sung, and see how that solid old tune brightens up and shows forth its grandeurs. Here, in my judgment, is one of the prime secrets of successful congregational singing."

Like the Englishman who agreed with Mr. Burke, I say "ditto" to Dr. Parker.

Your friend,
FRANCIS E. CLARK.

THE MINISTRY OF SONG.

BY CHARLES N. GOODRICH.

There are many avenues leading to the highway of the Great King, and to the child of faith song is a most favored approach. It is the natural expression of our very being, and accepted as a common pathway by the heavy-laden, as well as the joyful ones of earth; but the young people fail to appreciate in its fullest degree the inspiration of melody. We do not make enough of music in our meetings. There is an appeal in it which touches many responsive heart-chords, when other means have failed. In the matter of song there is a fine chance for us to give it an element of power to which it most surely aspires.

The hour of meeting having arrived and the young people all ready, what part shall song have during the coming hour? Leadership in song, according to my way of thinking, is just as necessary as leadership in devotion.

If your society is large enough, have a quartette, double quartette or chorus, which shall always be seated facing the other members of the society. Apart from their help in leading the general singing let there be some special contribution from them during the course of the meeting, a solo, duet, trio, quartette or something which will give a distinctive feature to the thought of the evening. Have something different in the line of music every time as far as expedient; for the unexpected will serve to excite an interest which cannot fail to be of benefit. A song which has a swing to it will, as a rule, be a good opening piece either for the leaders or those led. Is it best to have the unconverted numbered among the leadership of which I have just spoken? I am inclined to doubt the wisdom of it; for how can we tell the story of the Cross to others in song or otherwise, unless we first know it ourselves? Mr. Moody's chorus singers owe not a little of their power to the well-known fact that they believe what they sing, and thus their worship is sincere.

Impromptu singing is worthy of great commendation, and wisely used will be a spiritual lever, which will wondrously lift us up in thought and deed. I think it is conceded that no musical instrument is capable of such rich expression as the human voice, and the latter stands without a peer in the realm of music. With such a gift at our command, why not employ it alone, as occasion serves?

Let opportunity be the tuning-fork, which shall give the key-note. For instance, a boy has given, with extreme embarrassment, his first testimony for Christ. Every one is moved by the confession. Now is just the moment for some one, who knows the difference between a sharp and a flat, to begin singing some familiar and appropriate song, such as, "Am I a Soldier of the Cross," "O Happy Day that Fixed My Choice." "All Hail the Power of Jesus' Name," and the like. The response will be very hearty, and every one will speak a word of cheer to the young convert, through the happy medium of song. A lady has passed through some very trying experience, and is troubled beyond measure. She cannot understand the why of it. The brightness of life has become overcast by clouds of seeming adversity. It may be that a crisis is upon her. Lend a hand to her by singing very softly a verse or two of "Rock of Ages," "My Faith Looks up to Thee," "Jesus, Lover of My Soul," "Nearer My God to Thee," songs which have stood the test of time, and been to countless numbers of sorrowing children, "as the shadow of a great rock in a weary land." It will bring a relief to her beyond compare. The spirit of the song will follow her for weeks, perhaps years, and that meeting above all others will be held in most grateful memory. There are times when the very air is tremulous with expectancy. The Christ is near by. Hearts are turned to Him by the magnetism of His presence, as the mariner's compass points to the north star. Plead for the unconverted one by your side in "Pass Me Not, O Gentle Saviour," "Just as I Am," or "What a Friend we Have in Jesus."

Song may be our one talent; if so, shall we be voiceless? A young lady became an active member of a Christian Endeavor Society. She was timid by nature, and had never taken part in the prayer-meeting. What could she do? When she assumed the pledge of membership, she took the Lord into her confidence, and He said to her, "You have a very fine voice, consecrate that to My service, share with others your wealth of song." She responded to the divine suggestion, and sang with such sweetness for the dear Christ that it was thought by many that one soul after another was sung into the kingdom.

When I was a little boy, the Prince of Wales visited the city where I lived and every one gave him a right hearty welcome. Residences were beautifully decorated with flags and bunting, arches spanned the streets, and all the school children were drawn up on either side of the way through which the procession was to pass, the girls dressed in white, and the boys radiant in their Sunday clothes. When the carriage containing His Royal Highness approached, we, with uncovered heads, saluted him with acclamations, waving of flags and handkerchiefs. But, as I recall it all now, it seems to me that song was most acceptable, and capped the climax of the greeting; for, as he passed through the lines, with the dignity of a coming greatness resting upon him, we voiced our gladness at his presence in songs, and as soon as he heard the songs, he smiled upon us most graciously. And I have often thought that we can give no grander or more pleasing tribute to Him, who calls Himself the Prince of Peace, than in our service of song. Heaven and earth sometimes come very near together, never more so than when the redeemed, peopling two worlds, unite in singing the praises of the Redeemer Himself.

"OVERWORKING THE HYMN-BOOK."

The hymn-book is immensely overworked in some of our societies. We were in a meeting once where it seemed as though, after every testimony or verse of Scripture or brief prayer, a verse of a hymn was called for, and it was evident that many of the hymns were given out simply as the easiest way of "taking part." Any such participation is as bad as none at all. It is not in accordance with the spirit of the pledge. The leader of the meetings can usually give out the hymns with better judgment of the needs of the meeting than any one else. In no case should the cheap get-off, " Please sing No. 57," be offered or accepted as a substitute for a genuine word of testimony or a prayer or passage of Scripture. It is manifestly unfair and ungenerous for an unfaithful member to keep a whole audience singing, to enable him to escape a duty. It is often better to read a verse of a hymn than to ask to have it sung. We want singing enough, but not too much.

A CHRISTIAN ENDEAVOR CHOIR.

BY REV. CHARLES A. NORTHROP.

For many years the First Congregational Church, Norwich, Conn., had had no choir to lead the singing of the congregation. Leadership in song was in the hands of the pastor, who acted as precentor. His successor in the pulpit could not sing. No available precentor was to be had. The singing continued to be congregational in the sense that some in the congregation considered themselves permitted to sing, if they chose. It was a little relief when a few of the singers took their places on Sunday in the choir gallery, and, without previous practice of the tunes, sung with the congregation; familiar tunes flowed peacefully; an unusual tune wrought woe. Things went on in this way for three years or more, until one day the Y. P. S. C. E. of the church appointed a committee on music, pointed to the choir gallery, but spoke no word.

The committee understood, and went on to select from the congregation a double quartette choir, including a musical director. All these, with one exception, were members of the Christian Endeavor Society. This action was reported to the Endeavor society and approved by it. It had also the approbation of the standing committee of the church, and ultimately the approval of the Church itself, not only as respects the existence of the choir, but also as to its composition. The hearty approval of the congregation put the choir before the people as their leader in the improvement of public worship.

It was a condition of the appointment of the members of the choir that they should be willing to attend weekly rehearsals. A few months' trial of this Christian Endeavor choir has shown a decided interest on the part of its members in the necessary preparation for the fulfilling of its function as leader of public song, and attendance upon rehearsals has generally been constant. Freely and cheerfully, time and study have been given to the service of the church in this respect. There has been an enriching of public worship, on the side of song, by the introduction of the "Gloria," the chanting of the Lord's Prayer, an anthem or equivalent, and the prayer is sung at the reception of the weekly offerings.

The consciousness on the part of the choir that it has promoted true worship in song, and the consciousness on the part of the congregation that it is being led by those whose hearts are responsive to the words sung, have constantly tended to raise the musical part of the public service to its proper place among the forms of worship. Now the congregation listens to the singing, when it does not itself participate vocally, and feels that the song speaks the united prayer and praise of all the worshipers. It may be added that the improvement in the Sunday singing, consequent, partly, upon the stated rehearsals, has made itself felt in all the other public meetings of the church.

The experiment in this particular church was simplified, perhaps made possible, because there was no choir to be reorganized or displaced. The field was open. It was entered by Christian endeavor in the name of the Lord. It is being cultivated in the service of Christ.

TEMPERANCE.

WORK OF THE TEMPERANCE COMMITTEE.

From a Paper read at the Chicago Convention, by Rev. J. C. Cromer.

At its last convention, our society put itself on record for temperance in the following words: "*Whereas*, the evils of intemperance are the most momentous and gigantic that now impede our work among young men, therefore, RESOLVED: That we express ourselves as intensely opposed to this evil, and pledge our labors and our prayers to its banishment from among us." These are noble, strong words. They at once set our faces against the foe. They put prayers into our hearts, and weapons into our hands, and send us out, thus equipped, to do valiantly for humanity. It perhaps remains only for me to indicate a few doors of usefulness that stand open before us; to point out a few elements of power that belong to us as a Young People's Society of Christian Endeavor.

First, then, we are strong for this work on behalf of humanity, because we are Christian. Let it be accepted at once that we cannot do the work of a regularly organized temperance society. This exists for temperance alone. But cannot we do a work for temperance which such a society cannot accomplish? Have we not a vantage-ground of power which it does not possess? We are distinctively a Christian body. Whatever we do for temperance will be winged with the love of Christ for men. It will have these two characteristics, the vision of Christ in its methods, and the power of Christ in its performance.

Again, we are strong for this work for humanity because

we are young. Being young, we have a position of power, because we stand just where we can fight hand to hand with the enemy. I need not here state what we all know to be true, that the great majority of the recruits to the ranks of intemperance comes from the young, and that the most efficient work for temperance can be done among young men. For an old man, the chances for reformation have decreased inversely as the square of the distance that he has come down in life. In young manhood character is forming, habits are beginning, streams are starting from their sources. Now think of these three hundred and twenty-five thousand Christian endeavorers throughout the world. They stand as young men among young men — aye, as young women among young men, with power imperial. Fired with zeal and love for Christ, with hands ready and willing, and with hearts full of sympathy for their fellows, who shall be able to set bounds to their power and influence in staying the tides of intemperance just here where they begin to flow?

To do this work successfully, much depends upon a wide-awake, efficient temperance committee. First of all, by pledge or otherwise, the committee should bring the society itself to the position of total abstinence; for to stand in any other position will be to lose the very crown of its glory and power. Afterward, plans and methods of work which will reach out to the world can be devised. The saloon should be equalled, if possible surpassed, for social attractions. Individual young men should be prayed for and gone after. At times the whole thought, prayer and endeavor of the society should be directed, for weeks and months, toward some one young man, until he is brought in and saved.

But does some one remark that this work is necessarily slow and hopeless? That while one is snatched as a brand from the burning, hundreds are being caught of the fire? Then we reply that, so long as our banner floats on the breezes, bearing the inscription, "For Christ and the church," we can undertake none other than this practical, Christian temperance work; that for these talents, distinctively and peculiarly our own, we shall be held accountable in the end; and that, for hopefulness and promise in the future, we shall find, in their use and development, that the darkest skies above us will be streaked through with light, because of Him whose are the eternal years of God, and who has said, "Lo, I am with you alway, even unto the end of the world."

THE TEMPERANCE COMMITTEE.

BY SIGMA.

The temperance committee of our Christian Endeavor Society, West Haven, Conn., has been trying to evolve something practicable and efficient along its particular line. In addition to the circulation of literature and conducting an occasional meeting in the interests of temperance, the members have now drawn up a form of triple pledge which I wish to submit both as to form and as to the advisability of pledges of this kind in the society. This will be likely to call out the temperance work of the societies, and of the temperance committee in particular.

The form submitted by our committee is this:

(1) I promise that I will not use as a beverage anything that intoxicates, including malt liquors and cider.

(2) I promise to abstain from all profanity.

(3) I promise to refrain from the use of tobacco in any form, until I have passed the age of twenty-five.

Should I from any temptation break my pledge, I will still consider it binding upon me, and, seeking strength from my Heavenly Father, will strive to keep it afterward.

It is the plan of the committee to have a permanent enrollment book, and to solicit signatures from all sources, outside as well as inside the membership. The time limit in the third was inserted, as I understand, from a conviction that many boys would be likely to sign some such pledge with reference to tobacco, who would not sign an obsolute pledge; and that if they would abstain until twenty-five they would not be likely to fall into the tobacco habit; at least, they would fall with their eyes open. This time limit suggests that the use of tobacco is not to be considered as a sin *per se*, as profanity and drunkenness are, but that each one must answer to his own conscience, as to cost, effect on health, etc. It will be conceded, without debate, that the tobacco habit, when formed at all, is generally formed by boys in their teens, or even before; as likewise that remnant of old-time barbarism, now happily becoming obsolete, the ear mutilation of our girls for purposes of jewelry. Personally, I have never known a young man over twenty-five falling into the tobacco habit, nor a girl out of her teens having her ears pierced. And for that matter, the habit of drinking and profanity take root, generally, if at all, in early years.

MISSIONARY.

CHRISTIAN ENDEAVOR AND MISSIONS.

A Familiar Letter from the President of the United Society.

If there is any one thing which appeals to the heart of every true Christian endeavorer it must be the work of missions at home and abroad. This is only saying that the true Christian is always a missionary. He may not go to Africa or to New Mexico, but the moment he becomes a Christian he must receive into his heart the same spirit that sent Judson and Carey and Patteson on their missions. A hundred years ago a celebrated Roman Catholic historian taunted the Protestants with the fact that theirs was not a missionary religion, and predicted the speedy overthrow of Protestantism on that account.

To-day, thank God, that taunt is no longer true, and it is a wonderful fact that during the four-score years since Protestantism sent out its first missionary, it has gained more in numbers, wealth and influence than during all the previous centuries of its life.

If our society lives and grows, as we all hope and pray that it may, it will be because it has within it the real missionary spirit. Every committee is a missionary committee — the lookout, and the prayer-meeting, and the social, and the temperance, and the good literature, and the Sunday School committees, no less than the so-called missionary committee. They have different branches of missionary work to be carried on; but the very same spirit should pervade the committee that provides flowers for the pulpit, or brings new members into the Sunday School, or calls on a new family, that should animate the committee that provides the missionary meeting and seeks to interest the members in foreign missionary matters.

THE MISSIONARY UPRISING.

It is a significant fact that soon after the Society of Christian Endeavor began to make itself felt as a power among the young people of the land, a remarkable missionary uprising also became evident among the young people. Through the eloquent words of Mr. Wilder and those associated with him, the work has gained force, until we read with amazement of two thousand young men and women in our schools who are ready to pledge themselves to mission work abroad. Now let all the four hundred thousand active members of our Christian Endeavor societies pledge themselves to mission work at home or abroad as God shall call them, not waiting to begin their missionary labors until they get to India or out on our own frontier, but beginning it with their next neighbors and widening their sympathies until they learn the lesson Christ came to teach, that all the peoples of the world are our neighbors.

BE INTELLIGENT ABOUT MISSIONS.

But, speaking of missions, either home or foreign, the great reason why so few people care much about missions is, that so few know much about them. No one can become interested in a subject of which he is ignorant, and our interest in missionary work will be just in proportion to our knowledge of it. There are excellent missionary periodicals published by all the denominational boards. If you are a Presbyterian, read carefully *The Church at Home and Abroad;* if a Methodist, *The Gospel in All Lands, The Heathen Woman's Friend;* if a Baptist, *The Baptist Missionary Magazine, The Baptist Home Mission Monthly;* if a Congregationalist, the *Missionary Herald, Life and Light,* the *Home Missionary* and the *American Missionary.* In fact, read your denominational missionary magazine. Money cannot be expended better than in subscribing for one or more of these periodicals that represent the missionary work of your own church. There, too, is the capital *Missionary Review of the World,* and others of like nature, which give a wider view of missions in all denominations. Few people have any idea of the amount and value of missionary literature: books, pamphlets, leaflets, etc. Write to the denominational missionary headquarters and you can find out what is published and get the literature at very low rates.

GIVE.

Another requisite to a genuine interest in missions is a benevolent interest, as well as an intelligent interest, in them. We are likely to follow with our prayers and with our affectionate interest any cause or person to whom we give our money. The same principle applies as in the prayer-meeting. If we take part in it, we are interested in it and we say to each other as we go out, "What a good meeting we did have to-night!" So if we have part in sending the gospel to the heathen at home or abroad, and give our own hard-earned dollars or dimes for this purpose, we cannot well help being interested, and we shall follow the money with our prayers. As I have said before, I hope it will not be long before every Christian endeavor society, where the church approves, will raise some money every year through the envelope method, for missionary purposes. By this method, money is given deliberately and conscientiously and not simply in response to an appeal to the emotions, and we can educate in our societies whole generations of future givers.

GIVE TO A DEFINITE OBJECT.

I think many societies might wisely assume some definite object of benevolence; for instance, to support a native teacher in Turkey, or to build a schoolhouse in India, or to support a colored student in Georgia, or to help build a home missionary parsonage in the West. Get into correspondence with those to whom the money goes; consider them your missionaries, or your students, or your missionary helpers, and the joy and interest in giving will be increased fourfold. Our missionary boards always have special objects of this sort which they are glad to have you help, and concerning which they will give you all necessary information.

The United Society does not receive money for these missionary objects; it should be sent directly to the proper board and designated for the special use to which it is designed. Pastors and church committees will give all necessary advice in this matter. May the contributions be liberal and may a great blessing go with them and a great blessing come back to all who give!

Your friend,

FRANCIS E. CLARK.

HOW TO GIVE.

A Familiar Letter from the President of the United Society.

We expect that our societies will be training schools in Christian liberality as well as in all other graces. It is worth quite as much to the Christian to know how to give as how to speak or pray in public. Many Christians, I believe, grow up grasping and penurious, simply because they have not learned how to give; their education in this direction has been neglected.

Now the essential things in cultivating the spirit of benevolence are warm hearts, information concerning the world's needs, and some systematic and regular method of contributing to those needs. I can take for granted the warm, generous hearts. Few young Christians who have had their hearts touched by the love of God are not ready to listen to the world's appeal, but they too seldom hear it. They get little time to read; they have not as yet found out how thrillingly interesting is the appeal for the world's evangelization. Here is the province of the missionary committee and the missionary meeting of our society. Such meetings should be held regularly at least once a quarter. They can be and should be made of the deepest interest.

A SYSTEMATIC PLAN.

The remaining element in cultivating the gift of benevolence is some systematic and regular plan of giving. I know of no better plan, in fact none so good as the weekly envelope plan. I have tried it in the two churches of which I have been pastor, and have found it in every way admirable if properly kept before the people, and if the interest in the cause of missions is not allowed to flag.

WHAT PASTORS SAY.

I have recently, for a special purpose, sought the testimony of hundreds of pastors who have tried this plan, and in nine cases out of ten they speak favorably, most of them enthusiastically, of it. It can be used in raising money for necessary expenses and for home and foriegn missions. Many of your churches already use this plan, and you can subscribe something every week upon the regular church card, and you can use it also in your society if you desire. The United Society prepares envelopes and also the following benevolent pledge-card, to be used for these systematic offerings:

MONTHLY OFFERING.

Young People's Society of Christian Endeavor.

I hereby pledge myself to contribute MONTHLY for one year, from . . . . the sum marked below; the payment to be made at such times as the Society shall decide.

1c. 2c. 3c. 4c. 5c. 6c. 7c. 8c. 9c. 10c. 25c. 50c.

Name, ...

(This pledge being voluntary, may be withdrawn at any time by notifying the Treasurer.)

Mr. R. P. Wilder, whose addresses have thrilled so many hearts, sends a similar plan of systematic giving, and writes:

"The 'Plan' can be used by any denomination. It does not interfere with existing missionary agencies. The money raised is to be sent to the Board of foreign missions with which the society is connected. If each Endeavor society would support a missionary according to the enclosed 'Plan,' our church boards would be in no lack of funds for foreign service."

Here is the plan, and an admirable one it is:

1. An opportunity will be given to all who so desire to subscribe to the following pledge:

"I promise to give $ . . . and . . . cents each week during a period of five years from date, toward the support of a missionary in the foreign field, this sum to be over and above my present offerings to the cause of foreign missions."*

* This pledge is not legally binding.

(Instead of weekly payments, quarterly or yearly payments may be made if so desired.)

2. The weekly offerings shall be placed in envelopes furnished by the church treasurer to those who subscribe to the pledge, and these envelopes shall be collected on each Sabbath in connection with the usual collection.

3. It is suggested that a committee be appointed by the church to assist the treasurer in the work of collection and in obtaining new subscriptions.

4. If the amount pledged in any church is sufficient for the annual support of one or of several missionaries, that church shall report to the foreign board with which it is connected, that such a sum has been pledged for five years, and request that the board appoint one or more missionaries to represent that church in the foreign field.

5. If the amount pledged in any church is more than sufficient for the support of one missionary, and not enough for the support of two, the surplus shall be sent to the foreign board to be applied to the cause of foreign missions in whatever way may be thought best.

6. If the amount pledged in any church is insufficient for the support of a missionary, that church may unite with neighboring churches of the same denomination in the support of a representative. If this is impossible, the amount raised shall be forwarded to the Foreign Board to be used as the board may direct.

7. This plan is to be so carried out as not to interfere in any way with existing missionary agencies, but with the hope and earnest prayer that it may result in larger contributions than have ever been made to the mission cause.

I wish that all our societies might enter into some such effort, and that the missionary treasuries might be re-enforced by hundreds of thousands of dollars during the coming year. It is something for the missionary committees to consider carefully and prayerfully. If they do this, I believe they will also act energetically.

Your friend,

FRANCIS E. CLARK.

SOME METHODS OF RAISING MONEY.

The following hints from a valuable little tract by Mrs. Caswell, published by the American Home Missionary Society will be especially suggestive to young people:

THE SABBATH PENNY, NICKEL OR DIME. — Have a home missionary mite-box. As a part of your Sabbath morning worship, put into it, regularly, a penny or nickel or dime, with a prayer for the special object to which you contribute. If this offering is for your home missionary, you will ask God's blessing upon his labors for that day.

THE SACRIFICE GIFT. — Through some special self-denial you may be able to lay an extra offering at the feet of Jesus. How He loves such gifts!

SABBATH EGGS, etc. — In the country are those who have Sabbath eggs, Sabbath milk, Sabbath fruit, etc., turning all such articles that come on the Sabbath into offerings for God.

GARDENS, etc. — There are missionary hens, gardens, apple-trees, rag-bags, berries, etc.

FANCY BAGS. — A young lady makes a couple of fancy bags exactly alike. Perhaps she embroiders the words, "Our Country," on one side. She keeps one and presents the other to a young gentleman friend. Each hangs the bag in a place where it will not be forgotten, and throws into it all loose change that can be spared. At an appointed time the two compare notes. By a little competition, the missionary treasury is thus replenished.

INVESTMENTS. — We are familiar with penny investments. With some the plan has reached the dollar.

They find that as one penny was made to yield two, so one dollar will double itself, and with careful management grow to five.

THE CHRISTIAN ENDEAVOR SOCIETY AND YOUNG PEOPLE'S MISSIONARY ORGANIZATIONS.

BY MRS. JAMES L. HILL.

Such facts as these have now been much observed, and are extremely suggestive:

1. There is evidently among young people an enlarged desire for missionary intelligence. A librarian in the public library of one of the largest cities of Massachusetts said to a prominent Christian endeavor worker, "What is it that you have been doing to awake so much missionary inquiry among young people? We have been obliged to add several missionary volumes to our library, and in some cases to obtain duplicate copies." An increased number of periodicals — and these are quick to detect what the religious public want — are supplying missionary information.

2. Much of the incitement to missionary interest and effort among young people is from young people. Young hearts fire with enthusiasm other young hearts. Those who heard Mr. Wilder at recent Christian Endeavor State Conventions, and at the national gatherings as well, will understand what we mean. Yet such addresses are only indications. Proofs of this have accumulated without effort in such abundance and variety that they must be left to appear incidentally in these missionary columns as the weeks go by.

3. The officers of existing missionary organizations may well become the missionary committee of the Young People's Society. Of what advantage is this? Much every way. It gives to the society a missionary flavor; and the society gives to the missionary work numbers and

momentum. Certain recent years of our society's growth have been pleasantly marked by the affiliation in work of these various organizations. In many churches there exist such organizations as Missionary Cadets, or Chips from the Old Block, or Fireflies, or Standard Bearers, or Seek and Save Circles. Let these have recognition, co-operation, aid.

4. The society exists for forth-putting work in the extension of the kingdom. This is its whole pith and point. It is written into its very name by the use of the word "Endeavor." This is the particular thing that distinguishes it from the ordinary prayer-meeting. That society that in unselfish devotion is not praying "Thy kingdom come," and laboring and giving in accordance with its prayer, is recreant. Such a society has sad need of baptism into the missionary spirit. It does not see the unevangelized world as Christ viewed it. A society thrives best that prays and works for others as well as for its own self-centred prosperity. Young friends, lift up your eyes, and look on the fields!

5. Definiteness of form must be given to missionary work, if it is to enlist young people. A strong correspondent, whose labors in endeavor society circles have been conspicuously fruitful, writes to us, voicing the common desire that our young people, in blocking out their work may have the guidance of those who, by reason of opportunity, have wider and riper experience. If we are to lay hold of work, the handle of it must be turned toward us. Another person expresses the same idea in homelike phrase, to the effect that missionary work given over to young people ought to be first "cut and basted." The support of a dispensary, or Bible-reader, or missionary physician, or even of an entire school, ought to be undertaken in conjunction with the other organizations of the local church.

6. It is great unwisdom to assume any breach between

old and young in matters of missionary or other enterprise. Distinctions unrecognized fade. Charitable natures do not strain their eyes to discover such chasms. If in the past they have been talked into existence, cut off now their reason of being. The greatest effectiveness is secured where all the parts of a church come solidly together. A society of endeavor has no independent life. As it has relations, they must be recognized in all its work. Much that we would like to say is briefly comprehended in our society motto, " For Christ and the Chnrch." If we adopt this sentiment, it means labor in planting the church in new fields. It signifies, moreover, that we are "many members, yet but one body," and "that the member should have care one for another."

FOR THE MISSIONARY COMMITTEE.

Here is a hint for the missionary night which may help some committee to make its department more popular. As nothing is accomplished so well as when planned, let four members be chosen to report on some particular mission field, say Japan, or upon work among the freedmen, or work in cities. Let each reporter appointed choose, or be given, the branch of the topic he will speak upon. Information upon the subject can be secured, if not at hand, by writing to the secretary of any missionary society. And as young people are wide-awake, they will, without doubt, find something in the newspapers, during the month, on their topic. Mission fields from the ends of the earth may be reviewed, but the home field should not be overlooked. It is astonishing how interest grows as one studies a subject. Limit the reports, which should be spoken rather than read, to ten minutes; and let each speaker secure his successor on penalty of substituting himself. The plan has been tried with increasing success at several missionary meetings.

MISSIONARY WORK.

The society of the Green Hill Presbyterian Church, Philadelphia, has recently undertaken a novel form of missionary work, which many of our city societies might profitably adopt. They employ a Bible reader to work in the immediate vicinity of the church. A special committee has charge of this work, to which the reader reports the result of her work.

The various committees supplement her work, the relief committee looking after cases of destitution, the Sunday School committee bringing the children to Sunday School, and the lookout committee issuing invitations to attend the church services. Already they have accomplished much good, and recommend this plan to other societies. This society has also given a scholarship in the Ramona Indian school at Santa Fé, New Mexico.

HOW ONE MISSION CIRCLE WORKS.

The secretary of a missionary circle in Boston recently sent out, a few days before the date of its meeting, letters to members and friends, reminding them of their causes for thankfulness and inviting them to join in its thank-offering service. As a substitute for presence in person, if for any reason that should be impossible, they proposed the anonymous sending of the offering in an envelope enclosed for the purpose, and a reason for thankfulness, an appropriate verse of Scripture or any other expression of gratitude. Each letter closed with the appropriate quotation from Deut. xvi: 10:

"Thou shalt give unto the Lord thy God according as the Lord thy God has blessed thee."

PRACTICAL QUESTIONS CONCERNING THE WORK OF THE MISSIONARY COMMITTEE.

Question. What is the best method for raising funds?

Answer. The weekly or monthly envelope method. Let all who will, pledge one, two, five or ten cents each week or month, and all the money necessary will be raised and there will be a surplus for missionary purposes.

Ques. What is the "Envelope" plan of raising money?

Ans. Every one who enters into this plan agrees to give one, five, ten or twenty-five cents, or more, each week or month for a year, designating, if he desires, the objects for which his money should go. A package of envelopes is given each one who makes this pledge, the amount is deposited in the envelope each week or month and then placed in the contribution box when passed.

Ques. Should not all the money of a Y. P. S. C. E. be held by the treasurer of the society, and not by the committees who may have raised the money?

Ans. Yes; that is the duty of the treasurer.

Ques. How can we have an interesting missionary meeting?

Ans. Get full of missionary information and the missionary spirit, and there will be no trouble about having a good meeting. The reason that some missionary meetings are poor is, that those who attend them know little and care less about missions. Let the missionary committee distribute information among the members. Then have them give it in their own words. Have an interesting missionary story read. Let the prayers be specific and definite for the missionaries and their work. Occasionally get a live missionary to address the society, if possible. The missionary boards of the different denominations will send leaflets, statistics, stories, etc., if desired.

SUNDAY SCHOOL.

HINTS FOR THE SUNDAY SCHOOL COMMITTEE.

THE SUNDAY SCHOOL LIBRARY FUND.

Among the many schemes of work for the Sunday School committee that have been sent to us, this from Duluth, Minn., seems to us one of the most practical. Rev. E. M. Noyes writes:

"You may be interested in the way the Sunday School committee of the Y. P. S. C. E. looks after our Sunday School library fund. There are five members; each has a little book containing the names of ten people in the congregation who have offered to give ten cents a month for this fund. Thus we have five dollars a month steadily coming into the library fund, and get one new book each Sunday. We mean never to have to 'raise money for a library' again. Nobody feels the trifle given; it gives the Sunday School committee something definite and continual to do, aside from their other work; it helps teach them in turn something of the value and choice of books, as they are interested in the selection."

CO-OPERATION.

An excellent method of securing the co-operation of the Y. P. S. C. E. and the Sunday School has been devised by the Presbyterian Society of Decatur, Ill. The Sunday School committee of the society gave a six o'clock tea to the teachers and officers of the Sunday School, and discussed the relation of the two organizations, and pledged mutual support.

RESERVE TEACHERS.

The Sunday School committee of the Second Parish Church of Portland, Me., has, for a part of its duties, to obtain a reserve corps of teachers who may be called upon by the superintendent, at any time, to take a class. They have twenty reserve teachers on their list.

WORK FOR THE SUNDAY SCHOOL.

From the Sunday School committee of the Y. P. S. C.

E., West Spruce Street Presbyterian Church, Philadelphia, a circular and diagrams have been received, detailing a plan which that society has conceived for systematized work for the Sunday School, in outline as follows: To each member of the society a diagram is issued of a square of the city, which that member is expected to cover, going from house to house and ascertaining what children do not attend Sunday School, and to all such, sending cards on which are printed invitations to attend that of the Presbyterian Church. On the back of the diagrams are blanks to fill out, showing the result of the canvass. Once in two months the committee calls for special reports from the members.

PART XIII.

MISCELLANEOUS COMMITTEES.

GOOD LITERATURE COMMITTEE.

A unique feature of the Y. P. S. C. E. of Trinity M. E. Church of Charlestown, Mass., and one that we heartily recommend to the good literature committees of Christian Endeavor societies, is the "Young Christian's Library." This consists of books selected with especial care for the development of Christian character and the upbuilding of Christian graces. On its shelves are found such books as "Holy Living and Dying," "Imitation of Christ," "Kept for the Master's Use," "The Christian's Secret of a Happy Life," "Natural Law in the Spiritual World," "Prince of the House of David," Geikie's and Farrar's Lives of Christ, and Sermons by Whitefield, Payson, Moody and Phillips Brooks.

At present the library has about two hundred and fifty books, but of course this size has been reached gradually. No society need be discouraged from forming the nucleus of such a library if it has but one book. Begin, and others will soon be added.

1. Let this committee gather up second-hand papers, magazines, books, etc., and distribute them where they will do the most good.

2. Let it accumulate a Christian Endeavor Working Library, consisting of all the publications of the United Society. Let it pass this collection along, from term to term, holding it for reference by officers, committees, and Christian workers generally. Procure and keep, if pos-

sible, a complete file of *The Golden Rule*. It is of the greatest possible value for its working hints.

3. Let this committee interest itself in securing denominational papers, missionary magazines, and other religious periodicals of which the Church and pastor may approve. If possible see that a good religious paper gets into every family.

4. If the society is able, let the committee order papers of various kinds to be sent directly from the offices of publication to worthy persons. A dollar or two may often help greatly to brighten the home of an invalid for a year. Raise a Literature Fund by a concert, lecture, festival, or something of the sort.

THE "OMNIBUS COMMITTEE."

BY W. L. AMERMAN.

Our standing committees all hold their regular monthly meeting after the Monday night prayer-meeting the week before the monthly business-meeting of the society, and we have been trying to utilize the energies of the remainder of the members by calling them together for an "omnibus committee" meeting at the same hour. The president takes the chair and a free discussion of some phase of our work follows; *e. g.*, "Good Features in To-night's Meeting," "How We can Improve Our Prayer-meeting," "How to Prepare for the Meeting," "How We can Supplement the Social Committee's Work," etc. Great pains are taken to interest and draw out newcomers and less experienced members. A temporary secretary makes careful notes of each point, reading them before adjournment, and sometimes presenting them at the monthly business-meeting in the shape of a committee report. Special care is used that the suggestions take definite form, indicating clearly what service the members **present** may render, and at subsequent meetings a report on such work is called for.

CALLING AND FLOWER COMMITTEE.

BY H. HOWARD PEPPER.

The society of the Cranston Street Baptist Church, of Providence, R. I., has adopted the following method for finding out who are sick: In the rear of the church hangs a neat box upon which is a rack containing cards reading as follows:

Any one knowing of the sickness of any member of the Church, Sunday School or Y. P. S. C. E., will please fill out this card and drop it into the box.

NOTICE.— If the name is on the "Reported List," which hangs above the box, do not fill out a card unless you know that the case has not received attention.

After filling out the card, write the name of the sick person upon the "Reported List."

Name ....

Residence ....

Disease ....

Remarks ....

The size of this card is 4 x 5 inches.

The "Reported List" card is 4 1-2 x 8 inches, and reads as follows:

REPORTED LIST.

CALLING AND FLOWER COMMITTEE.

The following persons are reported sick.

Name.   *Remarks.*

The committee collect the cards after service, call upon the sick, or send to them fruit or flowers, with the attractive card issued by the United Society Christian Endeavor.

PASTOR'S COMMITTEE.

Another committee is suggested to us by Rev. E. R. Loomis, pastor of the first Congregational Church of Walla Walla, Washington. This, though not exactly a new idea, is new in name, we believe, and worthy of thoughtful consideration. We hear from him:

"Recently I read a communication from Rev. C. H. Smith, advocating Pastors' Informers in the Y. P. S. C. E. His idea has been carried out in our own society for several months past, but under a different, possibly a better, name, viz.: Pastor's Committee. This was added to the usual list at the beginning of the year. The officers of the society, with the chairmen of the committees, are its members. They meet at my call, and through them it is easy to find out about the workings of the whole society. Every pastor should have this body-guard of young people about him. This same committee plans for the open meetings of the society, which take the place of the evening services once in two months. By all means let every Y. P. S. C. E. have its Pastor's Committee."

MESSENGER COMMITTEE.

To meet the needs of a society in Chicago, this new committee was introduced, and most appropriately, we think. Mr. Otto C. Bruhlman writes: "They have put the very young men on this committee and also the very young ladies. Their work is to run errands and deliver messages for any of the committees or officers. This provides work for the associate members."

CHRISTIAN ENDEAVOR CLASSES.

The Y. P. S. C. E. of the Lafayette Square Presbyterian Church of Baltimore has added to its work a unique feature in the form of various educational classes. Last fall a committee of five was appointed to arrange for classes in telegraphy, phonography, calisthenics and drawing. These classes were formed and have proved a valuable addition to the purely religious work of the society. Short lectures on hygiene and physiology are also given under the auspices of the society. This seems to us a valuable suggestion for societies in city churches. Most city pastors are anxious to extend their work, and would, we have no doubt, be glad to know that their young people were willing, under pastoral guidance, of course, to attend such educational work.

FOR THE HOTEL COMMITTEES.

These committees are gaining favor in the societies of so many city churches, that we give for their benefit the following invitation sent each Saturday evening to the guests at the various hotels in St. Louis by the Y. P. S. C. E. of the Second Presbyterian Church, Rev. S. J. Niccolls, D. D., pastor:

DEAR SIR: During your stay in the city, we should be pleased to see you at any of the meetings of our church, mentioned below, especially at the young people's meeting and Sabbath School, where we make special effort to bid strangers welcome. Services on the Sabbath are: 9.30 A. M., Sabbath School; 11 A. M. morning service; 7.45 P. M., evening service.

Services during the week are:

1. Young People's Society of Christian Endeavor, every Monday at 8 P. M. in the lecture-room.

2. Weekly prayer-meeting on Wednesday at 7.45 P. M. in the lecture-room.

Hoping to see you, with as many of your friends as will come, and assuring you of a cordial welcome,

We are, yours very truly,

WELCOMING COMMITTEE,

Young People's Society of Christian Endeavor, Second Presbyterian Church.

N. B. — Please present this at the door and the usher will be pleased to show you to a seat.

On the reverse is a plan of the city, showing the position of the various hotels, the Second Presbyterian Church and the Y. M. C. A. building.

PART XIV

MISCELLANEOUS.

A CHRISTIAN ENDEAVOR PARLOR FOR YOUNG MEN AND BOYS.

All such efforts as those described below are movements in the right direction. We are glad to record and commend them. We will let an enterprising society tell its own story. Here is the statement it sent out:

The Young People's Society of Christian Endeavor of the Presbyterian Church of Jamesburg, N. J., has been deeply impressed with the following facts: While their work has been greatly blessed of God in the upbuilding of their own souls "in the nurture and admonition of the Lord," their influence upon the masses has been but slight. Their meetings are well attended, but largely by their own members. Surprised, upon reflection at the large number in the community, especially of the young men and boys, who are wholly indifferent to religious matters, and aroused by the Master's words, "Why stand ye here all the day idle," they have resolved to push forward. They accordingly ask your careful consideration of the following plan: They intend to open a Young People's Society of Christian Endeavor parlor for young men and boys. This room shall be open each evening, Sundays excepted, from 6.30 to 9 o'clock. Any one will be admitted to the privileges of the parlor who shall present each evening a ticket of admission which shall be furnished free, by the parlor committee. This parlor committee shall consist of fifteen members, and shall be appointed by the society at its regular business-meetings in March and September. Three members of the society shall be appointed by the parlor committee to take charge of the parlor on certain designated evenings.

The privileges of the parlor may be summed up as follows:

(1) Reading-room, where the leading daily and weekly papers and magazines shall be distributed. On Sabbath, only religious papers and literature.

(2) For the boys, a variety of games will be on hand for their use each evening. These games shall be innocent and instructive, subject always to the approval of the parlor committee.

(3) A singing class, which will teach not only familiar gospel songs, but national and popular airs.

(4) An evening of entertainment, consisting of readings, recitations, dialogues, music, etc.

(5) A library containing suitable books for our youths. This shall be open each evening for use in the room, and on Saturday evenings for the loan of books.

(6) To cultivate a literary taste, a paper shall be published by the parlor members, once a fortnight, which shall be edited by those of the parlor members, under the supervision of the committee for that evening. This shall consist of original articles, newspaper clippings, local jottings, etc., and shall be read before the parlor members on the second and fourth Saturday evenings of each month.

(7) To all who may wish to avail themselves of it, a savings system shall be arranged by which small deposits may be made from time to time, and when a sufficient sum is reached, it will be deposited in a suitable savings-bank, there to accrue interest to the profit of each individual depositor.

Besides these privileges of the week, the parlor will be thrown open to all men and boys on Sunday afternoon at four o'clock for a brief evangelistic service.

This parlor has already been opened under most favorable auspices. Rev. B. S. Everett, pastor of the Jamesburg Church, and Mr. F. B. Everett, secretary of the New Jersey Christian Endeavor Union, are prominent in this new enterprise.

AN INVITATION.

A very pleasing invitation to society membership has been received. On one side of a card is printed: "You are invited to the Young People's Society of Christian Endeavor," together with the name and address of the church with which it is connected; on the other, the reasons for desiring the attendance of those to whom it is sent, as follows:

We need You

   We need your Prayers

      We need your Sympathy

         We need your Counsel

           We need your Earnest work.

FOR YOUNG SOCIETIES.

The Society of the First Presbyterian Church of St. Joseph, Mo., recently held an unusually interesting and beneficial conference-meeting. Thinking that the plan might be of use to other societies, the president, Mr. James Canfield, has kindly sent a report of the meeting for our use. As the society is young, the committees have experienced some difficulty in doing their work promptly, sympathetically and effectively. Accordingly, the whole society was invited to the home of one of the members, for the purpose (to quote the invitation) "of consulting together in regard to practical plans for immediate work in our committees and to enable all to become better acquainted with what is expected of us as individual workers." The subjects for conference were suggested as follows:

1. How to work on a definite line to accomplish some definite aim?

2. How can we be made to feel more personal responsibility in the prosperity of the society?

3. The pledge — do I understand it? How can I successfully fulfill it?

4. How keep in mind that the spiritual work of the society is always paramount?

5. How best promote social feeling in both our society and church?

6. How feel more responsibility as a member of the committee for the work of that committee?

7. How interest in the Master's work young people of church and congregation who are not members of our society?

8. How can we be of more help to our pastor?

9. How can we add to the members and interest in the Sunday School?

10. Why not consult with our pastor regarding the work of the society?

11. How best use our musical talent?

12. How make our business and social meetings more of a success?

13. How "Be instant in season — out of season?"

Two hours were spent in earnest conversation, the chairman presenting the needs of the various committees and their plans for the coming months. Much help was afforded by the free discussion, and the idea of personal responsibility was made especially prominent. Light refreshments were served during the evening. We are glad to recommend this plan to all new societies. The mutual help thus afforded will prove invaluable for effective work.

CORRESPONDENCE BETWEEN SOCIETIES.

From a friend in Baraboo, Wis., we have received the details of a plan for correspondence between the societies of a district or State. The letters should contain reports of successful committee work, approved methods of conducting socials, accounts of interesting meetings, and any news that would tend to stimulate a Christian fellowship between societies. The letters should be written by the corresponding secretaries once a month, and those received should be read at the regular meetings of the societies. The first month, secretary No. 1 would write to secretary No. 2, No. 2 to No. 3, etc. The next month, No. 1 would write to No. 3, No. 2 to No. 4, etc. In this way letters would be received from different societies each month, and new and valuable hints would be constantly exchanged. In order to assist the secretary in making up his letter, the written monthly reports of the committees should be given to him for reference.

SAVING TIME.

Many societies which suffer from a temporary paralysis of activity, just after each election of officers, will be glad to know of the plan followed by the First Presbyterian Y. P. S. C. E. of Bath, N. Y.

This society holds its election two weeks before the expiration of the term of office, thus allowing time for the organization of new committees, while the old ones are doing active service. In this way they save nearly a month, which has previously been used in organization and trial work.

A GOOD WORD FOR THE BADGE.

A friend in Elgin, Ill., sends this hearty recommendation of the custom of wearing the C. E. badge:

"I have been wearing one for nearly two years, and I have found it useful and gratifying many times; useful in the way of stimulating to constant watchfulness, as it is always a silent reminder of the pledge; gratifying, as on several occasions, when in Chicago and elsewhere, I have been recognized there-by as a Christian Endeavorer, and pleasant and profitable acquaintances have followed."

This testimony is echoed by many others who have gained like advantages from the little gold or silver emblem.

SUGGESTIONS FOR ANNIVERSARIES.

A friend who has recently attended many anniversaries and union meetings has sent us the following suggestions, evidently borne in upon him by experience:

First, It is better to have the meeting in a small room that is full, or nearly so, than in a large room or church auditorium where the number is just sufficient to give a scattered, unsocial appearance.

Second, The leaders of the meeting, and all delegates who are to speak, should be impressed with the necessity of speaking so that they can be heard. As a rule, the speaking delegate cannot be heard over twenty-five feet away, and the exercises become simply a pantomime of an exasperating character.

HOTEL INVITATIONS.

A friend who recently spent a Sunday in Waterville, Me., has sent us an invitation which he received shortly after his arrival at the hotel, on Saturday evening. The hotel furnishes the society a list of the persons who are to be in town over Sunday, and each guest receives an invitation like the following:

DEAR FRIEND: You are cordially invited to attend the services at the Methodist Episcopal Church on Pleasant Street, near Center, on Sunday, —— —, Rev. H. Clifford, pastor.

Preaching service at 1.30 A. M.; subject: ———————. Sunday School at 12 M.; prayer-meeting of the Y. P. S. C. E. at 5.45 P. M.; subject: ——————, preceded by a song service of fifteen minutes; church prayer-meeting at 7 P. M. Come.

Fraternally yours,
Pleasant Street Y. P. S. C. E.

A CHRISTIAN ENDEAVOR SAVINGS BANK.

The Y. P. S. C. E. of the Congregational Church of Saugerties, N. Y., has recently added a novel annex, in the shape of a savings bank. The deposits are received after the regular Wednesday evening meeting and can be made only by members of the society. A merchant, who is a friend of the society, pays six per cent. interest on deposits which have been in the bank for a year. The enterprise has been very successful in inducing the younger members of the society to save their money; some of the boys deposited as much as five dollars within the first three months. Certainly anything that teaches lessons of frugality and economy to young people is well worth trying.

PRACTICAL QUESTIONS.

Question. What is the so-called "Christian Endeavor benediction"?

Answer. The old "Mizpah" benediction of Gen. xxxi: 49—"The Lord watch between me and thee when we are absent one from another." This was used first at the second Saratoga Convention, seemed particularly appropriate, and has been adopted by many societies. The members often unite in repeating this at the close of their meeting, and thus invoke a blessing upon each other.

Ques. How would you arrange for anniversary exercises which shall interest young Christians who are not yet members of the society, and others who, though members, do not appreciate its value?

Ans. Every society must exercise its own ingenuity in regard to such a matter. Be inventive, enterprising, wide-awake, and you will have an interesting anniversary. Perhaps you can get a good speaker to address the society on the principles of the organization. Don't get some one, however, who will pretend to give a Christian Endeavor address, and will then talk on the Hegelian Philosophy or on Witchcraft or the Sin of Ananias. Sometimes the best way is to have a quiet anniversary, employing only home talent. Have two or three bright, spicy essays or addresses on the essential features of the society; the prayer-meeting pledge, the consecration meeting, the committee work. Show how reasonable and hopeful such work is, and arouse the enthusiasm of all to engage in it.

SUGGESTIONS FOR SUMMER MISSIONARY WORK.

The following valuable hints for summer work are printed by a hectograph process, and sent out by one of our societies:

Wherever you go, bear "The Standard."

How?

First, Be present at the local prayer-meeting.

Second, Attend the Sabbath School, either as a scholar or teacher, not simply a looker-on. Take your "lesson helps" along, and study as at home.

Third, Take a supply of religious literature — books, tracts or papers; the latter, even if back numbers, may be new and acceptable to persons you may meet. Take your singing-books, also.

Fourth, If scholar, write to your Sunday School teacher, or, if teacher, write to your Sunday School scholars, during your absence, once, at least.

Fifth, Come back prepared to give some account of your summer's work at our first missionary-meeting in the fall.

NEWSPAPER EXCHANGE.

From Rev. A. F. Newton, of Marlboro', Mass., we have received the following suggestion, which may be useful to other societies:

"We find it a success. Several months ago our Young People's Society of Christian Endeavor chose a newspaper committee. A table was purchased and placed in a convenient place in the vestibule of the church. Over the table was hung a large card, on which was printed the following:

NEWSPAPER EXCHANGE.

Members of the congregation are requested to contribute papers to this table, and also to take away any paper they may wish for themselves or others. Please use this exchange generously.

Newspaper Committee Y. P. S. C. E.

"We announced from the pulpit the facts about the Newspaper Exchange, and occasionally call attention to it. After reading them, the people bring their religious papers and magazines quite freely and carry away others. We send papers to new families, and in this way spread hundreds of pages of Christian reading matter where they will do much good. Let there be a Newspaper Exchange in every church."

A PRAYER-CIRCLE CARD.

The Young People's Society of Christian Endeavor of the North Church, Springfield, Mass., for the purpose of aiding each other and of bringing souls to the knowledge of Christ, have organized a prayer-circle, and, by the use of the following card, they make the prayer regular and systematic:

Ways and Means.

"FOR YOU I AM PRAYING."

THE . . . . *PRAYER CIRCLE.*
Formed . . . . 18 . . . .

NAMES.	DAY OF REMEMBRANCE.
. . . .	Sunday
. . . .	Monday
. . . .	Tuesday
. . . .	Wednesday
. . . .	Thursday
. . . .	Friday
. . . .	Saturday

Each member of the circle has his day of remembrance when all others will pray for him. The first person named will act as secretary and see that each member and the pastor has a correct list. The pastor asks a special blessing on the day of the weekly meeting and Sunday. Keep this card where it will be seen daily.
John xvii: 21.

On the back of the card are printed directions and explanations:

"Select a name for your circle and write it in the space at the top of the card. Seven members compose a circle. A monthly meeting of the seven, for social prayer, will prove helpful."

The card was prepared for the society by Rev. F. Barrows Makepeace, is copyrighted, and may be obtained, postpaid, of Robert F. Warren, 72 Pearl Street, Springfield, Mass., at the following prices: Single set, eight cards, 15 cents; ten sets, or more, per set, 12 cents.

A MONTHLY CONFERENCE.

A friend in Scranton, Penn., sends word of a conference meeting that has proved of much benefit wherever tried. Once a month, the officers and committees of the society meet with the pastor for prayer and consultation. God's especial blessing is asked for the work of the society, the committees hold short meetings, and then all together discuss with the pastor new methods of work.

SOCIETY VISITATION.

Many societies feel the lack of acquaintance with societies in their immediate neighborhood. The local unions somewhat obviate this difficulty, but as they hold but four or five public meetings each year, personal intercourse between members of the different societies is plainly impracticable. The executive committee of the Christian Endeavor Union of Dayton, Ohio, has devised the following plan of society visitation :

Each society sends two members to visit the other societies in regular weekly order, the first two going one week to visit one society, the second two the next week to visit another, and so on. These visitors take some part in the meeting they attend, announcing the name of the society from which they come, and offering words of encouragement as they may be able. On returning to their own society, at its next meeting, they give brief reports of their visit, being careful to mention any new idea that was gained. When the round of societies has been completed, the list is to be gone over again with new visitors. In this way, every society will soon be visited by every other one. The amount of good which will be done by such a commingling of Christians cannot be estimated. It will put all into possession of what is enjoyed by all the rest.

PART XV.

BUSINESS MEETINGS.

A FAMILIAR LETTER

From the President of the United Society.

The business meetings of our Society have not received the attention which they should receive, I think. Sometimes they have been given the go-by altogether, at other times there has been altogether too much of them.

WORK ON BUSINESS PRINCIPLES.

It is needless to say that our Christian Endeavor work should be done on business principles. More and more it is coming to be seen that the business affairs of a church or of a missionary organization must be run on business principles. The Lord does not help the lazy and shiftless church out of its difficulties, any more than the lazy, shiftless grocer. Accumulated interest and debts oppress, and unwise financial management cripples a church as well as a cotton mill. One of the minor results of the Society of Christian Endeavor should be to train its members to do their business judiciously, expeditiously and with the least friction possible. It should pay its debts promptly, elect its officers properly, and transact its business legally and according to the rules of parliamentary law, and yet all these things should be made subordinate to higher aims.

BUSINESS A SECONDARY MATTER.

It should never be forgotten that the main object of our Society is not to teach parliamentary law, or the best methods of debate, or to develop a race of acute statesmen in every village. Just as little time should be taken up with business matters as is consistent with doing the business well. On this account, it is wise to have an executive committee, consisting of the officers and the chairmen of the various committees, who can bring the business into shape, hear the pros and cons, and save the time of the Society, which is so much more needed for other things than to discuss trivial matters of business. A good executive committee can prevent all friction and "keep things sweet" in any society. For this reason, too, at the semi-annual election it is well to have a nominating committee, to propose officers and committees for the ensuing term. This committee is not for the purpose of limiting the choice of members, but for the very obvious reason that in selecting a large number of persons for different positions, a few wisely selected individuals, sitting down quietly by themselves, will be likely to choose more carefully than a crowd, acting hurriedly and without concert of action.

ACCEPT THE WILL OF THE MAJORITY.

When the election has been held and the new officers fairly chosen, let the result be cheerfully accepted by the society at large. One of the most encouraging things connected with the whole movement has been the remarkably little trouble which has been experienced in these frequent elections. I do not remember having heard of a single society that has been seriously divided or injured by any internal quarrel. I believe this happy state of things is due to the devout Christian spirit which prevails, and which seeks not place or power, but only opportunity for usefulness.

DUTIES OF OFFICERS.

1. *President.* The president of the society shall perform the duties usually pertaining to that office. He shall have especial watch over the interests of the society, and it

shall be his care to see that the different committees perform the duties devolving upon them.

2. *Vice-President.* The vice-president shall perform the duties of the president in his absence.

3. *Corresponding Secretary.* It shall be the duty of the corresponding secretary to keep the local society in communication with the United Society and with other local societies, and to present to his own society such matters of interest as may come from the United Society, from other local societies, and from other authorized sources of Christian Endeavor. This office shall be permanent, and the name shall be forwarded to the United Society.

4. *Recording Secretary.* It shall be the duty of the recording secretary to keep a record of the members, and to correct it from time to time, as may be necessary, and to obtain the signature of each newly-elected member to the constitution; also, to correspond with absent members, and inform them of their standing in the society; also, to keep correct minutes of all business-meetings of the society; also, to notify all persons elected to office or to committees, and to do so in writing, if necessary.

5. *Treasurer.* It shall be the duty of the treasurer to keep safely all moneys belonging to the society, and to pay out only such sums as shall be voted by the society.

6. *Executive Committee.* This committee shall consist of the pastor of the church, the officers of the society, and the chairman of the various committees. All matters of business requiring debate shall be brought first before this committee, and by it reported either favorably or adversely to the society. All discussion of proposed measures shall take place before this committee and not before the society. Recommendations concerning the finances of the society shall also originate with this committee.

WHEN TO HOLD BUSINESS MEETINGS.

Usually they can be properly held at the close of one of the regular prayer-meetings of the month (once a month is sufficient in any society). As a rule, they need not occupy more than fifteen or twenty minutes, and the business which needs to be brought up (if all discussions are held before the executive committee) ought not to interfere with or spoil the effect of the most devout spiritual prayer-meeting.

Sometimes when the meetings are held on Sunday evening it may be best to bring up some items of business at the monthly social gatherings, or some other time. Still, let us not get the idea that our prayer-meetings are sacred and our business meetings purely secular. If carried on in the right spirit the business part may be as sacred as the prayer part.

One of our friends, Mr. E. Richmond, formerly of Delaware, but now an earnest worker in Philadelphia, has sent the following order for a business meeting, which seems to me very good:

1, Singing. 2, Prayer. 3, Reading minutes of previous meeting. 4, President's report. 5, Secretary's report. 6, Reports of Standing Committee; reports of Lookout Committee; reports of Prayer-Meeting Committee, Pastor's Aid Committee, social, etc. 7, Unfinished business (special committees, etc.). 8, New business. 9, Election of new members. 10, Presentation of cards for membership. 11, Closing service.

THE REPORTS OF COMMITTEES.

The most important part of the monthly business meeting in my opinion, is the report of the various committees. As has before been said, these should be submitted in writing, and should never be omitted. Every committee should make a report, whether it has accomplished anything or not. If nothing has been done, that should be said and put in writing, and every effort made to have a better report next month. These reports should be taken by the Secretary and placed on file, and they will, in course of time, form a tolerably complete history of the society. If your society has not adopted these written monthly reports from each committee, will you not try it, and see what interesting, stimulating and profitable occasions these monthly business meetings will become?

Your friend,
Francis E. Clark.

PRACTICAL QUESTIONS CONCERNING BUSINESS MEETINGS.

Question. I would like to ask if, when a society has adopted the "Model Constitution," which says, "Business meetings shall be held once a month," a change can be made by vote of the executive committee to have them once in two or three months, when there is no business to call us together oftener? It is hard to arrange entertainment as often as once a month, when there is little business, but the social committee feels it must provide *something* when the meeting is called.

Answer. Such a change as indicated can be made at any time, if the society votes it, on recommendation of the executive committee. The executive committee by itself is not competent to make such a change unless the society desires it, but its recommendation to this effect would usually be accepted. Every society, we think, however, should have a short business meeting every month, to hear the reports of the committees, but these reports can be given at one of the weekly prayer-meetings.

Ques. Can a question which has been voted upon by the executive committee and reported to the society adversely by that committee be then voted upon by the society?

Ans. Certainly. The recommendation of the executive committee is *only* a recommendation, not a final decision.

Ques. Can the pastor, as a member of the executive committee, if he is not an active member, vote with the other members of said committee?

Ans. Yes, the pastor should have a vote. The whole Christian Endeavor movement proceeds upon the assumption that the pastor of the church is pastor of the society by virtue of his office, and has voice and vote in all things. We hope he will always be an active member when possible.

Ques. Do you think it is for the interest of the society to combine its meetings with the regular church prayer-meeting?

Ans. Usually the young people need a separate meeting as their training school. Sometimes, for a little while under exceptional circumstances, as during the summer vacation, it may be well to combine the two meetings.

Ques. Should each of the committees have a committee meeting each month regularly?

Ans. Yes.

Ques. Should new members be voted in at the prayer-meeting or only at the monthly business-meeting?

Ans. Usually at the monthly business-meeting?

REPORTS OF COMMITTEES.

Many Societies do not yet appreciate the vital importance of monthly written reports from each committee, which, after being read, shall be kept and filed by the secretary. The following are specimens of actual reports which have been given, which show what we have in mind:

Monthly report of the Lookout Committee of the Y. P. S. C. E. of the First Congregational Church of Oregon City, Oregon.

A meeting of this committee was held on Tuesday evening, July 30th, all the members being present except one. We discussed some plans of work, and are trying by individual effort and personal work to increase the interest and faithfulness of the members of the society, and also to interest others in the work. Since the last business-meeting Miss —— has been received as an associate member, and the name of Miss —— has been proposed for associate membership.

We have tried to induce the leaders of the meetings to make the opening prayer, believing it to be part of their duty, and feel encouraged at the success of the effort though some of the leaders have not done so.

At one meeting we decided to have a hundred or more copies of our constitution and by-laws printed, as we have on hand no extra copies now. We would urge upon the other committees the advisability of holding a meeting at least once a month to plan for the work and seek our Master's help and guidance in His work.

   Respectfully submitted,
     GEORGE BLANK, Chairman.

November report of the Missionary Committee of the Y. P. S. C. E. of the First M. E. Church of Greensburg, Ind.

Within the past month one evening was given to the subject of missions; several selections were read, appropriate songs sung, a short address given by our pastor, and a letter from our district missionary, Miss Ella Shaw, was read. It was a meeting tending to inspire us with new zeal for the work.

Miss Shaw stated that the greatest need at present for her work in China was an organ.

Our society immediately voted her the amount required, thirty-two dollars, and instructed the missionary committee to devise ways by which the money could be raised. So stirred was every heart that, before any plans were made, the proposed sum had been secured by volunteer contributions, and in less than a week from the time of the action of the society, the money was forwarded.

A small surplus remains in our treasury.

May the Lord increase our zeal; and may the organ prove a blessing to Miss Shaw in her work of winning souls to Christ.

   Respectfully submitted,
     MISSIONARY COMMITTEE.

Semi-annual report of the Prayer-meeting Committee of the Y. P. S. C. E. of the First Congregational Church of Bridgeport, Conn.

Since our last semi-annual meeting, we have held twenty-eight Sunday evening meetings, viz.: Six consecration services, two character studies, one praise-meeting, and nineteen prayer-meetings. The average attendance has been eighty-seven; the largest, 114, on Feb. 3d; the smallest, thirty-one, on Nov. 25th, a stormy evening. We have used the topics as given by the united society, with the exception of two evenings, when the character studies of Daniel and John were substituted. The meetings have been well sustained. One encouraging feature is that the ladies have more frequently taken the leadership of the meeting, several having taken up the cross for Jesus for the first time. Also, some of our members have been encouraged to make an advance from repeating verses to offering prayer. Our pastor has generally been present with us, and closed the meeting with a brief, earnest talk to the young people of his flock. On the whole, we may thank God and take courage, believing that the presence and blessing of the Master will always be with us, and that He will accept the service, imperfect though it may be, which we offer Him from week to week.

Respectfully submitted,

PRAYER-MEETING COMMITTEE.

F. B. SAMMIS, *Chairman.*

Monthly report of the Helping Hand Committee of the Y. P. S. C. E. of the Bedford Reformed Church of Brooklyn, N. Y.

DEAR FRIENDS: Your committee wish that they might come to you to-night with a record of great things done in the name of our society, but as that cannot be, they assure you that the little things you have done through them have been fully appreciated. From us went a book of daily readings to an active member of another Y. P. S. C. E., who has been afflicted with a long, tedious illness. He writes that the book has given him both pleasure and comfort, and that he wishes his warmest thanks given to the society. To another young lad whom God will soon call to pass through the ever-open gates of that beautiful city whose inhabitants never say, "I am sick," we have had the pleasure of sending a dainty basket of fruit and flowers combined. Eight bouquets of wild and garden flowers have been taken to the Old Ladies' Home, where they have doubtless caused the inmates to "see visions and dream dreams" of the country which we have seen in reality this summer. A pot of ferns and some cut flowers have been sent at different times to sick friends in our own congregation. During the month there has been started a loan library of books and magazines. This will be under the care of the helping hand committee, who will gladly receive additions of suitable matter at any time. We have expended ninty-eight cents, and have the sum of two dollars in our treasury.

PART XVI.

THE UNITED SOCIETY—LOCAL AND STATE UNIONS.

THE UNITED SOCIETY.

A Familiar Letter About Matters More or Less Personal.

Pardon me for taking a little space to speak of some matter of history connected with the United Society. Almost every week, I have had scores of requests to tell more about the United Society and how it does its work. It is not out of place, I think, to tell you how there came to be a United Society and how *The Golden Rule* came to be adopted as the National Christian Endeavor paper, especially as so many thousands have joined the Endeavor family since anything has been said on this subject.

WHY THE UNITED SOCIETY EXISTS.

If you could come into the office at 50 Bromfield Street any morning at about 9 o'clock, as the office boy brings the mail, you would very soon realize why the United Society exists. His big leather mail-bag is running over with letters. Forty or fifty or perhaps seventy-five he brings to my desk. Another pile goes to the business agent; still a larger lot, a hundred, more or less, to the general secretary. This is only the first mail of the day. There are half a dozen more clerks, all Christian Endeavorers, and all *active* members, who are kept as busy as bees, filling orders, doing up samples of literature, sending out the free information which is still called for by the ton, etc. All these letters are the direct and legitimate descendants of that first letter that came a little more than seven years ago, asking for information concerning the first experiment, called a Society of Christian Endeavor.

THE LETTERS.

Multiply this pile of letters by three hundred and seven, the number of working-days in the year, throwing out Sundays and holidays, and you will have at least 75,000 of them and a very sufficient reason, were there no other, for the existence of the United Society. Then there is all the organizing work and the writing and supervision of literature and the efficient work of the general secretary, for all of which the United Society is responsible. Every month the trustees of the United Society have a meeting and give a good part of a day to consultation concerning the work. And yet no authority is claimed, no allegiance is asked for the United Society, no taxes are levied. The United Society exists for what it can give, and as soon as its mission is ended it will be very glad to give up its commission and go out of existence.

THE GOLDEN RULE.

But the well being of *The Golden Rule* seems to be an affront to some people. They cannot understand its prosperity or the growth of its subscription list. They think it has thrust itself upon the societies, and that somehow it compels the innocent and unsuspecting young people to subscribe. Thousands of the more recent societies do not know how this paper came to be adopted as the organ of the societies. Let me tell them: For several years one of the "burning questions" at every convention was, "Shall we have a newspaper representative?" One scheme after another was proposed only to be rejected. The United Society had no money to buy or establish a respectable newspaper, and no one was brave enough to put his money into such an enterprise. At length, in response to repeated requests from the societies, five gentlemen obtained a controlling interest in *The Golden*

Rule, a paper which had had a checkered existence for several years. They were willing to risk their own money in a scheme which promised much for the society but offered at the best little prospect of pecuniary return. This paper was adopted very heartily at the next national convention as the national Christian Endeavor paper. Every national convention and very many State conventions since have repeated the indorsement. One or two of the brethren in the ministry and one or two religious newspaper editors are very much exercised over the fearful thought that somebody is getting rich out of the paper. If they can figure a great profit out of such a paper as *The Golden Rule*, furnished as it is to most of the Christian Endeavor readers for a dollar a year, I think the proprietors will be willing to divide any such imaginary profit with the distinguished mathematician. Moreover *The Golden Rule* has a field of its own, and seeks to occupy that alone. It does not interfere with denominational and other religious papers, but is rather a help to their circulation, as more than one editor has testified. It simply stands upon its own merits as a religious journal for young people.

A MONEY SAVER.

One thing I know, and that is, that *The Golden Rule* saves the United Society thousands of dollars every year. It prints a great deal of literature that otherwise would have to be put in pamphlet form; it enables the president of the United Society to give his services to the cause; it reaches over two hundred thousand readers every week with the freshest news and the latest methods of work, as they could not possibly be reached in any other way.

MUCH SERVICE FOR NOTHING.

No one connected with the society, I am sure, desires to make any appeal for sympathy and no one appears in the rôle of the underpaid official or the martyr to the cause; but I can assure you that, so far as I know, there is no organization in America where so much service is freely rendered on the part of officers, trustees and friends alike, for which no penny of pay is ever asked or received, as in the Society of Christian Endeavor. It has been characterized by this from the beginning. No one has ever been connected with it in any section of the country for "what he could make." No State officers have ever received any salary, though many of them have done much work, and it is an unwritten law that all this work is to be done gratuitously by busy men who have other means of support. Every night in the week, in all parts of the land, scores of Christian Endeavor addresses are made without any pay by speakers, many of whom could command a large price for their services. I know that it is unnecessary to say these things to those who will read this letter, but it will, at least, give you the facts to reply to those who may make ill-natured and unjust attacks. No cause can expect to make the headway that the Christian Endeavor cause has made without exciting the jealousy and opposition of some. Our society has met with surprisingly little opposition and it has always been profited rather than hindered by it. If we are humble, faithful and true to our great purpose, this will always be the result.

Your friend,

FRANCIS E. CLARK.

CHRISTIAN ENDEAVOR UNIONS.—THEIR HELPFULNESS AND POSSIBILITIES.

BY REV. JUSTIN E. TWITCHELL, D. D.,

Pastor of the Dwight Place Church, New Haven.

Young people's meetings are nothing new. For many years they have been held in numerous churches of the land, and universally have been helpful, not only to the young people who have attended and sustained them, but also to the churches of which these young people have been members, or in which they have been worshippers.

No room for argument here, nor call for illustration. Union meetings of these young people from different churches in various localities are nothing new. They have been held statedly or occasionally in more than one city for several years, and they have always been of interest.

It remained, however, for a certain church in Portland, Me., to perfect the organization known as the "Y. P. S. C. E.," and for a certain church in New Haven, Conn., to organize the "Christian Endeavor Unions."

That the Y. P. S. C. E. has been wonderfully blessed and prospered, its growth and power abundantly attest. At first, by some, it was looked upon with suspicion. Now, however, no pastor can afford to fail of encouraging it and no church can afford to be without it. It has increased the devotion of the young people everywhere; has marvellously developed the working forces among them, and, in many cases, has put new life into the church itself. Originating at a time when the churches of the land had grown comparatively undevotional and inactive, it has been owned of God in quickening the love, increasing the zeal and setting in motion the dormant energies of many an adult follower of Christ.

As a natural and almost inevitable result of the multiplied and fast-multiplying local Societies of Christian Endeavor, these separate organizations have sought fellowship one with another. Thus the "Christian Endeavor Union" was born, upon which the abundant blessing of God has been bestowed.

The helpfulness of these unions is already found to be great:

1. IN THEIR SUGGESTIONS. If the members of the local society never look or go beyond themselves, they are in danger of growing short-sighted, narrow in their conception of duty and privilege, formal and routine in their "endeavor," and are liable to languish, if not actually die, of discouragement. All Christians, and especially the

young, need to know what others are thinking about, along Christian lines; what their methods of worship and work are, and how this or that method has succeeded.

The Christian Endeavor union brings together for consultation a dozen or more representative young Christians from as many different local societies. Matters of mutual interest are discussed, plans reported, difficulties considered, advantages weighed and results given. Each local society, therefore, has the advantage of the projects and experiences of all the rest.

2. IN INSPIRATION. — Bring together three or five hundred young Christians from twenty or thirty churches; let them look into each other's faces; let them warmly grasp each others' hands; let their voices unite in song; let them hear each other pray; let them report the Lord's doings with them in their several societies and churches; let them listen to personal testimony; above all, let them bow in humble confession and consecration; the inspiration is untold. Those who are present usually go back to their local societies and churches quickened and equipped for aggressive Christian work.

3. IN FELLOWSHIP. — Young Christians especially, need this. Living in comparative isolation, as many of them do, working in their own local field, which is often, as they feel, limited and little hopeful, the danger is that they will become lonely and disheartened. Bring them into contact with fellow-Christians of their own age and "endeavor;" they will see that a common bond of sympathy unites them, that the family of God is of an uncounted membership, that real Christian love pulsates in the heart of every true disciple, that there is a real fellowship among those who love the Lord and are endeavoring to do God's work in the world, whatever be their church home or their church surroundings.

Along these three lines, suggestion, inspiration and fellowship, Christian Endeavor Unions are wonderfully helpful. Let every local society seek union with others, and make much of the stated union meetings.

As to the possibilities of these Christian Endeavor Unions, who shall venture to name them? I can see that they are immense and immeasurable. They are to develop and intelligently direct the activities of a great host of our young people in the nearly one hundred thousand Christian churches of the land. They are to suggest to them and largely shape forms of worship and of work. They are to train young men and women to take up their cross, bear personal testimony, and make personal endeavor for the winning of souls to Christ. They are to have large influence on the conception and character of the prayer and conference meetings of the churches. They are to be the means of increasing the activity and zeal of older church-members. They are to develop a noble band of Christian young men and women for the responsibilities of church management, and bring into play forces that will be felt for good in all our churches when the fathers and mothers shall give place to the sons and daughters in the direction of church affairs and in worldwide evangelizing efforts.

No tongue shall assume to tell, or pen to write, the possibilities of Christian Endeavor Unions. The prophecy, however, is plain that brighter days ere long shall dawn on the church and world, largely ushered in through the instrumentality of agencies which quicken and combine the young in our churches.

CONCERNING LOCAL UNIONS.

A Familiar Letter from the President of the United Society.

I wonder if we have yet learned, in our Christian Endeavor work, the power of union effort? We have been largely emphasizing the other side, the individual element, and we have not by any means said the last word on this exceedingly important theme. The great object of our organization is accomplished when each local society is doing its utmost to strengthen the church with which it is connected. The fact cannot be over-emphasized that the Y. P. S. C. E. is permanently (more, perhaps, than any other society ever formed) a church and pastor's aid society, and that its work is largely done when it has aided to the utmost its own particular church.

And yet, for the sake of doing this special work most efficiently, we must look beyond our own little, narrow horizon occasionally, and hear some other sounds than the singing of our own individual tea-kettle on our own family hearth.

THE OBJECT OF CHRISTIAN ENDEAVOR UNIONS.

To make each local society most efficient and most helpful in its own church have Christian Endeavor unions been established, and union meetings held, and very largely have they accomplished their purpose. Like everything else connected with our work, they have had a providential origin and development. It was felt that something was being lost because the societies could not oftener inquire after each other's welfare, and compare notes, and talk over methods of work, and so, at the instance in the first place of Rev. J. E. Twitchell, D. D., of New Haven, some of our zealous Christian Endeavor Societies in that city formed themselves into a local union. The example was contagious, as, fortunately, a good example, as well as an evil one, often is. Other unions in the vicinity were at once formed, and, though Connecticut has heretofore been the banner State in this branch of our work, her good example has been copied far and wide.

DOES YOUR SOCIETY BELONG TO A UNION?

Perhaps it is not feasible. Yours may be isolated from others so that you may be obliged to get along without this source of inspiration. But if yours is one of a little group of six or eight societies in city or country, there is no reason why you should not form a union, and gain great help from it. You are deliberately giving up one real and accessible "means of grace" by neglecting to form it.

HOW TO FORM A UNION.

Let some one call together some representatives from all the local societies who are interested in this matter; adopt a simple constitution, without much machinery (a model which has worked well in many societies will be furnished by the United Society, if you desire), have every society in the vicinity that will join represented on the executive committee (perhaps by its president), choose a president, secretary and treasurer, and your craft is all built and rigged, and ready to be launched.

Since the sole object of these unions is fraternity, fellowship, good feeling and mutual help, care should be taken that no society, however small or weak, has occasion to feel slighted, and that no clique or ring controls the union; while, on the other hand, the super-sensitive, who are always getting "grieved" if they are not sufficiently consulted and deferred to, should remember that very little can ever be done in this world unless some one goes ahead and does the work, and that it is a great deal better to fall into line and help make those things better that are not quite perfect, than to nurse wounded feelings and sore heads.

However, it is a work of supererogation to say such things as these to members of a Christian Endeavor Society, or at least — it ought to be.

WHAT KIND OF MEETINGS SHALL WE HAVE?

1. Have variety. Do not have two meetings in succession that are just alike.

2. Do not weary the audience with too many long reports from local societies. Have these reports once a year, have them crisp, short and meaty, not over two minutes in length from each society. Keep every speaker within the allotted time.

3. Bring out new and improved methods of work. Let each society in the union tell just how it has been able to do the best work.

4. Rely most upon home talent, but perhaps once or twice a year have some speaker from outside the union, who can arouse and inspire the members.

5. Occasionally have a union consecration-meeting (say once a year), a real, live, Christian Endeavor consecration-meeting, and I have little doubt that at its close you will say, "That is the best meeting we have had."

HOW OFTEN SHALL MEETINGS OF THE UNION BE HELD?

Not too often. The demands of the local society and the church for which it labors are numerous and exacting, and the meetings of the union should not be held often enough to interfere with them. Some unions hold monthly meetings, but most find that once in two months, or even quarterly, is often enough for the best results.

Hold the meetings with the different churches composing the union.

Go to get good, and not to criticise. Go to give as well as to get. Take away only the best things, and forget any mistakes or blunders, and remember that the true standard by which to measure the meetings is the spiritual standard. I will append a simple constitution which has been found to work well in practice.

FORM OF CONSTITUTION FOR A LOCAL UNION.

ARTICLE I. This society shall be called the ——————— Christian Endeavor Union.

ART. II. The object of the society shall be to stimulate the interest in Young People's Societies of Christian Endeavor in ——————— and vicinity. To increase their mutual acquaintance and to make them more useful in the service of God.

ART. III. Any Young People's Society of Christian Endeavor in ——————— and vicinity, whose Constitution in its aim and prayer-meeting obligations conforms generally in spirit to the "Model" Constitution, may join this Society by notifying the Secretary.

ART. IV The officers shall be a President, Vice-President, and

Secretary and Treasurer. The President and Secretary and Treasurer shall be selected from Active Members, and to serve one year, remaining in office until their successors are elected. All the Presidents of the Y. P. S. C. E. forming this Union shall be Vice-Presidents of this Society. The President, Vice-Presidents, and Secretary and Treasurer shall constitute an Executive Committee to provide for the general interest of the Union.

ART. V. This Society shall hold meetings at such times and places as shall be determined by the Executive Committee. The president may call special meetings of the Executive Committee when he may deem it necessary.

ART. VI. The duties of the President, Vice-President, Secretary and Treasurer shall be the duties usually pertaining to these offices.

ART. VII. This Constitution may be amended by a two-thirds vote of all the Active Members present at any regular meeting, the amendment having been submitted in writing, and notice having been given at least four weeks before action is taken.

Any local union, of course, is at liberty to enlarge upon or improve this constitution, but I think that the above will be found in the main, to answer the requirements of most societies.

Your friend,

FRANCIS E. CLARKE.

THE IDEAL PROGRAMME FOR A LOCAL UNION.

BY W. H. CHILDS,

Vice-President of the Connecticut Union.

There are four things that local union programems can legitimately aim at, viz.: Conversion, inspiration, instruction and sociability. Programmes should be arranged by the executive committee, after careful consideration of the needs of the societies to be reached. It is seldom wise to attempt to hit all of these points in one programme, and care should be exercised that one part of the programme does not neutralize the effect of another part. The social features of our union work are very valuable, and the friendships made in them and the ties formed between the members of different churches are solving, in many places, the problem of Christian unity. Make much of the social part, but make more of the other parts. As a rule, the social part should precede the programme proper, or else come in before the address or closing devotional service. Only in rare cases should the union meeting close with a sociable. Although we can closely unite sociability and prayer, yet the memory of the last hour is apt to stay with us longest, and it should be the memory of an uplift toward God.

The following programmes illustrate two of many ways of making up union meetings :

First. 6 to 7.30, supper and social greetings; 7.30 to 8, praise service, Bible reading (with reference to subject of meeting), prayer; 8 to 8.10, business; 8.10 to 8.40, address; 8.40 to 9, devotional service, following closely subject of address.

In this case, if the speaker can be depended upon to lead up in his address to a close full of inspiration, it might be well to put the devotional service just before the address.

Second. 7.30 to 7.45, opening service; 7.45 to 8, business; 8 to 8.20, paper on lookout committee work, with short discussion; 8.20, singing; 8.20 to 8.35, social recess; 8.35 to 8.50, address, "Pledges Made to God"; 8.50 to 9.10, consecration service, subject: "Keeping Vows."

These samples simply illustrate the statement that programmes should be made up in harmony with one central thought, and should aim at something.

CONCERNING THE IDEAL CONVENTION.

A Familiar Letter from the President of the United Society.

Within a few weeks I have attended more than a score of Christian Endeavor conventions and conferences of greater or less magnitude, most of them large and capitally managed meetings, and I feel moved to pass over to you some hints and suggestions that have come to me, which will perhaps help you in some future meetings.

AS TO PREPARATION.

Most of the meetings this fall have been, as I said, wonderfully successful; and it has been because *some one* has prepared for them beforehand. Who that some one has been, I have not always known; that some one has not always been most prominent in the convention; but, in sight or out of sight, he has been there, and without this some one the convention would have been a miserable failure. Some one, however, should not have all the work or all the responsibility. For an important meeting there should be various committees to do the work, and it should be parcelled out systematically among them: one committee on programmes; another on such details as ushers, badges, suitable tables for literature, etc.; another on hospitality, to welcome arriving delegates, and to direct them to their lodgings or the place of meeting, etc. I am aware that all these details often have to be attended to by one or two individuals; but, as our state and local work grows, and the number of workers increases, these matters should be subdivided, and no one overloaded with all the details.

AS TO THE PROGRAMME.

Have different denominations represented so far as the societies found in any locality are divided among denominations, remembering always that ours is an inter-denominational society. Know something about all your speakers. Do not take many chances in any speaker or leader of a meeting. We desire, of course, to develop the young and inexperienced; but a great convention is not the place to do this. Remember that every minute of a convention is precious. It will not do to run risks. For leading speakers get not only those who are well known, so far as possible, but get those who are bright, vigorous and forceful. A speaker who can be heard only half-way across the hall is much better off the programme than on. Our societies are developing plenty of bright young men and women who will make a capital impression, and commend the cause to all who hear them. Before any one is invited to appear before such audiences as our conventions bring together you should know what he can do. Give a good deal of time, also, to volunteer speakers from the floor. Have live questions that can be discussed; but do not choose those that will naturally excite controversy. Have a half-hour for brief, pithy reports from societies or unions, but do not spend too much time on this, or have simply figures reported (so many members, date of formation, etc.). Have each one tell, rather, what the society has done for the church. Do not overcrowd the programme. This is perhaps the most common danger of all. Be very careful who opens the question-box. Have level-headed, common-sensible, well-posted persons to do this.

BRING THE MINISTERS TO THE FRONT.

Since our society is so peculiarly and closely related to the work of each local church, and since it has no mission apart from the church, the pastors should have a prominent place at all these meetings. Get as many as you can on the platform. Give them a chance to give their testimony concerning the society; see that their influence is recognized on the committees, and in official positions; let every convention and union meeting be an object-lesson of the cordial, affectionate relation existing between the pastors and the societies. Whether a clergyman should be president of the convention must be determined by local considerations. Frequently their names and position in the community will help the cause, though sometimes they cannot give the time necessary to the position, and some capable young layman can fill it better on that account. Let it always be understood, however, that the co-operation, presence and advice of the pastors is desired and expected, just as it is in our individual societies.

AS TO THE CHAIRMAN.

The qualities needed in a good chairman are that he should be alert, wide-awake, sensible, and should know enough of parliamentary law to keep from getting into a snarl. Very little parliamentary sharp practice is ever known at these meetings, I am thankful to say; but the chairman should be enough at ease in his place to keep things running smoothly. By a few timely words, a pleasant manner, and with the exercise of a little tact, he can oil the wheels and prevent any possible friction. We have been, I think, for the most part, remarkably happy in these officers.

A FEW DETAILS.

Who should be invited to the conventions? In my opinion, all the members of every society in the State or district should be invited to come as delegates. Some, I know, think that the voting delegates should be limited to one or two from each society, and I only give my opinion for what it is worth. I think, however, that as a rule, we can do more good by inviting all, and by giving them all the privileges of delegates. In our meetings there is little danger of packed conventions, for we must remember that they are never for legislation, but only for spiritual stimulus and inspiration; so the more who attend as delegates, the better. Should delegates pay their own bills? I think so, as a rule. I know that some States have generously and freely entertained all delegates, and I appreciate the kindness of heart that prompts this entertainment, but in many of our States it is already impossible to do this, the numbers are so large. We wish to be no burden to the hospitality of any community; and if it costs a little more to go and pay our own way, we shall usually get enough more out of the meeting to pay the extra cost. The very lowest possible rates should be secured, and very cheap accommodations obtained, for those who can pay but a small sum. However, each convention will, I am sure, decide wisely all such matters for itself.

SOME TOPICS.

Here are some good fresh topics from recent programmes, with which I will close my letter:

"The Prayer-meeting of 1900," "Our Societies' Sentinels" (*i. e.*, the lookout committee), "Pledge Requirements," "Things that Hinder," "The Young Woman in Christian Endeavor," "Cure for the Neglectful," "Prayer-meeting Ruts." Of course these are in addition to the more common, but all-important, subjects of "Committee Work." "The Consecration-meeting," "The Society Interdenominational," "The Junior Work," "The Aim and Purpose of Christian Endeavor," etc., subjects which cannot yet be safely omitted from many of our convention programmes.

Your friend,

FRANCIS E. CLARK.

HOW TO PREPARE FOR A STATE CONVENTION.

BY REV. JOHN L. SEWALL.

1. Begin twelve months ahead to pray and plan. Note any failure or mistake in this year's meeting, any place for possible improvement, while freshly in mind.

2. Capture and imprison in memorandum book every bright idea which flashes upon your mind: a timely topic, the name of a good speaker, a new method.

3. As to place of meeting: see that the greatest possible Endeavor enthusiasm is previously aroused in the community and adjoining towns, as by a local union or similar meeting; local interest is a great help.

4. Secure as chairman of committee of arrangements a genuine business man, and let all local responsibility center in him.

5. As to programme:

(1) Arrange it three months before the meeting; this will give none too much time to secure a speaker for every part; six weeks before the convention the complete programme ought to be ready and printed.

(2) Have some reliable, "all-round" men ready to fill vacancies which are sure to come during the sessions.

(3) Use lay talent as much as possible, in a few ten-minute and more five-minute addresses; let those who take these parts understand that time limits will be strictly enforced; if they are inexperienced in public speaking, earnestly advise them to submit their papers to their pastors for criticism.

(4) For themes requiring special wisdom and discrimination, call to your aid the right kind of ministers; but never put any man upon the programme as a "compliment". Sometimes, ask the ministers to promptly follow, rather than lead in the discussions.

(5) Have every part of the State represented in the list of speakers, not slighting the smaller societies. Try to discover new talent by inquiry of pastors and local union secretaries.

(6) As to character of topics: divide about equally between those of instruction upon specific points of C. E. work and those of broader inspiration to better Christian service. Rely on the question-box for all matters of detail in the work of the societies.

(7) Take the work of some one committee, as, for instance, the social, subdivide and thoroughly discuss it.

(8) Secure, if possible, one of our trusted leaders from the National Society, and give him a fair chance, that is, if he gives an evening address, shorten the preliminaries, and have only one address (not exceeding thirty minutes) before his, so that he may have a fresh and not an exhausted audience.

6. Plan places for business where it will not find uninterested audiences; for example, put in a half-hour at the close of the afternoon, when the local audience, but not the delegates, will be anxious to get to their homes.

7. Have frequent devotion interspersed throughout each session, rather than concentrated at its beginning. For good singing, get the S. C. E. books, a cornetist (indispensable) and a chorus choir (very helpful).

8. Remember that the two best parts of the programme are the model C. E. prayer-meeting (an early morning one, if possible, led by the best leader in the State) and the

consecration-meeting. If you cannot have an eminent worker lead this last, do the next best thing you can.

9. As to finances: send out, two months before the meeting, a statement of the estimated expense of the convention to every society, with a blank pledge to be filled and returned to the State treasurer, and to be paid at the meeting. This plan will obviate any word of begging in the meetings, and will probably leave a comfortable surplus for the next year.

10. Do not be afraid to use the printing-press; advertise the convention well; send preliminary announcements, programmes, appeals, bulletins, a week or ten days apart, until every society in the State is positively sure that there is to be a convention; it will cost something, but it will richly pay in enthusiasm and large representation.

AN IDEAL STATE CONVENTION PROGRAMME.

BY REV. H. N. KINNEY.

President of the Connecticut Union.

1. It will be a *State* programme, in dignity and design, as contrasted with a local union programme; in subjects and speakers, in distinction from a national conference programme. Yet the United Society will be recognized.

2. It will characterize and epitomize the work of Endeavor in the State.

3. It will suggest and emphasize what it ought to be in the future.

4. It will answer the question, for members and societies, "How?" for pastors and the public, "What?" for wide-awake workers, "What next?" in that state.

5. It will grow out of the programme of the year before, and into the programme of the year to come.

6. It will be based on a knowledge of the condition of the societies, of the principles of Endeavor and of the

place of Endeavor, in the work of Christ and the church at large.

7. The committee of arrangements will be Brains, Forethought, Spiritual Purpose, Executive Ability and Good Judgment.

8. The local committee will be Obedience to Orders, Perfections in Details, Willingness to Work, Prayerful Preparation and Cordial Welcome.

9. In main outline, it will be thought of and thought out during the year preceding crystallizing in solution.

10. Amid diversity will "our increasing purpose run." It will not be a witch's cauldron, a crazy-quilt or even the chance combination of a kaleidoscope; rather a mosaic — "as the world, harmoniously confused."

11. The first session will be Introduction; the second, Routine Discussion; the third, Elucidation and Inspiration; the fourth, Climax and Consecration.

12. Its model will be a Christian Endeavor prayer-meeting.

13. Its motto will be: "No long speeches. Many to hear from. Every one on time."

14. It will recognize lay talent as well as ministerial, male and female, sections and sects, in due proportion.

15. It will proceed on "schedule time" and be carried out as planned, yet will be flexible for discussions from the floor. *It will have a bell!*

16. It will allow no choir-singing on the last night of the convention.

17. It will give frequent place for prayer.

18. It will subdivide its topics on occasion, in the morning, for discussion by groups in different rooms.

19. It will make all announcements on a printed programme.

20. The printed programme will be, though plain, attractive.

PRACTICAL QUESTIONS CONCERNING UNITED SOCIETY LOCAL UNIONS, ETC.

Question. In order to belong to the United Society of Christian Endeavor, is it absolutely essential that a society should adopt word for word the common pledge?

Answer. No. If the idea and spirit and obligation are the same, that is sufficient, but uniformity is pleasant and desirable.

Ques. Is there not some danger to be apprehended from banding these local societies together in national and State organizations?

Ans. No danger will be apprehended when the nature of these unions is understood. These organizations demand nothing of the young people. They exercise no control and lay down no laws. They exist only to give information and to aid the local societies, and one way in which they do this is by constantly urging to greater love and loyalty for the church.

Ques. How shall one go to work to form a local union?

Ans. Call a preliminary meeting of all who are interested in such a project in the various societies. After voting to form such a union, if this is the desire of the societies represented, adopt a simple constitution and elect officers and arrange for the first meeting of the union, or leave it in the hands of the executive committee. All the societies of the union should be represented (through their presidents, perhaps) on the executive committee. A sample constitution, which has been adopted by many unions will be sent on application to the U. S. C. E., 50 Bromfield Street, Boston.

Ques. When a county convention is held, whose duty is it to notify neighboring societies?

Ans. It is the duty of the secretary of the union.

Ques. Should the corresponding secretary report regularly? If so, how often, and what items should be included in the report?

Ans. Blanks will be sent to the corresponding secretary once a year to be filled out.

Ques. What Helps does the United Society publish and at what price?

Ans. A complete price-list will be sent on application. Here are some of the publications: "The Society of C. E. What It Is and How It Works," "The Model Constitution," "The Element of Obligation," "Junior Societies," "Reorganization," "What the Pastors Say," "The Work of the Committees," "The Beginnings of a Society of Christian Endeavor." These pamphlets are by Rev. F. E. Clark, except the last, which is by Rev. S. W. Adriance, and are published for two cents, except "The Work of the Committees," which costs three cents. Besides these, pledge cards for active and associate members, invitation and introduction cards and others for the Sunday School and flower committee are published at an average price of 50 cents per hundred. Uniform prayer-meeting topic cards cost from $1 per hundred upward, according to style. The solid gold C. E. badge costs 75 cents or $1, according to weight, and the silver one, 25 cents. A handsome lithograph copy of the prayer-meeting pledge, suitable for framing and which can be read across the vestry, costs 50 cents.

The revised pledge suspended from rod with roll attached, price 75 cents.

PART XVII.

JUNIOR SOCIETIES.

A FAMILIAR LETTER

By the President of the United Society.

A providential outgrowth of the Christian Endeavor movement has been the Junior Societies, which are now being formed so rapidly. Many churches desire to do more for the younger boys and girls than seems quite practicable in the average society of Christian Endeavor. Most societies hold their prayer-meeting as late as half-past seven o'clock in the evening, and at the best it is difficult to get through and home again before nine o'clock. For the boys and girls, from eight to twelve or thirteen, many parents have thought these hours too late, and as they cannot wisely be changed, this very fact has made the Junior Society or something that answers this purpose almost a matter of necessity.

Moreover, the same sort of a meeting is not always the most appropriate for the younger ones and for the older ones alike, since more in the way of instruction can be introduced to the advantage of the Junior Societies.

In the regular Christian Endeavor meeting the leader should take up very few of the precious minutes; in the Junior meeting, which should be led usually by some older person, more time can be appropriately taken in this way.

TEACH THEM TO PRAY.

In these meetings the boys and girls should be taught to pray aloud, and before their companions. The eight-year-old boy can offer a prayer which is exactly as appropriate for him to offer as the prayer which his father, the fifty-year-old deacon, may offer. If the boys and girls begin in the Junior Societies to offer these prayers, and it becomes a part of their religious lives thus to pray, the time will never come when they cannot perform this Christian duty. I know of some homes where the little ones at the table ask the blessing on the food, and it always seems to me a delightful recognition of God's willingness to listen to a child's prayer.

In one church with which I am acquainted, one of the leading young men, the president of the society of Christian Endeavor, gets a company of boys together every Sunday afternoon, talks and prays with them, and gets them to pray for themselves. No formal Junior Society of Christian Endeavor has yet been formed in that church, but the work thus done will help the boys wonderfully, and before many years their voices will be heard, I believe, in prayer in the weekly meeting of the society.

A COMBINATION OF WORK.

These Junior Societies, too, while they should not forget their especial mission of training the boys and girls for the older society, and thus for the church, can frequently combine and render more effective various scattered branches of church work for children. For instance, one branch of the work may have reference to temperance effort, and one meeting each month may be used to inculcate temperance principles, and to pray for this great cause. Another branch may be the mission circle division, with a monthly missionary meeting, and an afternoon, as often as may be deemed best, for the girls to sew or pack the missionary box. Still another branch might be for the many admirable lines of work taken up by the King's Sons and the King's Daughters. Thus, instead of increasing and multiplying organizations, the Junior Society may simplify and make more effective the work of many existing organizations, while at the same time the spiritual side of all this work is made prominent by the Junior prayer-meeting, which may be made very short, but should never be omitted.

ANOTHER ADVANTAGE.

Another advantage of combining the different branches of work and centering them around the prayer-meeting is, that thus many more children can be interested in the great movements of the day.

For instance, in many churches only a dozen or twenty of the girls are in the mission circle, but through the Junior Society all the boys and girls might be led to take some interest in missions and in the work of the circle. So with temperance and other branches of Christian work. They are all important, and all necessary, and the Junior Society, if rightly managed, may bring a multitude of children to become interested in these things, and greatly increase their efficiency. Mrs. Alice May Scudder has written an admirable book for Junior Societies called Attractive Truths in Lesson and Story, to which I would refer you for further information on the snbject.

Your friend,

FRANCIS E. CLARK.

WORK AMONG CHILDREN.

BY MISS MARY F. DANA.

I suppose that none of us question the advisability and importance of interesting the children in Christian work, and it is perfectly apparent in most Endeavor societies that there is no opportunity for the active participation of children. "Even a child is known by his doings, whether his work be pure and whether it be right." We believe it, and we desire to see Christian Endeavorers among the children. It is early training in the Scriptures and in the principles of right action that is essential to the development of a strong and pure youth. If in some homes the children are fortunate enough to receive the desired training in these things, in others they are not so blessed, and, moreover, the meeting together, the assuming of some slight responsibility and the taking part in some public exercise, teaches them a ready application of their powers to active Christian service. In educating children for citizenship, the State does not rest upon the supposition that parents will see that their children are suitably prepared for their duties. We know very well that many parents will do nothing of the kind, and we make a certain degree of education a compulsory matter. In many countries children and youth have been, and still are compelled to undergo a certain amount of physical training. Should not the church then, by every means in its power, supplement all possible home-training, and provide for the lack of it, by organized endeavor for the development of the pliant spiritual powers of its children? Most Sunday School teachers know how impossible it is to give much time to the memorizing of Scripture, to instruction in missionary and temperance matters, in the one short hour of the Sunday session. A Christian Endeavor meeting is a good place to take up much work of this sort. These meetings are also invaluable opportunities for additional efforts in the exercise of singing.

METHODS OF ORGANIZATION.

If we are to bear the name of Junior Y. P. S. C. E., we should, as a matter of course, preserve, so far as possible, the distinctive characteristics of the Christian Endeavor movement; but some modifications are necessary. In our own society we did not feel that we could work a children's society successfully by the Model Constitution. We did not divide into active and associate members. Our acquaintance with the children was, in the beginning, too slight to enable us to make such distinctions among them, and they themselves had too little understanding of the requirements, and would have taken the pledge thoughtlessly. But a pledge is required of all, a pledge of constant attendance and assistance in promoting the ends of the society, and as acquaintance with individuals increases, endeavors are made to obtain from the more thoughtful an expression of Christian purpose, and we intend that when they join the older society they shall not be afraid to take the strictest sort of a pledge.

Officers and committees can be substantially the same as in the senior society, with the same terms of office and the same methods of election, provided they be under the supervision of adult officers. Let the connection with the older society be as close as possible. Let the superintendent of the juniors be chosen from the active members of the other branch, and let this branch always be reported at the semi-annual business-meeting, then they will naturally pass into the older society when they have reached the age limit of the juniors.

VARIETY.

Greater variety in the meetings is, of course, necessary with the children. We hold one temperance-meeting a month, one missionary-meeting, one Bible-reading and a consecration-meeting, as we call it. Although this is somewhat different in character from the consecration-meeting of the older members, it is conducted in a similar manner. As the roll is called, each one responds to his name by some Scripture quotation, prayer, song, story, or by simply naming a hymn to be sung. One month we ask some one to address the children on the subject of temperance or missions; another month the boys arrange for a temperance meeting and the girls for a missionary meeting, and *vice versa*. There is a grand chance to teach the young people to work for others. Let them raise money in some way, adopt a new plan as often as possible, and let it be devoted to various objects. We raise every year money for foreign missions, send something to home missionaries, and assist in filling the Christmas-tree at the Mission Sunday School or the Children's Home.

Of course we find difficulties in the way, the work will not always run smoothly; we learn as often by our failures as by our successes. Patience, perseverance and enthusiasm, with a love for children, and some experience with them, are the best qualifications for a leader. Time and money are necessary factors in the successful result.

NOVELTIES

To maintain the interest it is necessary to introduce novelties as often as possible. At one time furnish badges at another a banner; again distribute picture-tracts or papers. We have promised this year a social every two months, while the society is holding its meetings. These, with the exception of the regular parties at Christmas and at the "jug-breaking" festival, are for those who have attended the other meetings during the two months, and are informal, with games arranged by the social committee, and with a basket-supper. We have just had one of these sociables, which passed off very pleasantly in spite of a hard rain.

We find that all these things help us in maintaining order. Excite first the members' interest and desire to remain in the society, and, by steady persistence, the proprieties of the place and of the work in which they are engaged will be impressed upon the most restless and light-minded. If there are any whose interest cannot be aroused, they will soon take themselves away.

It has been said that there is a constant call for patience in the work, but there is also a certain reward and pleasure. The enthusiasm of the children is contagious; their eagerness to begin the meetings again, after every vacation, the growth manifested in the points of self-control and quiet attention, are all very gratifying. To any who contemplate entering upon this work, I can confidently say from my own experience, that you will find great joy in doing it, and can feel that it is a work upon which the Master will gladly bestow His blessing.

THE JUNIOR SOCIETY OF CHRISTIAN ENDEAVOR.

BY REV. NORMAN PLASS.

This organization is a later development of the Christian Endeavor movement. It exists for the benefit of our younger young people, or boys and girls under fifteen years of age. It becomes for them a training school, with afternoon or early evening sessions, where they can be instructed in the Bible and Christian doctrine, taught to perform the duties of the Christian life, and thus be prepared for membership in the senior society and the church. To make sure of

A RIGHT START,

don't give any notice. If you do you will get a lot of little children and only a few of the older ones, and your endeavor will result in failure. Do your first work in private. Specially invite to meet you the ones you want for a nucleus of the society. Start with five or six. Don't speak of organization at first. Meet them again and again, talk and pray with them. Give each the privilege of inviting one more. When you are sure that you have material for organization, then speak of it, and ask the children to talk it over with father and mother and report next time. Then organize. Obtain of the United Society a pamphlet entitled "Junior Societies of Christian Endeavor." That will furnish you a "model constitution" and suggestions regarding organization. Consider what special features a society in your church will demand. "Have it as much like the older society as possible, while at the same time the needs of the children are remembered."

If the pastor is himself unable to lead the society, let him search out one of the older young people — I might almost say one of the older young ladies. He should choose a member of the senior society of Christian Endeavor, or one who has the true spirit of Christian Endeavor, a good manager, one who loves children and whom the children love, who has tact in dealing with them, is wise in winning them to Christ, and believes that they can be "genuine Christians and live children at the same time."

Most often the senior and junior societies are wholly separate and distinct. Would it not be well, at least, to have in the constitution of each a clause looking toward the other, and expressing the expectation that, at a proper age, members of the junior society will become active members of the senior society? A union still more vital, I believe, would be wise. The control of the junior society should be vested in the senior, and not be left to the one person temporarily in charge. It would seem to be advisable to have one Endeavor society in a church, with two branches, and to have in the senior branch a standing committee of five, called the junior branch committee, to be appointed with great care and with the co-operation of the pastor. The chairman may be designated as leader of the branch, another member as assistant, and the other three as special directors of the prayer-meeting, lookout and social committees of the junior branch. Reports of the junior work should be submitted by this committee at the business meetings. Occasionally there should be joint prayer or consecration-meetings and union entertainments. If other juvenile societies are incorporated into the Junior Endeavor Society, the leaders of these will be the best additional members of the junior branch committee. Don't let the committee do the work of the juniors, but simply superintend it.

In the junior society

WE MUST HAVE THE PLEDGE.

It is the backbone of any endeavor society. The idea of obligation is the secret of strength in the movement. The pledge in the junior society must be the same in substance as in the senior — a promise to try to lead a Christian life, to perform its duties, and to attend and take some part in every meeting of the society. Have the object of the society and the pledge printed on a stiff card, with a space for the name of the child. Below, with a space for the parent's name, have printed this sentence: "I am willing that —— should join this society, and will do all I can to help him (or her) keep the pledge." When the signatures are obtained, punch the card in a corner, tie in a pretty ribbon, and give it to the child to hang up at home as a constant reminder. Rather than to divide the juniors into active and associate members, would it not be wise to have a section for recruits and another for advanced members, the conditions of promotion being based upon conduct, regularity of attendance, evidence of right Christian purpose, etc.?

As to whether the children or others should lead the meetings, all seems to depend upon the character of the boys and girls. The child-leadership is the ideal. Let the superintendent have entire charge at first. Suitable leaders will be developed among the children. Let them be taught and in reality feel all the responsibility of leadership, and under judicious direction they will become true leaders.

Have weekly meetings whenever you can with success. Where the meetings must be held Sunday afternoon, twice a month may be best.

THE MONTHLY CONSECRATION-MEETINGS
are the ribs of a society, as the pledge is the backbone. It is not beyond the experience of children to "renew their allegiance to Christ." They will appreciate the meeting, if rightly conducted, and profit by it more than by any other meeting of the month.

To maintain the interest, every meeting must be fully planned with the greatest care, and no two should be alike. Have neat printed programmes, with blanks for the child's record of attendance and part taken. Choose simple subjects. Have occasional Bible-readings, temperance and missionary meetings, "promise" meetings, services of song, and meetings to which the parents shall be invited. Give the children work to do in preparing for the meetings. Appoint two who shall each tell a Bible story at the next meeting. Put the meetings occasionally in the hands of committees.

Instruction should have large place. Drill the children in finding places in their Bibles readily. Have Scripture passages memorized and recited in concert. Teach Christian doctrine by means of a catechism. Give out profitable Bible questions to be answered. Use the blackboard. Have the children state proper objects for prayer, and put these down on the board. Early in the meeting have the children kneel, and ask that a number lead in prayer. Encourage sentence-prayers. After prayer, have responsive reading of the lesson. Tell a Bible story, and let the children guess who the characters are. Give opportunity for Bible texts and personal testimony. Close by repeating in concert the pledge or the Endeavor benediction. With such methods, most of the children cannot help taking part.

There may be various accessories to the meetings, but bend all to the aim of winning the children to Christ and training them for His service. It will be hard work, to be sure; but what that is worth having do we get in this life without hard work? I know of no other line of work that pays as good dividends.

HOW ONE PASTOR MANAGES HIS JUNIOR SOCIETY.

We take the following from an excellent article by Rev. H. W. Pope, in *The Congregationalist*. Mr. Pope has a flourishing Junior Society in his church in Palmer:

We have a very simple constitution, and also use a pledge card which reads as follows:

Trusting in Jesus for strength, I promise Him that I will strive to do whatever He would like to have me do, that I will pray to Him every day, and that just so far as I know how, I will try to lead a Christian life.

Signed, —— —— —— —— —— ——.

I am willing that —— should join this Society, and I will do all I can to help —— keep the pledge.

Parents' name, —— —— —— —— ——.

Our meetings are held each alternate Friday, for half an hour, at the close of school. They are usually led by the boys and girls, though the pastor sits beside the leader and does most of the talking. A topic is always assigned beforehand. After the roll is called and the meeting opened, the pastor takes up the topic and questions them upon it. For instance, if the subject is "Sin," he will ask, "What is sin?" "Who commit sin?" "Why do they do it?" "What are the consequences of sin?" "What is the cure for it?" and so on. Sometimes we have a temperance-meeting or a Bible-reading or a praise service. Occasionally we have a newspaper-meeting, when the children bring in clippings to illustrate the subject. Sometimes we go on a missionary tour, look up the route, the price of tickets, the manners and customs of the people we are to visit. Occasionally we have a consecration service, when the children are encouraged to offer prayer, and speak in a personal way of their Christian hope and purpose, and their helps and hindrances in the Christian life. Now and then we have a social or pack a box of clothing for missionary use. The main object is to teach them the meaning and value of the Christian life, and to show them not only from the Word of God, but also from their own experience and observation, that "the way of the transgressor is hard."

PART XVIII.

REORGANIZATION.

CONCERNING REORGANIZATION.

BY GEORGE M. WARD.

Amongst the many letters asking for advice, that daily come to the general office, we frequently find the query: "What can we do with those active members who do not and will not take part?" Examination in nearly every case leads to the discovery that these so-called active members were allowed to join the society without first obtaining any adequate idea of what would be required of them in such capacity, in some cases even without a thorough reading of the constitution. This fact at once points out a warning to our lookout committee. You all realize how much easier it is to start a person right, than it is to correct him after a wrong advance has been made. Once admit to active membership a young person who does not fully understand and appreciate the responsibilities incurred, and the result is that before us. Just think for a moment of the situation. First, you have pledged him to work he was not aware of, and perhaps is not ready to undertake. Second, you have set for the associate members an example which cannot be approved, and which cannot but do great harm. And again you have lowered the standard of your society. In many instances this state of affairs is due to the fact that, previous to the organization of the Christian Endeavor, there had been in existence some other society, whose aim had been of a social and literary character, and whose work had not been of a distinctively religious kind. In such organizations the requirements for admission are usually of a merely nominal character, and the work demanded, if there be any, is not such as calls for the acknowledgment, tacitly or otherwise, that the participant is a Christian.

In many such instances the pastor or interested friends are anxious to turn the young life thus interested into religious channels, and to bring out for the benefit of the church itself the talent, often considerable in amount, that is latent here. But how to accomplish this? The Christian Endeavor plan is examined and approved, but the wide difference between its requirements and the absolute freedom of the old institution is plainly noticeable, and at once the fear arises that the contrast will prevent many of the young people from joining, and will cause them to drift away from church influences entirely. The result is that the constitution is modified or weakened, the pledge is omitted, and one and all are welcomed without regard to adaptability or fitness. The outcome is the state of affairs outlined at the beginning of this article — a society, Christian Endeavor in name only, a membership pledged to nothing, and consequently doing nothing, and a pastor and lookout committee at their wits' end.

What is to be done? Experience gives an answer: Reorganize! Let some Christian, your pastor if possible, state plainly to the young people the aim of a true Christian Endeavor Society, show to them the privilege which may be theirs if they will enter in earnest into the Master's service, and show to them, in a kindly spirit, the fact that they must stand on one side or the other in this matter, they must be either with the Lord or against Him, there can be no middle way — and then ask them to choose, for "His sake," on which side they will stand. The decision will impress the most sanguine. One pastor wrote, that the young persons of whom he had scarcely dared hope for a response came out on the Lord's side, saying that they could not be counted against Him; while member after member who had failed of performing his duty, through carelessness, was brought to a standstill by the mere thought of what his neglect really meant.

It is not an intentional neglect of duty, only the result of thoughtlessness, and it needs only a kindly and Christian reminder of the fact to arouse the latent energy to renewed action. Start right. Place the standard high, and strive to live up to it! Remember that the rules are for the many, and not for the individual cases. Where in single instances the rule seems hard, try by personal effort and assistance to smooth over the difficulty, but do not lower the standard. The Society of Christian Endeavor is a society of workers, a society to advance the kingdom, a society, not of idlers who would carry the Lord's name as His followers and do nothing to deserve their Leader, but a society of earnest young soldiers, whose oath of allegiance has been taken to serve in any situation or duty where the commander shall station them.

HOW TO REORGANIZE.

BY REV. F. E. CLARK.

1. Do not reorganize your society unless there is real need of it. If almost all your members are faithful to their vows, let the lookout committee see the few delinquents, and in a kindly and brotherly spirit bring them back to their duty, or show them the harm they are doing while active members, and induce them to leave the active membership, if they are incorrigible.

2. If you have omitted the prayer-meeting pledge from your constitution, or have so weakened it that it means very little, or have omitted the consecration-meeting, and, in consequence, find that there is little vitality in your society, and that the meetings are languishing, then change your constitution, until it contains the main fea-

tures of the Model Constitution, which is adopted by nine-tenths of the societies throughout the world, and which contains this prayer-meeting clause: "Every active member is expected to attend every weekly prayer-meeting, unless detained by some absolute necessity, and to take some part, however slight, in every meeting." "Absolute necessity" the revised Model Constitution defines as "some reason which the young disciple can conscientiously give to the Master, Jesus Christ, for non-attendance or non-participation."

Then when you are sure that all the members understand the constitution, and know what they are doing, give out the regular active membership pledge cards.

3. If your society already has adopted the right constitution, but contains many members who are not faithful, and who are really a hindrance to the spiritual life of all present, then give to every active member the following card:

AS AN ACTIVE MEMBER,
I HAVE PROMISED

1st.—To be present at every meeting, unless detained by absolute necessity, meaning by this some reason which, with a clear conscience, I can present to my Master, Jesus Christ.

2d.—To take some part in every meeting, aside from singing.

3d.—If absent from the monthly consecration-meeting, to send if possible, a verse of Scripture to be read to the society.

I hereby renew this covenant with God, and by His grace will fulfill its requirements.

DATED, ...

SIGNED, ...

When thou shalt vow a vow unto the Lord thy God, thou shalt not slack to pay it: for the Lord thy God will surely require it of thee; and it would be sin in thee.— Deut. xxiii: 21.

Those who will not sign this card thus drop themselves from membership, and the active list is thus relieved of unfaithful ones, and the society, even though reduced in size, is really stronger than before.

By this process of reorganization no one, of course, is excluded from attending the meetings, or from associate membership. In scores of cases this method has worked admirably.

Cards like the above can be printed by each society, or can be obtained of the United Society of Christian Endeavor.

A PRACTICAL EXAMPLE.

A correspondent in Los Angeles, sometime since sent us the following characteristic account of the reorganization of his society. This experience has been duplicated by hundreds of societies.

The Y. P. S. C. E. of the First Congregational Church of Los Angeles, Cal., is one of the societies that have seen the effects of reorganization. Two or three years since it had a membership of eighty-five, all nominally active members. Its prayer-meetings were well attended, its monthly socials noted for their sociability, and its help to the church acknowledged by all members of the church. But it had no pledge, and it seemed to those most deeply interested that there was a lack of results, though plenty of endeavor. After much discussion it was voted to reorganize, and a new constitution, including the "cast-iron pledge," was adopted. There was much opposition, and one member expressed the opinion that "the society would be dead in less than a year."

The new society began its life at one of the regular consecration-meetings, with about twenty names on the roll.

It was indeed a trying time for the young society. The church was without a pastor; the summer, proverbially a dull season for churches, was just beginning, and many members were about to leave for their vacations. About the same time the president removed from the city, and it seemed as if the prediction made might come to pass. But it did not. The society grew, and at the end of three months had a membership of forty-six active and one associate, with the objecting member above referred to, on the list and leading the meeting. Since then, absent ones have returned, and the society is growing every week. Our President is an earnest worker, and is well aided by good committees; good work is constantly being planned, and we are sure will be accomplished, for now we are a true society of Christian Endeavor.

PRACTICAL QUESTIONS CONCERNING REORGANIZATION.

Question. When organizing our society we were not as particular as we should have been regarding the election of new members; now, on entering work for a new year, we find that there are some that are very lax in their attendance, and in taking part in the meetings. What shall we do with them?

Answer. The old plan, frequently before suggested, is the only one we can recommend; reorganize your society by presenting to each one the prayer-meeting pledge, and have for members only those who intelligently and voluntarily sign this "reorganization card." Do not make any other changes, except to incorporate the pledge in the constitution, if it is not there already. It is a very simple and easy thing to do. Reorganization cards will be furnished by the United Society, or can be printed by any local societies.

Ques. Are reorganization cards to be used only when a society has not lived up to its pledge?

Ans. They are to be used only when needed, and if the members live up faithfully to their pledge, we can hardly conceive of the necessity of using them.

Ques. In the case of a society of which at least sixty per cent. of its membership either do not know or do not intend to fulfill their obligations, and who make a majority at the business-meetings, thereby barring out reorganization, what can and should be done?

Ans. If you cannot reorganize drop the Christian Endeavor name, and have the best sort of a society possible without the Christian Endeavor principle

PART XIX.

THE SOCIETY IN A REVIVAL.

A FAMILIAR LETTER

From the President of the United Society.

The special revival effort to be put forth by each society of which we have been talking for a few weeks, must be largely determined, of course, by the needs and opportunities of each society, after much prayer and consultation with the pastor and others. Here are some suggestions which have certainly proved useful in many places.

THE SUNDAY SCHOOL PRAYER-MEETING.

Scarcely any line of evangelistic work is more hopeful than the Sunday School prayer-meeting. If the pastor is willing, and, better still, under his leadership and guidance, call such a meeting. Ask all who will, teachers and scholars, to remain after the Sunday School, and then for twenty minutes conduct as earnest a gospel meeting as is possible. Do not leave it too much to chance, but have it arranged beforehand, so that the warmest prayers will be offered from the warmest hearts, and the most urgent, sensible and heartfelt invitations given to accept Christ. Let it be clearly understood what accepting Christ means and involves, and give the invitation to any who would be Christians to express it in some way. Have four or five of these meetings on successive Sundays, and, if they are of the right kind, it is almost certain that some will declare themselves as desiring to begin the Christian life.

THE WORK JUST BEGUN.

Then the work is just begun, and just there comes in the especial opportunity for the Christian Endeavor Society. Then take these boys and girls, these young men and women, follow them up, get them to the weekly meeting, see that they take some further stand for Christ, set them at work, put the arms of loving interest around them, and it will not be long before they have taken the second and third steps in the Christian life, and soon they will be active members of the church of God.

The great thing is to take the first step, and this the Sunday School prayer-meeting enables them to do naturally and appropriately. Moreover, we have the younger people at Sunday School, if nowhere else, and until their interest has been aroused and their hearts touched, we cannot always get them into our society meetings. But be very sure not to drop them after they have expressed an interest and a desire to follow Christ, or else their latter state may be worse than the former. However young and apparently thoughtless they are follow them up after this entering wedge has been driven, in the Sunday School prayer-meeting, until they are thoroughly committed to, and identified with, the right side.

THE AFTER MEETING.

Another most effective evangelistic method which can be used in many churches, is the "After Meeting." Following the Sunday evening service, let the invitation be given to all who will to remain for a short prayer-meeting. At this meeting have everything — singing, praying, speaking — short, crisp, earnest, full of heart. At the end, give the invitation to acknowledge Christ, and even if none accept it the first evening, repeat it the second and third. Very likely, however, many in your church are waiting for just such an opportunity which they have not yet had.

"DRAWING THE NET."

Do not be afraid of drawing the net, or, in other words, of giving the unconverted an opportunity to express their decision for or against Christ. I do not by any means say that this invitation should be given at every meeting through the year, but in these special meetings of a revival nature, it can seldom safely be omitted. Many, I know, shrink from this invitation, and not unnaturally. They fear that if not accepted by any one it will result in more harm than good. It is easy to reason one's self out of it and to give a score of good reasons for not extending it, but these are often temptations of the enemy to neglect a duty.

By a few judicious words, any evil tendencies may be avoided, the real nature of, and reason for, the invitation can be explained, and the burden of accepting or rejecting it can be rolled heavily upon the hearts of those who have never said, "As for me, I will serve the Lord."

I should not dare, at such a time, to neglect this invitation, lest the blood of some souls at last should be found on my soul. At the same time, it must be given simply and quietly and with the utmost solemnity, and only after and accompanied with, heartfelt prayer.

Thus given it can never do harm, and no soul can say, "I did not have the matter presented to me clearly and definitely by the Christians who ought thus to have presented it."

VARIOUS METHODS.

There are various ways of drawing the net; no stereotyped method can always be followed, but in some way each soul should be faced with the question: "*Will you now and here decide for Christ and express this decision?*"

There are also many other special methods of evangelistic work which can be devised, but I will only mention one more.

ASSIGN INDIVIDUALS TO INDIVIDUALS.

This is being done in some societies, and I am sure the importance of this method can hardly be overstated. To each warm-hearted, active member assign some one or more associate members, or some one outside of the society altogether. Do this quietly and discreetly. Do not parade it, and, if possible, do not let the associate members know that it has been done.

Then let the active member rest not until the one specially committed to him has had every good influence thrown around him which may bring him to Christ. This, too, must be done wisely and judiciously with sanctified common-sense, but it must be done if we would see the results for which we are praying this winter. These are only some of the methods. The evangelistic efforts which Christian Endeavor Unions may make have been, and will be, described elsewhere. But in some way, dear friends, shall we not so pray and labor, that the angels' song, as the months and years pass on, may mean more than it does now to thousands of our associate members, "Glory to God in the Highest, on earth peace, good-will to men." God grant it!

Your friend,
Francis E. Clark.

OUR SOCIETY AND OUR REVIVAL.

BY REV. JOHN L. SEWALL.

Two good things have come to us this winter: a Society of Christian Endeavor, starting last November and growing steadily ever since; and a revival of religion in connection with special meetings during the latter part of January. The connection between the two is worth noticing.

1. Our society *before* the revival. There was no special religious interest at the time of its organization, only a feeling that something must be done for the youth of this community, and an expectation that a blessing was not far distant. The active membership brought together the younger members of our church, and because of the responsibility, now felt for the first time, greatly increased their activity. Our weekly church prayer-meetings, while far better than the average, were marked by long pauses,

lack of heartiness, and a total absence of unconverted young people. These meetings soon showed improvement. The younger members of the church took more part, and young people not Christians began to drop in, having first found their way through the society meetings. A surprisingly large associate membership joined us at the start, and their presence was a strong incentive to active members to faithfulness and earnest, specific prayer.

2. Our society *in* the revival. The revival began, if at any one point, in our first consecration meeting, at the close of the old year. This was anticipated by us all with much anxiety; but it proved to be one of those meetings where, with wise leadership and the Spirit's presence, a new power appears in one and another Christian heart. When Mr. A. L. Parsons, the evangelist, came to us, we were ready from the first to listen and to labor. Our active membership furnished willing and efficient workers; those who could be depended upon for song, for prayer, for testimony, for private personal work, for help in the inquiry room. And our associate membership — here was the material for conversions. It was noteworthy that the first fifteen or twenty conversions were wholly among these members, or others who were expecting to join them.

3. Our society *after* the special meetings. I am glad I need not say after the revival, for that time has not yet come. Although we have come back to our ordinary services, the Spirit is still working in individual hearts. Twenty or more associate members have come over to the active list, and find in their new obligations just what they long to do for their newly-found Master. All who were active members before the meetings have learned new meanings in that word "active". Some who felt that they "could never pray in public or lead a meeting," now rejoice to do both. The possibilities of work which the special meetings taught, are to be realized in coming days in our

society, which furnishes a most natural and effective place for the exercise of those gifts which are equally cause and effect of revivals.

Lesson First. If you want a revival, get together all the young Christians you can find, whether there be six, sixteen, or sixty, and let them organize into a regular Society of Endeavor, and live up to their obligations. Sooner or later the revival will come.

Lesson Second. If you have had a revival, start without delay a Society of Christian Endeavor. It will keep the young life alive, and help it to grow by exercise and sympathy. It will hold young converts till a pastor's training-class can make them ready for church membership. There may be other ways of accomplishing this same end, but can any one mention a way which has been proved to be better?

PART XX.

THE SOCIETY AS A PART OF THE CHURCH.

SUSTAINING THE CHURCH SERVICES.

A Familiar Letter from the President of the United Society.

I have frequently had something to say about the duty of Christian Endeavorers in sustaining the other services of the church with the same fidelity that they sustain their own meetings. It is a subject worth emphasizing, and you will do me a favor by giving special attention to the matter, for the honor of our society depends upon the faithfulness of its members to the services of the church quite as much as to the meetings of the society.

From what I learn, from a very wide correspondence with pastors in all parts of the country, I am convinced that all the services are recruited and reinforced by the influence of the society, and the few exceptions which relate to the Sunday evening service, are scarcely enough to prove the rule. However, none of us want the rule proved in this way, for, throughout all the land, we would have no exception to the uniform rule that every society aids and reinforces every service of its church.

THE MORNING SERVICE.

Let me remind you again how much your regular presence in your own place and your interested attention will help your pastor. You who have always sat in the pew and never in the pulpit, can have little idea how a minister's heart sinks within him when he glances over the congregation and sees one-half or one-quarter of the family pews vacant. He may have been laboring half the week over a sermon for your special help, and then to see that you are not in your place to hear is more than a disappointment, I assure you; it is almost a mortification. Nor can you understand how a pastor comes to rely on a few "stand-by's." They are always on hand, and during the sermon have their eyes fixed on him, while he gains more inspiration and courage for his message from those persons than from all the rest of the congregation put together. Be one of those few, let me beg of you, my friend, and if your pastor doesn't rise up to call you blessed, he is a different man from what I take him to be.

AT THE SUNDAY SCHOOL.

Then there is the Sunday School service! An excellent place and time to put Christian Endeavor principles into practice is that. Let the superintendent count on you just as the pastor does. If you are a teacher, do not be one of those nuisances who can be depended on only to be absent half the time without any good excuse; and if you are a scholar, do for your teacher, when the Sunday School hour comes, just what I have been urging you to do for your pastor during the church service.

AT THE WEEK-NIGHT PRAYER-MEETING.

Another place where we can all be of special service is at the week-night church prayer-meeting. The quality of your Christian life and the value of your society will be gauged even more by your helpfulness in this meeting than by your fidelity to your own. Older people are very apt to say, "Well, those young folks seem to have pretty good meetings for their society, but before I approve of it, I am going to see how much they help our regular church meetings." Show these doubters, as thousands of societies have shown, that since you have learned to be faithful to one duty you have learned, at the same time, to be faithful to every duty, and that the weekly prayer-meeting has more young people and more help from the young people than ever before; and then the last lingering objection to the society will disappear.

AT THE SUNDAY EVENING SERVICE.

I speak of this last, for this Sunday evening service, when it follows the Christian Endeavor prayer-meeting, is often the greatest test of our loyalty to the church. On some accounts, the hour before the evening service is a good one for the Christian Endeavor prayer-meeting; on other accounts it is an unfortunate one, because their is a great temptation to run away and leave the evening service. It is not enough to say that more young people stay to it when it follows the Christian Endeavor service than would come out to it if there were no such service; that does not excuse those who ought to stay to it and do not. It is not enough to say that the children cannot stay to the later evening service. I am not writing to the little children or to invalids just now, but to the strong, hearty boys and girls and young men and women who make up the rank and file of our societies. It is sheer nonsense for them to say that they get so tired that they cannot attend a second evening service after sitting an hour in the Christian Endeavor meeting. Those same boys, next Saturday afternoon, will sit three hours on the hard side of a pine board to watch a base-ball game, and will be sorry then when it is over; and those same girls, on the same Saturday afternoon, if common rumor does not slander them, will spend three hours on their feet, in crowded stores, matching a piece of 'ribbon and buying a new hat; and both boys and girls will sit three hours at a time in the schoolroom, five days in the week, with only a ten-minutes' recess.

SUGAR OR SALT.

A bright article which once appeared in *The Golden Rule* was addressed to older people who took the text " Ye are the salt of the earth " too literally, and stayed away from church when it rained a little, for fear of being dissolved. I sincerely hope that none of the robust young men and women who compose our Christian Endeavor societies will consider themselves as made of such fragile stuff that they cannot attend two meetings, on the same evening, of an hour's duration each. If you are so frail, then I have no hesitation in saying, "Attend the church service if only one." Get excused from the Christian Endeavor Society on the ground that you are too feeble to attend its services, which, if true, is a perfectly legitimate excuse; but a plan better still for every young person in average health is to embrace this opportunity to show that he can "endure (a little) hardness as a good soldier of Jesus Christ" by attending both services. For His sake suffer a little weariness, if need be. For His sake help the church, aid the pastor, strengthen your own Christian purpose, and exemplify the true character of our society by being present at every regular service of the church, "unless detained by some reason which you can conscientiously give to the Master, Jesus Christ."

Your Friend,

FRANCIS E. CLARK.

GAINING THE CONFIDENCE OF THE CHURCH.

A Familiar Letter from the President of the United Society.

In the course of a month I have a good many letters of about the same purport; namely, how a society can obtain or increase the confidence of pastor and church in its purposes and plans. Evidently, among our twelve thousand societies there are quite a number whose churches have not yet learned what a royal and loyal helper a Christian Endeavor Society may be. According to a well-known story, these churches regard the societies as the little boy in the Sunday School class regarded the camel, as chiefly "good for circuses." In real distress or anxiety more than one correspondent writes: "How can we interest our older friends more in our work?" Let me suggest one or two ways.

THE HONORARY MEMBERS.

First remind the honorary members of their membership. Perhaps the pastor and deacons and elders and Sunday School superintendent do not know of the almost universal rule in our societies, which makes them, by virtue of their office, honorary members.

While you possibly have considered them a little distant and offish, they may have thought you exclusive and self-centered, and the very first thing to do is to break down these imaginary barriers, for I am sure they are only imaginary. If it has never been understood by your society that these officers are honorary members, put that clause distinctly into your constitution, and then let the honorary members know of their relation to the society, and invite them to come occasionally to your meetings.

GET THEM INTO THE MEETINGS.

After all, the great thing is to get together. When you have once persuaded them to come into your meetings a few times, and when they see what you are really trying to do, and how the young people's meeting has been quickened and revived by the society, there will be no more distance on their part. It is a very old story about the man who saw his own brother through the fog, and, thinking that he was some horrible monster, was dreadfully scared until he got near enough to see that it was only his own brother John, after all. If we see the best Christian brother through the fog of prejudice, he is apt to look distorted, but it all comes right when we get near enough to each other. If the invitation is not at first accepted by the honorary members, renew it and renew it, until at last they come.

Perhaps it would be well to tell one of them that you want a five-minute talk from him at the close of the prayer-meeting. See if he is not on hand to give it.

GIVE NO CAUSE OF OFFENCE.

Possibly some pastors and churches have just reason to think that the society is less thoughtful than it ought to be of the other interests of the church. Then remove that rock of stumbling. Perhaps your pastor has seen some of you go away from the Christian Endeavor prayer-meeting when he thought you had no good reason for not staying to the evening service. Next Sunday evening let him see you all in your places, listening to his sermon; follow this plan week after week, and see if his last prejudice does not disappear.

Do you say, "More of us go to the evening service now than ever before, far more than would go if the Christian Endeavor meeting did not come first?" This is not to the point. Our principles are that *every one* should go to the second service, "unless detained by a reason which he can conscientiously present to the Master." Give your pastor and all the other church-members an ocular demonstration of this principle of the society every Sunday evening.

OFFER YOUR SERVICES.

Then let me say once more, offer your services in any way available. Do not take it for granted that all the church-members know your intentions, but ask if there isn't something more you can do. Let the lookout committee send its chairman to the pastor to find out if there is not something more it can do. Let the Sunday School committee propound the same question to the Sunday School superintendent; then let the music committee tender its services, if the pastor would like the singing in the weekly prayer-meetings reinforced, as I warrant you he does. In fact, let every committee remember that its duties are not ended until it has done the last thing that the church desires to have done in its line. Try these different plans, and see if the imaginary barriers, should any such exist, between your society and the rest of the church, are not burned away by the kindling flame of Christian love between old and young.

Your friend,
Francis E. Clark.

FOR THE BEGINNING OF THE CHURCH YEAR.

A Familiar Letter from the President of the United Society.

CONCERNING BEGINNINGS.

In my estimation one of the most critical seasons of the year is just upon us, for the early fall is the beginning of the society year with many of us. The church calendar has of late years re-arranged itself, and the first month of the church year is September. January is early harvest time, May is late in the fall, and midsummer, so far as church activities are concerned, is barren midwinter. I am not saying that this is as it should be, but in this topsy-turvy world we frequently must take things as they are, and try to make them better. And certainly we are obliged to recognize the fact that the annual vacation from school and business implies, in a great many churches, a vacation from certain forms of church activity. So long as people go away from home in large and increasing numbers, at one particular season, the work in those churches from which they go must in some measure be curtailed.

Our societies, while they stimulate and aid, also reflect the life of the church to which they belong, and it is inevitable that if the activities of the church suffer during the vacation season, the society will suffer too.

But I will take it for granted that we have at last come together again. Only the late stragglers are still away. As we came out from this week's meeting, we said to each other, "It looks like old times, doesn't it?" and we took courage for a new year of work. This is just the time, then, for us to take to heart two or three invaluable lessons; by learning these lessons thoroughly we can almost

BEGIN.

Frequently an immense amount of valuable time is frittered away at the beginning of the church year, simply because instead of actually going about our work we think about it and talk about it and plan for it, possibly, but practically say, "We can't expect very much just yet, the meetings will be rather thin and not very interesting for awhile, we cannot expect too much at once; about the first of January we may look for results." In this way we feel quite comfortable, and delude ourselves that we are really doing all that can be expected at this time of the year.

The summer vacation would be by no means the disastrous thing it is in the church, did it not take so long to recover from it. Obviously, the only thing for us to do in beginning our society work is to begin, just as one of our greatest statesmen told us, when gold was at an immense premium, that the way to resume specie payments was to resume. The first of October, or the first of November, or the first of December, is no better time for vigorously commencing all branches of our society work than this very day of grace; in fact, not nearly so good a time.

BEGIN HEARTILY.

Let the president call all the committees together, if this has not yet been done, and let each committee lay out its campaign for the coming six months, and begin that campaign the same day. The trouble with some of our generals in the Civil War was that they never found the convenient time to *begin* their campaigns in good earnest. They were most excellent strategists; they could plan to a nicety just how things ought to be done, but the trouble was that the time never seemed to come when they could carry out their admirable plans. Either the roads were too muddy, or the streams were too swollen, or the enemy had too many troops, or the Union army had too few, and so precious years were wasted, and the cruel war dragged its slow length along. This policy of " masterly inactivity," I fear, is imitated by some of our societies at the beginning of the new year of work. If we belong to such society, let us remember that our Captain sends us orders to "push things," and to do it at once.

Our vacation has done us little good unless we have come back from it healthier and heartier than we went away. Let us show this gain in the hearty, earnest way we take hold of our work. Let us resolve that the best meetings, the most earnest work for souls, the most efficient committee work that our societies have ever known, shall be characteristic of this year's service, and remember that to-day's service is a very important part of the year's service. If our work in September is begun in a careless, indifferent, nonchalant way the whole year will suffer in consequence. But it is necessary not only to begin our work, and to begin it heartily, but it is especially important to

BEGIN RIGHT.

There is no better time to shake off the incubus of bad methods and past mistakes than just at the beginning of the new church year. If there has been carelessness about the pledge, now is just the time to tone up the conscience of the society, being very careful that each one of us begins with his own individual conscience.

If some of the committees have been inefficient and practically worthless, find out what the trouble is. Perhaps there is no reason for the existence of these committees in your particular church. If so, disband them promptly; but if they are needed, as most likely they are, see that they do their work and do it well.

Perhaps you have not monthly reports from the committees, and this little addition to the monthly business meeting may make all the difference between earnest, hearty, persistent effort, and slipshod methods that never have any report to give of themselves, because nothing is ever done. Then introduce this change at once, and see if it does not revolutionize some branches of the work.

Possibly the members of your society have not been as regular in their attendance at the church prayer-meeting, or as ready to participate in it as they should have been. Here, then, is a place to begin. Bring up this matter in the society meeting, stir each other up, "by way of remembrance," and see that you individually turn over this new leaf, if there is need of it.

Perhaps, last year, through the agency of your society, very few, possibly none, of the associate members were brought to Christ. If so, see that no such thing can be recorded of your society next September, by beginning now, vigorously, earnestly, affectionately, to bring your companions to Christ.

If, as the poet says, "Every day is a fresh beginning," surely, every new church year is a capital time for a fresh beginning. We need not be hampered by last year's failures and shortcomings. We can put off the old year with its deeds, as well as the old man. There is no time to do this in all the twelve months nearly so good as *just now*.

Your friend,

FRANCIS E. CLARK.

THE ALUMNI OF Y. P. S. C. E.—THE CHURCH OF THE FUTURE.

BY A PASTOR.

The "graduate" idea occurred to the writer many months ago, as doubtless it has suggested itself in some form to others who have thought, in connection with the future of the society, of those who soon will possess only in memory the days of their youth.

The distinctive feature of this movement consists in the fact that though the society was started by the church and for the church, it is of the young.

As the idea above alluded to has been lately brought to the front, and as it is a subject which must inevitably come to the surface, as the years go by, it is worth more than a passing glance.

While persons who join by profession the church of Christ, become members for life, the hundreds of thousands who now belong to the Young People's Societies of Christian Endeavor, in a score or more of years, will be no longer members, for the obvious reason that they will be no longer young.

If the older members of our churches, and the older persons in our communities do not, from the nature of the case, join the society, although occasional attendants upon the meetings, when these hosts of young people who now constitute the membership of these societies shall themselves have become elderly people, they will necessarily pass the reins and the membership of the organization into the hands of the younger generation; graduating from the institution, like the students of a college or seminary, who hold the relation of alumni to their *Alma Mater*. But a graduate from one of the colleges of Christian Endeavor, while he will ever cherish filial affection and a special interest in its behalf, will not only hold some sort of a relation to it, not now determined, since the time has not arrived for any "Alumni Association," but will also have entered more fully upon the great work for which these "colleges" are founded, the more rapid development of the kingdom of heaven on earth, through a disciplined church, where every one is armed and equipped for establishing the reign of the Redeemer in the hearts and lives of men. It is this grand foundation-work for the church of the future, which the society is doing in its devotional and missionary spirit, that warms the faith of every lover of the kingdom of our Lord. When these young people of one score and five and under, shall have reached the years of three score and ten and over, what golden harvests will be gathered from the ripeness of their Christian experience, growing richer and richer from the days of their youth.

Had such a movement as this, for the special training of young people in the Christian life, been started a third of a century ago, and God certainly was ready for one, there would not be so many lock-jawed members as there are to-day in some of our churches.

An old minister of the last century, a predecessor of the writer, in a Massachusetts parish, observing, one Sunday, that a person in his congregation had gaped his jaw out of joint, and was listening with mouth wide open, descended from the pulpit and adjusted the man's jaw. But in some of our churches to-day, pastors find it more difficult to pry open the mouths of the members than to shut any whose owners cannot do it themselves.

The adult members in some of our churches, who are active in the prayer-meeting, who are zealous in missionary enterprise, whose hearts yearn for the conversion of the world and the universal dominion of the Redeemer, these form the exception rather than the rule. But the adult members in our churches, in the next century, who will be inactive in the prayer-meeting, listless in plans for benevolence, and hindrances instead of helps, will constitute the exception, and, in most of the churches, they will be very rare.

For, if from these many scores of thousands, during these seven years of plenty, so much has already been gathered to feed the church of God, how much more may yet be expected from the great numbers who are to enter these societies during the years of still greater spiritual plenty, ere the new century shall have dawned upon us!

As the acorn contains, in embryo, the material for the great tree that is to weather the storms of the centuries, so these societies of Christian youth hold the forces for that church of the future, which will be built up in the strength and beauty of a complete spiritual maturity, able to meet the social and moral conflicts awaiting the country and nations in the coming century.

The Lord baptize with the glory of His power, His kingdom of young people, who hold in their hands the destinies of the church that is to be!

PART XXI.

SOCIETIES IN CITY AND COUNTRY.

CONCERNING A LARGE SOCIETY.

A Familiar Letter from the President of the United Society.

A few weeks ago the question was sent in to the question-box as to what should be done when a society became too large; whether it was best to form two societies, or restrict the membership. I was able to answer it very briefly at that time, and promised to take up the subject again. I should be glad of the experience of those who have met and vanquished this practical difficulty, but perhaps I cannot do better than give my view on the subject, in this familar corner.

OBJECTIONS TO A LARGE SOCIETY.

It is said with some plausibility, that after a society reaches a certain limit, it is impossible for all to fulfill the prayer-meeting pledge. Or that, if it is attempted, only a minute or half a minute can be taken by each one, and so no one will have a chance to speak "to edification." But, after all, these objections are more plausible than real. The effort should not be to curtail the society, but to curtail the length of the speeches. Very few have any idea how many can take part in a single hour, and do it intelligently, reverently, helpfully.

Often a radically

WRONG IDEA OF THE PRAYER-MEETING

lies at the bottom of this objection. Let it be said and repeated and re-repeated, the prayer-meeting is not the place for a speech, or for eloquent periods, or for practice in oratory, or even for what are generally termed "edifying remarks." This idea has very nearly been the death of the prayer-meeting, and it is the hardest idea possible to eradicate. There are plenty of other places for the exercise of eloquence — the pulpit, the platform, the stump — let the prayer-meeting be sacred to something better and higher. It does not require five minutes, or three minutes, or two minutes to offer an earnest prayer, or to give a helpful testimony. The Publican could offer his prayer in one-tenth part of a minute (time his petition, and see), and yet it was one of the most effective prayers ever offered. The Pharisee's prayer was a good minute in length, but though it was ten times as long, it was quite ten times as weak.

A SUM IN ARITHMETIC.

Let us do a little sum in arithmetic. Here is a society of three hundred active members (I have never heard of a society as large as this, and there are very few that will ever have half as many active members); supposing that five-sixths of them are present at every regular meeting — a very large proportion — then there would be time for every one of them to "take part" to the extent that the Publican did in the Temple, and then leave one-half of the hour for the long pauses which are so familiar in many a prayer-meeting.

But the fact is, very few societies number now, or ever will number, over one hundred and fifty active members. (There is a limit to the number of young people in any church.) Not more than three-fourths of them, on the average, can be present at the prayer-meeting at one time, then it will rarely happen that there will be many more than one hundred present who are pledged to take part in any meeting. For this one hundred, or one hundred and twenty, who will usually constitute the outside limit of participants in a large society, there will be ample time in the course of the hour, for a sensible, unhurried, reverent participation. Many will offer sentence prayers; others will repeat brief verses of Scripture; to others, who have a longer message, can be accorded a little more time; but, if there is promptness and a true conception of what constitutes a good meeting, there will be no lack of time for the participation of all. The fact is, a great many people have never learned the possibilities of a Christian Endeavor prayer-meeting, or know how much of earnest, sensible testimony and prayer can be crowded into sixty minutes.

If you had been with me at Chicago, or at the recent Christian Endeavor days at Round Lake, or at any one of a dozen other assemblies, where I have been of late, and had enjoyed those meetings, where a hundred and fifty participating in the course of an hour would be a very moderate estimate, you would not talk again about limiting your membership.

THE LEADER.

But much depends upon the leader. If he gives out four hymns, and sings six stanzas of each; if he reads seventy-nine verses of Ezekiel, offers a prayer ten minutes long, and takes another fifteen minutes in "opening" the meeting, of course there will not be time for all to fulfill their pledge. The meeting will be so thoroughly opened that every one else will be shut up. I was in a meeting not long ago where the leader took up thirty minutes of the precious forty-five in the opening exercises, and there were at least fifty in the room who had pledged themselves, and were ready to take part. This was simply an outrage upon the meeting. A leader with no more common-sense than that ought to be labored with, or, at least, never appointed again. An eight-year-old boy, who could only give out the number of the hymns, and read two verses of Scripture, would make a better leader. Too much time is often taken up in singing, also. It is a sign of weakness if some one is constantly giving out a hymn "to take up the time." "Don't work the singing-book too hard," is good advice.

DR. DUBIOUS.

Now do not shake your head, my dear Dr. Dubious, and tell me that you are very fearful that such a meeting will be "a mere scroppy patchwork of disjointed thoughts and vain repetitions." You are talking from theory now, and not from experience, I am sure. Attend a genuine prayer-meeting, where five hundred are anxious to give their testimony, and where two hundred succeed in the course of an hour, and you will not talk about limiting the number of your members again.

THE INTENT OF THE PLEDGE.

Besides, it ought to be said that if one goes with his heart prepared, and with his mind made up to fulfill his prayer-meeting obligation, and to do it promptly, and then gets crowded out (something that will very rarely happen), he has, to all intents and purposes, performed his duty.

But let no one lightly ease his conscience in this way, by saying that the time was well occupied, and there was no room for him. I have frequently heard young people say that there was no opportunity for them to take their part, when several minutes went to waste at the beginning of the meeting. The truth was, they were not ready *at the beginning* to help the meeting, where it most needed help, and so they lost their chance; but because the last few minutes were well occupied, and they found no chance just then, they cannot be held free of the charge of breaking their pledge. The trouble with all such is, that they do not light their torch before they come. They wait for the heat and fire that is generated in the meeting. No wonder they lose their opportunity, and break their word.

In a very large society it may be well to give opportunity, at the close of the meeting, for those who have not taken part verbally, to do so by rising, thus declaring that they are Christians. But, after all, there is no real difficulty on this score. The real difficulty is in the lack of personal, individual influence upon each member, active and associate, which it is much harder to exert in a very large society than in a small one; but even this difficulty can be overcome by persistence, patience and grace.

Your Friend,

FRANCIS E. CLARK.

CHRISTIAN ENDEAVOR WORK IN THE COUNTRY.

BY MRS. E. M. WINSLOW.

One of the questions often asked concerning a business is, "Does it pay?" or, in other words, "Is it a success?" To the question, "Is the Young People's Society of Christian Endeavor a success in the country?" the answer is, Yes. That there are disadvantages connected with a country work is true, but, taking the year through, they are no greater than those found in the centres of population. In cities and towns, the theatre, opera and dance, together with card-parties, socials and lectures, are almost constant sources of temptation to neglect the work and the meetings of the society, and, no doubt, are often allowed to keep many away from its direct influence, who would become associate members, and, in time, be brought into the fold of Christ. Nearly all of these things have but slight influence in the country. The theatre and opera, of course, are not there. The dance, at times, with some, has an influence in the wrong direction, but as for socials and lectures and such gatherings, they can generally be so arranged as not to conflict with the society's meetings.

NATURAL DISADVANTAGES.

The disadvantages incident to this kind of work in the country seem, to a great extent, to be natural, and their influence over the spiritual life is neither so powerful nor so deadly as those disadvantages found in cities and towns, which are the result of men's inventions. The cold of winter, the heat of summer, the rain and mud, are factors which must be frequently considered. In a certain community, the same subject and leader were advertised from the pulpit four successive Sundays, owing to the fact that every Friday night there was a storm. The same storm would not have prevented the young people from gathering, had they lived in town, but the darkness and mud were obstacles which could not, in the country, be easily overcome. This, to be sure, is an exceptional instance in its successive recurrence, but it indicates one of the disadvantages of country work. Distance must also be taken into consideration. There are regular attendants of this society of which I write, who live nine miles apart, the place of meeting being half-way between. During the busy season of the year, especially when the days are long, it seems almost impossible for the young people from the farms to get together before half-past eight; and the consequence is that they do not start for home till hard-working people should be asleep. But when it is remembered by these same young people that they can meet at a party and stay till midnight, and go right on with their accustomed duties the next day, they generally conclude that a little self-denial, for the cause of the Master, will not seriously injure them, and they are usually found at their post of duty.

ADVANTAGES OF COUNTRY SOCIETIES.

It is sometimes said, "There is no rose without its thorn," so it may be said that there is no work without its drawbacks and hard places. As it is not wisdom to always be looking for thorns, neither is it wise to look only at the obstacles to be met by a society in the country, for there is another, brighter side. The advantage of not having the world's most fascinating allurements to contend with has already been mentioned. There is a community of interest in the country, and a feeling of fellowship, which is not found in our cities and towns until much time and labor have been expended to bring them about; and happy is that church or society which gains them even by diligent effort. This interest in one another makes young people more ready to do just such work as the society demands. An incident, not given because such incidents are rare in the community in which it occurred, will illustrate with what promptness this feeling manifests itself along the line of Christian effort. Not long since, a young lady came to the home of a friend in one of the rural districts of Kansas. After a few days, she said, "The people around here are nearly all religious, are they not?" On being answered in the affirmative, she said, "Well, I am not; but the people need not know it." Her friend said, "They will find it out." "How?" she asked. "They will ask if you are a Christian," was the reply. She thought her distant bearing would keep them from so personal a question, but it was not long before her fancied secret was known, and the young people began to work and pray that their God might be her God. The end is not yet.

The Young People's Society of Christian Endeavor proves itself a success in the country in that it secures the object for which it was organized; it strengthens and develops the Christian life of its members; and not only does it do this, but it is one of the important helps in bringing souls to Christ. It is customary in a certain country society, as it is, doubtless, in many others, to have those who are diffident and weak lead the meetings, as well as those who are more active. During the thirteen months since its organization, no person has been appointed leader more than twice, and only a few have been thus privileged. To lead the meeting seems almost to revolutionize some members, at least so far as their activity in meetings is concerned; they have learned how much the leader needs the help of every one, and their individual responsibility can no longer be lightly thrown upon others. The spirit of criticism, sometimes seen in religious gatherings, and which is as much to be dreaded as a blast from the frozen zone upon a garden of flowers, is absent, and a feeling of sympathy and kindness manifested in its stead. Mr. Formality, in his starchiest suit, has not been admitted; it is thought advisable that he remain outside the fold. Sincerity and earnestness are very noticeable features of this country work. Among the number of those who have been brought into the church within the last year, is a young man who has experienced the benefits and disadvantages of city life. He attributes his change to the earnest way in which the gospel was presented, and said that it was "through the mercy of God that he was led to attend the meetings of the society."

IMPORTANCE OF THE COUNTRY WORK.

Christian endeavor work in the country should not be lightly esteemed. The tendency of the people of this land, it is true, is toward cities, with a feeling that the desired and desirable things of life are there. The country is too apt to be looked upon as a necessary evil, which must be endured till sufficient means are gained to move to town. But history repeats itself, and what has been true will be true, and in the country to-day are to be found a large proportion of the men and women who, in after years, will be moulding and shaping the destiny of this nation, and, through it, the destiny of the whole world. It is not an insignificant matter that the power of religion of the Lord Jesus Christ be brought to bear upon the young people of the country in its most effective way. Country parishes ought, wherever possible, to have societies of Christian endeavor, for the society, properly conducted, will develop a true Christian life. Complaint is sometimes made about the monotony of country life. The meetings of the society, properly attended, do away with the cause for this complaint. By means of them the young people have an opportunity to see each other once a week, and enjoy one another's presence in the best and most advantageous way.

Country life, while it has many benefits, is not the one of ease and freedom that it is sometimes thought to be. A young man told the writer that, two years ago, he ran a harvester day and night, and that one week he slept but fourteen hours in all. He would work till he could not go any longer, and then fall over and sleep an hour, and then get up and go on with his work. This seems to be the spirit in which much of the farm work is carried on in Kansas; get just as much done as possible, with as little time spent in eating and sleeping as nature will permit. Country life must be experienced to be fully appreciated and understood. It is a good thing for a people so pressed down with work, to throw off their burden for a time and come together in a social meeting. It is a wonderful strengthener for both body and spirit. So say they who are Christians, and practise it. The Society of Christian Endeavor gives this opportunity to the young people, and to those whose hearts have not grown old.

PART XXII.

WOMAN'S WORK.

WOMAN'S WORK IN CHRISTIAN ENDEAVOR.

BY MRS. ALICE MAY SCUDDER.

"It is not good that man should be alone." Thus saith God in the Garden of Eden, thus He saith in Christian Endeavor.

God created man first, but only for a few brief days in the entire existence of our race did God allow him complete possession and mastery of all that he surveyed.

As soon as God paused a moment in creation to view His work, he recognized the fact that man could not live alone. God recognized it, experience is constantly echoing it, and man, willingly or unwillingly, must give his assent to it.

The world would have been very incomplete without womankind. Her ministrations are constant. From the moment that man utters his first salute to the new world which he has entered, until his voice is silenced by death, he is dependent on woman. The food he eats, the clothes he wears are largely the work of her hands. Not infrequently he leans on her for no small share of his support. I heard of a man once who, when questioned as to how he could afford to marry on so small a salary, said, "Why, John, I'll tell you how I did it. Before I was married, I could almost support myself, and now, that I have a good likely woman to help me, I can do so entirely." This man put a proper estimate on woman's work, and so do most men. There are a few dwarfs here and there who never get beyond valuing themselves — men of the pinch-penny type, who think only of their own existence. It was one of this sort who wished to bestow a gift of approval on his wife, and so decided, after long deliberation, to make her a present of twelve yards of cloth to make him some new shirts. This man, however, is an exception to the general rule. Most men love and value these helpmeets whom God has given them.

The ministrations of woman are as varied as the figures in a kaleidoscope. The combinations change at every turn. In the home she is an example of constant and untiring devotion. Who can weigh or measure the influence of a Christian mother? Day after day she chisels away, often discouraged, but never content until she gives to the world a noble Christian son or daughter, made by her own hand in the image of God. Most of the great men who are standing in the niches of time were thus fashioned.

If woman is needed in the home circle, equally is she needed in the social world. "It is not good for man to be alone." That portion of our social fabric that is content to do without woman's presence and influence often represents the more depraved side of men. "Stag parties" seldom conduce to man's highest good. Cards, liquor, tobacco — these are too often the food on which the "stags" feed. In the society of women, especially Christian women, the conversation is pure, the companionship refining, and the whole tendency uplifting. It is a great mystery how young men can substitute trivial amusements for woman's society. Some young men are too wise to do this. Instead of spending all their spare time and money in club-rooms, they seek organizations where they can enjoy their pleasures by the side of their sisters or some one else's sisters. This Young People's Society of Christian Endeavor is such an organization. Here a young man can have social enjoyments, literary pursuits, mental diversions, varied amusements and an opportunity to spend money. But, better yet, he can have spiritual advantages that shall lift him morally above his fellows. This organization should be the mental and spiritual centre of every community. It can be if every Christian young woman in our land will do her part. What is her part, do you ask?

1. *Be attractive.* How quickly the world recognizes an attractive woman! By her fascinations she can lead man where she will. Let a woman be thoroughly magnetized by the Lord Jesus Christ and she can draw people to the church, to prayer-meeting, and even to the foot of the cross. Some people object because a young man goes to a prayer-meeting to see a young woman (and it is not a very lofty motive for church attendance); but if a mother is not able to induce her son to attend church or prayer-meeting with her, she is very wise to encourage his acquaintance with any young lady who is able to draw him into the house of God. To catch fish you must entice them upon the fishing grounds within the reach of lines, and if men are to be caught for God, in some way they must be brought into the sanctuary. Young women must not think their work done until every young man over whom they have any influence is brought into the religious meetings of the church, and especially into this Society of Christian Endeavor.

2. *Be talkative.* This injunction may seem unnecessary, for women are so proverbially talkative that it is an ever-present source of jesting. Women are talkative, but they are not responsible for that. God made them so. Where their responsibility does lie is in taking this gift and using it everywhere for God's service. Woe unto woman if, with all her social qualifications, she can lay no trophies at her Master's feet! Woman's voice must be heard in the prayer-room. Thirty years ago, one might as well have expected to hear the dead speak as to hear a woman in a public assembly; but now our sisters sit in religious convention, and with cool nerves carry on the

meetings with as much capability as members of Parliament. Times have changed, and our young women must be ready to meet the demands of the times. They will find themselves in embarrassing positions if they are not prepared to express the thoughts that lie within them.

Make a firm resolve that you will speak or pray, even if, like a little child, you can say only one word at a time. If the right spirit is there, women cannot help speaking. Don't be discouraged if you do not edify the first or second time. Cheer yourself with the thought that men do not always speak to edification.

There is another reason why our young women must learn to speak and pray. The young women of our Christian Endeavor Societies to-day are to be the mothers ten or twenty years from now, and they must be praying mothers. If the boys of the future are to grow up strong enough to cope with the temptations of this wicked age, they must have mothers who can raise more than a silent prayer, and who are not afraid to speak the name of Jesus to their children.

3. The last injunction is, *Be spiritual*. This is, after all, the most important qualification. A young lady may be attractive and talkative, and yet be a long way from a successful worker. There must be added a deep-seated consecration. Each should examine herself and find her weak points, and then determine, with God's help, to correct them, for you may be certain that every defect of your personal character will hinder the work in your society. Ask yourself, Do I always keep my promises? Christian Endeavor has a pledge, do I keep it? Am I naturally tardy? Christian Endeavor wants no dilatory people on her committees. Am I charitable in my opinions of others, or am I imprudent in speech? Remember that the Social Committees require those who are "slow to anger" and "kindly affectioned one to another." Have

I the gentleness of my Master? If not, ask God to give you the mind that was in Christ Jesus our Lord.

In whatever you are deficient, endeavor to become proficient. Thus by carefully cultivating all the graces shall each be enabled to go from strength to strength and from glory to glory, until all shall appear in Zion, before God.

PART XXIII.

FAMILIAR LETTERS ON VARIOUS TOPICS

DOUBTFUL AMUSEMENTS.

A Familiar Letter from the President of the United Society.

I have a number of letters of late like the following: "Will you please tell us your opinion of theatre-going and card-playing"; or, "Is it right for an active member of the Society of Christian Endeavor to go to a dance? Please tell us what you think about these things." I do not know that I can do any better than say a few words in regard to them all in this letter.

They all belong to the same class of questions of Christian casuistry about which young people have more trouble than any other. The difficulty is, you always want an answer "yes" or "no" in regard to each particular case, and that is just the answer that ought not to be given. You want to shift upon somebody else the responsibility of deciding these questions for you which every young Christian ought to decide for himself. If your pastor or your Sunday School teacher would only say, "Yes, you can go to this doubtful place of amusement," then you would feel perfectly easy about it and think that you had no further responsibility in the matter. But supposing your pastor should not know what you ought to do, or supposing your Sunday School teacher is mistaken!

After all, this is not God's way. He leaves it for every person to decide such questions for himself. This is part of our probationary discipline, and it is a poor way to shirk out of the serious problems of life to get some one else to decide them all for us. Said a young lady to me one day, when speaking of one of these debatable matters, "Now, I don't want you to give me general principles; I want you to say that 'I may' or 'I must not'." But, as I said before, God doesn't treat us in this way. He might have proclaimed a hundred commandments instead of ten, and, instead of confining the decalogue to the great fundamental principles of right and wrong, He might have gone on to say:

"Thou shalt not go to the theatre, but you may once in a while go to the opera."

"Thou shalt not play cards."

"Thou shalt not go to the ball, but you may dance square dances occasionally."

I know a great many young people in America, in this nineteenth century who would be very much relieved if they could only find something of this sort written in the twentieth chapter of Exodus.

But instead of doing anything of this sort God has given us each a conscience, and said to us, "Guard it well, keep it tender, see that it does not get warped or twisted, and then follow it."

Instead of specifying every possible temptation into which the young American Christian might fall, he lays down certain grand, fundamental principles, which are just as good for His disciples in Jerusalem or Zululand as in America; certain principles which were just as good in the nineteenth century before Christ as they are to-day, and that will be just as good in the twenty-ninth century as they are in the nineteenth.

"If meat make my brother to offend"—you know how to fill out that verse; that is one of these verses. Read that whole chapter in which this verse occurs, and see how it answers almost every question which you can raise on these troublesome questions. Then there is another class of precepts which bears on these matters. For instance, "Whatsoever ye do, in word or deed, do all in the name of the Lord Jesus." "Whether, therefore, ye eat or drink or whatsoever ye do, do all to the glory of God."

Such verses are worth ten thousand specific commands, for they embrace all specific commands and give us a touchstone by which we can test every doubtful action. Such principles will always test character. Perhaps the young people of the year 2887 may not care much for progressive euchre or the German, but there will be some doubtful amusement whose indulgence will trouble their conscience, I am very sure, and these principles will be just as useful for them as they are for us.

It would not hurt our conscience, perhaps, to ring the bells or play "tip-cat" on the village green, for times have changed since the days of the Bedford tinker, and amusements have changed, too, but these games hurt Bunyan's conscience, and these same verses told him he was doing wrong when he was violating his conscience.

THE ONLY TEST.

This, then, is the only test. What in the light of God's Word will our consciences allow? Anything that our conscience disapproves, anything about which it troubles us, is wrong for us. "He that doubteth is condemned."

I cannot keep your conscience, or you mine. I know what is wrong for me, you know what is wrong for you. No matter what others do or do not do. What you are doubtful about, as to whether it is right or wrong, is wrong for you until you have decided that it is right. Then go ahead and do it whatever others say, if you have no secret qualms, and if you can ask and have asked God's blessing upon that thing.

A CHRISTIAN ENDEAVOR PRINCIPLE HERE.

After all, this is but the carrying out of one of our Christian Endeavor principles, which puts the burden for the performance or non-performance of every duty on the individual conscience. In the Society, we promise to do certain things unless prevented by some "absolute necessity," and every one's conscience must decide what is an "absolute necessity" for him. If he can conscientiously give a reason to the Lord Jesus Christ for absence or non-participation in meeting, or for non-performance of committee work, then he is absolved, but no other reason can excuse him. Just so is it in all other matters. Keep your conscience unwarped and tender, and then with prayer take every doubtful matter to that tribunal and you will not go far wrong.

TRY EARNEST WORK.

One more thing, earnest work is a great solvent for all these difficult problems, and here again the Society of Christian Endeavor comes in to help you. Enter into the work with all your heart; always be found in your place in the prayer-meeting; take up the committee work to which you are appointed as though you were called by God to do it, as assuredly you are; learn by blessed, practical experience something of the "joy of service," and all these other questions will settle themselves.

You will find a happiness and satisfaction in this whole-hearted devotion that you never dreamed of before. You will not continually be asking, "Can I do this?" "May I not indulge in that?" You will want to do the things you ought to do; and these doubtful matters will seem so insignificant and paltry that you will be willing to forego them until you are sure they are right for you. Try it and see.

Your friend,
FRANCIS E. CLARK.

CONCERNING INTERDENOMINATIONALISM.

A Familiar Letter from the President of the United Society.

One important matter which found expression at a recent inspiring Minnesota convention, I understand, was the interdenominational character of our societies, and we are informed that "whenever the interdenominational features of Christian Endeavor work were mentioned, prolonged applause resulted." This sentiment has been characteristic of other conventions. I have not said much about the matter in these columns, thinking that it would take care of itself, and that this feature of our work would commend itself to all fair-minded Christians. Evidently, however, the pastors and the churches and the young people themselves are not slow to see the great advantage of inspiration which comes from interdenominational co-operation, and it is a matter well worth dwelling upon. For my part I cannot see how any Christian, looking at the facts as they are, can help rejoicing in this aspect of a society which, while holding its young people loyal to their own churches and denominations, as one of its essential features, affords them such a chance to broaden their fellowship and increase their friendships among Christians of all denominations that honor Jesus.

SOME LOOK ASKANCE.

I can understand how some might look askance at the movement if the tendency was to obliterate all denominational lines and amalgamate all Christians into one great denomination, for there is much to be said in favor of denominations; they stand for ideas, and when denominational interests are conducted in the spirit of brotherly love, more can be accomplished for the common Master, I believe, when the army is thus divided into regiments and corps. There is nothing to be said for the spirit that would keep Christians, young or old, from coming together for mutual help and conference, and for the spirit that would say to them, "You must never step out of your own little corner of the vineyard, even to attend a convention of vinedressers, and even though it be for the sake of learning how to go back and cultivate and prune your own vines better." This is not the spirit that can prevail in this latter quarter of the nineteenth century, and it is not the spirit which is prevailing in any denomination, as a whole, so far as I know.

DENOMINATIONAL LOYALTY CULTIVATED.

It ought to be distinctly understood that love for and loyalty to one's own denomination is distinctly cultivated by the Christian Endeavor Society. Just as essential as the prayer-meeting pledge to a true Christian Endeavor society is the underlying idea that each society exists for its own church. Every principle of the movement is an index finger pointing in this direction. Its whole history, from the second day of February, 1881, to the present day, tells this same story. Unless facts are perverted, nothing else can be proved but this, that the whole tendency of the society has been to lead the young people to love the church of their fathers and mothers, and to support it with a hearty enthusiasm that they have never known before.

Let it be repeated once more: no society owes any allegiance to any organization except its own church. The United Society has been careful to disclaim any authority. It desires to exert none. It makes no assessments. It imposes no conditions. It does not seek for uniformity of methods or constitution. It advocates certain principles, but only because experience has proved that they are essential to continued success. It seeks to give information and help the societies in every possible way, and that is all.

UNGROUNDED FEARS.

It is amusing to see how much afraid a few pastors are of a harmless little blank sent out by the United Society, asking for information. They have societies of Christian Endeavor, which have helped them in their work, they get the idea and copies of the constitution and other literature from the United Society free of all charge, but now fear that something may be demanded of them, and they refuse even a courteous answer to the question, "Have you a society?" There are only half a dozen such in the country, however, so far as I know. Every society may be under denominational control; every society may study the history and doctrine of its own church; every society, along the lines of its own denomination, can best build up the kingdom of God. These are the principles and this the practice of the Christian Endeavor Society. Surely, when this is understood, no one would desire to prevent young Christians from coming together in conventions and union meetings for fellowship and mutual help.

A GREAT ELEMENT OF POWER.

Of how much would our great State and national gatherings be robbed if there were not this free communion of members of different churches! Presbyterians and Methodists, Baptists and Congregationalists, United Brethren and Disciples, Episcopalians and Friends, Lutherans and Moravians, as they meet together and pray and talk, one with another, learn to love not their denomination less, but Christ more. Let us never forget this important part of our mission, not to weaken denominational ties, but to show to all the world how "these Christians" (of all denominations) love one another.

Your friend,

FRANCIS E. CLARK.

CONCERNING ANNIVERSARIES.

A Familiar Letter from the President of the United Society.

Allow me to say a few words concerning anniversaries and conventions.

The work of our societies has been largely advanced by means of such public meetings, and it is of great importance that they should be properly managed, and made productive of the highest good. But conditions change with the growth of such a society as ours, and I am inclined to think that the time has come, in some places, for us to revise our notions on the subject of

ANNIVERSARIES.

I am not sure that it is wise to celebrate every anniversary of every society with a public meeting, to which all the societies in the vicinity are invited. It was a very good plan to do this in the earlier days of the work, when societies were few, and when the special principles of the movement could be explained at such meetings, and by this means interest be aroused. To hold such public anniversaries now is most desirable in sections of the country where the cause is little known, and when it can be advanced in this way, but ordinarily, I think it is quite as well for our societies, where Christian Endeavor unions exist, to celebrate their own anniversaries quietly in their own church families just as the birthdays of the children are celebrated at home, and let the unions have the public meeting, when all the societies can be brought together.

THE REASON FOR THIS.

It will readily be seen that, where there are a hundred societies in the same city and its suburbs (as there are in more than one city), and where each society holds a public anniversary, and invites all the others in the vicinity, that it is difficult to find delegates who can attend. The result is inevitable. The attendance from outside will become smaller and smaller, the inviting society will be disappointed, and perhaps think it almost a slight that its invitation is not accepted. And yet no slight will be intended and no indifference will be indicated. It is simply an impossibility for an ordinary society to find suitable delegates to attend a hundred anniversaries in the course of the year, or even fifty anniversaries.

Our work is to be done at home. Most of us have comparatively little time to give to meetings held in any other place than our own church. Four or five times a year we can go, and perhaps oftener, but we cannot send delegates to two or three anniversaries every week, strong as may be our feelings of brotherly interest in our neighbors.

Besides, it is difficult to obtain speakers for so many anniversaries. Some few are overcrowded already, and, with all their evenings occupied, are obliged to decline a score of invitations every week.

THIS APPLIES TO THE FUTURE.

I am not criticising any anniversary that has been held. Perhaps, so far, there has not been one too many. Certainly all that I have attended have been justified by peculiar circumstances; but in the future, as societies multiply, let us celebrate them just the same, but celebrate them in our own church families. In sections where there are but few societies, where our principles are little known, or where there are, as yet, no unions, by all means make the most possible of these anniversaries.

A few words about the programmes for these public meetings.

DON'T OVERLOAD THE PROGRAMME.

The great danger always is that the evening will be too much crowded. I have myself made this mistake in arranging a programme more than once, so that I am making a kind of confession in this advice. A programme-maker, like the leader of a prayer-meeting, is always fearful lest "the time will not be occupied," and so he loads it down too heavily.

Due allowance is not usually made for the time occupied by singing. Even a spirited congregational hymn takes usually five minutes; but when the choir must have a chance to sing the *Te Deum* and the *Venite*, and one or two long anthems beside, a half-hour is gone before one knows it. Then the reports from the societies, which are advertised to take one minute each, invariably take three minutes apiece, and another fifty or sixty minutes speed away. Then, if there are three speakers "from abroad," you can imagine how the last poor man feels as he sees the hands on the dial getting on to ten o'clock, and the audience all the time growing smaller by degrees and beautifully less.

Moreover, it is a kind of imposition on a speaker to ask him to come a hundred miles, give up one or two days of valuable time, and then crowd him so that he cannot begin to give what he has carefully prepared, without feeling that he is wearying the audience or trespassing upon some other person's time. At an ordinary anniversary or union meeting, one leading speaker is enough for the best results. When I was in England recently, the papers were complaining bitterly of this fault, that public religious meetings were degenerating because, instead of having one or two strong addresses, half a dozen ten or fifteen minute talks were crowded into the same evening.

A DIFFERENCE TO BE OBSERVED.

Do not misunderstand me. In the conventions where methods are discussed and where all-day sessions are held, have all the exercises brief, crisp, sharp; keep time with the bell, if necessary; in short, as has been said recently, conduct them on the principle of a Christian Endeavor prayer-meeting, at least until the hour comes which is set apart for the more elaborate address.

It has been whispered to me (I hope it is wholly unnecessary to repeat it), that it would be well to remind some societies to pay the expenses of their speakers who come from a distance, to take pains to welcome them cordially, and send them on their way again rejoicing.

If these laborers do not ask any other "hire" (and I do not know that they ever do), they are at least worthy of their "expenses," and the heartiest kind of a reception, and if they ever fail to receive it, it is only from thoughtlessness, which needs but a slight reminder to become thoughtfulness.

Your friend,

FRANCIS E. CLARK.

OUR SOCIETIES IN THE VACATION SEASON.

A Familiar Letter from the President of the United Society.

The time has come for the return of that "necessary evil," as it has been called, the summer vacation. That it is "necessary" in these high pressure days of American life, I do not think any one would dispute. The business man and the parson, the clerk and the school-boy, will all agree on that point. The proposition that it is an evil of any kind, necessary or unnecessary, would be received with a good deal more qualification, at least by certain school-boys of my acquaintance. From a religious standpoint, however, as our churches are constituted, I think there can be no question that the annual vacation is a serious drawback in the work of the year.

If it were only the loss of one month or two months in the middle of summer, that would be no inconsiderable loss; but in addition to this, vacation means a slow recovery in the fall and a slackening up in church work in the spring, which leaves only four or five months for the most aggressive kind of Christian work. So we must recognize and do our best to counteract not the vacation, but its incidental evils. I hope every one of my readers will have a holiday season, but not vacation from religious service, only a change of service which will fit them for better work when they get home. But there are two or three things appropriate to be said just now.

BEFORE VACATION.

First, don't let the work drag in anticipation of the vacation. It is very easy to say, "Well, there is only a month more before the Sunday School closes for the season; it will not make much difference if I am away." Or to say, "These short, hot evenings the prayer-meeting cannot be expected to keep up its numbers." Almost unconsciously we fall into the way of *expecting* the work to drag, and of not feeling very much condemned if it should. Now, he would be a poor engineer who should begin to slow up his engine two miles before he reached the station. He would certainly make no very good time. Let it be the ambition of every Endeavor society to have just as good meetings in July as in January, and let every member do his part to make them so. One's religious constancy is tested a good deal more at such times than when every one else is at the flood tide of enthusiasm. These are just the months when our Christian Endeavor pledge and principles should come to the front.

AFTER THE VACATION.

Then when you get back from your holiday excursion, throw yourself into the work again, *at once*. It may take an engine some little time to get up steam after leaving the station (to continue our railroad simile), but it ought not to take the Christian any time to get back into the spirit of work; for if he spends his vacation in the right way, he never gets out of the spirit of work. He should only come back fresher and stronger, and more ready than ever to do his part by reason of the rest and recreation that God has given him.

DURING VACATION.

And then during the vacation days how much can be done! I do not advise an evangelistic tour or a preaching circuit, but in a quiet way wherever our inclination calls us; at the seashore, at the mountains, camping out on the shores of the lake, you will be within reach of some church or Sunday School or school-house meeting. Let us see that there is one more present and one more helpful voice heard, and one more dollar or half dollar in the contribution box because we are spending a week near by. Think of it! Probably half of our Christian Endeavor members will go away from their homes somewhere this summer. There is an army of a quarter of a million, then, scattered here and there in almost every hamlet of the Union. Think of the opportunity! I have heard of many and many a church and Endeavor society formed during the vacation months by a "summer visitor" from some wide-awake society. There is no reason why our great army of vacationists should not leave behind them, when they return to their homes, at least a thousand societies. See if you cannot establish one of these thousand.

Your friend,
Francis E. Clark.

AN INFALLIBLE TOUCHSTONE.

A Familiar Letter from the President of the United Society.

There is only one excuse that is admitted in a Christian Endeavor Society, and that is, one that we can give with a clear conscience to the Lord Jesus Christ; and I am writing this letter to urge you all to bring everything to this touchstone. I remember finding, when I was a boy, a piece of sparkling iron pyrites. I did not more than half believe that it was gold, but I had a lingering hope that it might be; so, without saying much about it, for fear of being laughed at, I took it to a jeweller's, and he very soon dispelled my last lingering hope by pouring a few drops of acid on my "gold" and destroying it utterly. Now I think that we can always test our excuses by taking them to Jesus Christ.

APPLY THE TEST.

Our school, our business, our health, the weather — do they furnish good reasons for not performing some accustomed duty, for not going to church or Sunday School or the Christian Endeavor meeting, or for not performing any one of a thousand duties? Who can tell us? The lookout committee doesn't know; and our pastor may be inaccessible, or unable to tell us if we could get at him; and we ourselves are in doubt about it. What shall we do? Why, apply the test. Get down on your knees by yourself, in your own room, if possible, and ask yourself if there, in His sight, that excuse satisfies your conscience. If so, you need no other. But if not, beware how you tamper with your sense of duty.

A CONSCIENCE-QUICKENER.

Now, it seems to me that just here our society may be used as a wonderful developer and quickener of conscience. If you will read the revised pledge carefully, you will see that in effect it twice uses these words, "Unless hindered by some reason which I can conscientiously give to the Master." These words did not get into the pledge by mistake, or for the sake of rounding out a sentence, but because this is the only worthy excuse which a Christian can ever give, and because it puts the responsibility just where it belongs. Let me very earnestly beg the lookout committees and officers of our societies to make much of this. Insist on it. Keep it before your members. Do not try to decide too many matters for them; but throw them back hard upon this question, "Is your reason for absence, or for the non-performance of any duty, one that you can give to Christ?" "If so, you need not tell it to us unless you choose; but, if you feel that He accepts it, it is all right." Innumerable doubtful questions will this settle; and, better than all, it will develop, as nothing else can, a Christian character that is at once stalwart and strong and tender.

THE REASONABLENESS OF IT.

It takes away, too, the last vestige of unreasonableness that may seem to be involved in the pledge. It asks no more of any member than Christ asks of him. It imposes no duty that Christ does not impose. If He were standing by our side, He would demand just as much as our pledge demands, and every Christian ought to be ashamed to offer any poorer excuse.

DANCING, ET AL.

And would not this same idea of responsibility and accountability to Him for everything settle a thousand other perplexing questions? O, how many questions concerning dancing and card-playing and theatre-going I am asked to answer in the course of the year! I always refuse to answer them when I can, and always dislike to have them asked. Of what use is my opinion? Of how little use is any man's opinion! To rely upon the advice of some one else, instead of having an inward principle and an inward monitor to decide these things, is like sending a hundred miles for a cup of water, when you might go to the unfailing spring right in your own dooryard. The cup of water from the distance may quench thirst for a little while; but in another hour we shall be thirsty again. Why not go to the original spring and source of all living water? Ask Christ about the theatre and the ball. Would He have you go? Will He go with you? Will you feel easy and comfortable in your own mind while there? Can you go from there to a highly spiritual prayer-meeting and feel no incongruity? Please do not ask my opinion again. It isn't worth the asking. But do bring everything to this touchstone, and ask, "Can I do this, or can I refuse to do that, and not feel uneasy and conscience-stricken, with Christ's eye upon me?"

Your friend,
Francis E. Clark.

TO YOUNG CHRISTIANS WHO ARE NOT MEMBERS OF THE SOCIETY.

A Familiar Letter from the President of the United Society.

Let me write a few words to those of you who are not active members of the Society of Christian Endeavor, but who ought to be. I will take it for granted that a society exists in your church, that you are among the Christian young people of the community, and, perhaps, members of the church, and yet for various reasons you are not members of the society.

I am not blaming you at all for being slow and cautious about taking such a step. This is altogether commendable. Any obligations should be weighed before they are assumed. Yet many of you have had plenty of time to consider these obligations, and still you hesitate Your companions have often urged you to come with them into the society as active members, and you know that they need you and want your aid. Why do you hesitate? I wonder if I can suggest any of the reasons, and possibly remove your objections.

DOES THE PLEDGE STAND IN THE WAY?

It does with some conscientious young Christians, I know; but I think it is usually because they have not considered it carefully, or, possibly, even read it candidly. The part of it that relates particularly to the society reads, "I will attend every weekly meeting of the society, and will take some part, aside from singing, in every meeting, unless prevented by some reason that I can conscientiously give to my Master, Jesus Christ." Is there anything unreasonable to ask of a young Christian in that? You acknowledge, doubtless, that it is well to have a young people's prayer-meeting, and that somebody ought to sustain it. But who is that somebody? The other young Christians? But why should they do this if you are unwilling to do your part? But possibly you say again, "I don't like to promise all this. I am willing to do what I can, but I dislike to pledge myself to do it." If you say this let me ask you to

READ THE LAST SENTENCE AGAIN.

"Unless prevented by some reason which I can conscientiously give to my master Jesus Christ."

Does not this phrase make it possible for the most tender conscience to accept it? If the prayer-meeting is something which ought to be sustained, and if it is a Christian's duty to sustain it, then the only excuse which can be given by any Christian for not attending and doing his part in any particular meeting is some excuse which can be conscientiously given to the Master, Jesus Christ. There is no other excuse possible to any true Christian for the non-performance of any duty. Why, then, should you shrink from taking this pledge thus explained?

A MATTER FOR EVERY ONE'S CONSCIENCE TO DECIDE.

There are no inquisitors on hand to wring from you the exact nature of your excuse, unless you choose to give it. If you have one that satisfies your own conscience, it will be enough to say so to the lookout committee or to the society. You need not go into particulars except with your own conscience. Be sure that you have no doubt that you have an excuse that Christ would accept. Then you can be at rest. But if you have a doubt, lean to the side of performance rather than non-performance.

When the evening of the monthly consecration-meeting comes, it surely is not usually too much to send a brief note to the meeting, saying you cannot be present and expressing your interest in and thought for your friends, or, at least, to send a verbal message to the society by some one who attends.

But even here the pledge is carefully guarded, and the words "if possible" are introduced. "If obliged to be absent from the monthly consecration or experience meeting, I will, if possible, send an excuse by some one who attends." No impossibility is asked or promised. If you are suddenly taken ill, or if unexpectedly you find yourself a hundred miles or ten miles away from the consecration-meeting when the hour arrives, you have broken no promise by not sending an excuse.

THE SAME VOWS INVOLVED IN CHURCH MEMBERSHIP.

Some of you who hesitate about joining the society on this account are church-members, and yet I do not see how you can consistently be members of the church without taking just such vows. You promised, when you joined the church, to serve God with all your heart, and to sustain the worship and ordinances of the church. This prayer-meeting is one of her ordinances for the young in churches where Societies of Christian Endeavor exist. Of course, if you have a good reason for not belonging to the society and sustaining its meetings, you are excused; but if you have not, the vows of church membership embrace the vows of society membership and a thousand times more. In fact, the very first vow you uttered when you became a Christian, and without which you could not have become a Christian, involved everything which the most stringent Christian Endeavor pledge ever asked.

CAPTIOUS AND PETTY EXCUSES.

I feel confident that few, if any, of the young Christians to whom I write would offer any captious reason for not joining the society. And yet I have occasionally heard these reasons advanced. One young lady, with a toss of her curly head, said "she wasn't going to join any such absurd society, for then she could never stir away from home, even for a summer vacation!" She knew, as well as I did, that that was simply a captious excuse, and I think she must have noticed how silly it sounded. Others refuse to join because of love for some previous organization that once existed in the church, or because of some one in the society whom they dislike, or because of some action taken that they did not approve, but I am convinced that these objections, when seriously looked at, will not weigh an ounce in the mind of a faithful young Christian who will do all that he can for the Master. Such an one will not let private likes or dislikes or personal reasons of this kind keep him from any real service.

Your objections have been genuine and honest, I am confident, but have been founded on a misapprehension. Think the matter over again, pray about it earnestly, and I think you will soon gladden the hearts of your friends, and find new and large opportunities for serving your Lord, by enrolling yourselves as active members of the Society of Christian Endeavor.

Your friend,

FRANCIS E. CLARK.

INDEX OF SUBJECTS.

Part I.

A Short History of the Christian Endeavor Movement   PAGE 1

Part II.

Young People's Society of Christian Endeavor

    What it is and how it works 15
    The model constitution 22
    Specimen by-laws given as hints for the regulation of local societies 28
    The best way of training young Christians . . . 33
    Seven reasons for commending the Young People's Society of Christian Endeavor . . . 36
    Some eloquent indorsements 38
    A pastor's objections answered 40
    Distinguishing features 41
    How to start a society 42

Part III.

The Membership

    Practical questions concerning active membership . 43
    For associate members 44
    How can we help our associate members? . . . 48
    Practical questions concerning associate members . 50
    Concerning affiliated members 51
    The reception of new members 54

Index of Subjects.

PART IV.

The Prayer-Meeting

The new prayer-meeting	57
Notes and suggestions upon the prayer-meeting	64
Nonsense concerning the prayer-meeting	70
The prayer-meeting the test of a good society	72
A good prayer-meeting	75
Some little foxes which mar the prayer-meeting vine	79
Some more "trifles" that make perfection	82
How shall we take part in the Christian Endeavor meetings?	85
Two suggestions for the ideal prayer-meeting	88
Various kinds of meetings	89
A prayer-meeting programme	94
I couldn't think of anything to say	95
Ways, themes, sources	95
Hints concerning methods for the prayer-meeting	96
Practical questions concerning the prayer-meeting	98

PART V.

The Prayer-Meeting Pledge

For what does the pledge stand	100
Something more concerning the pledge	104
Magnetizing the iron-clad pledge	108
Invertebrate societies	108
The interpretation of the pledge	111
Practical questions concerning the pledge	114

PART VI.

The Consecration-Meeting

Concerning the consecration-meeting	117
Calling the roll	120
A successful consecration-meeting	121
Does an earnest Christian need the consecration-meeting	122
The personal element in the consecration-meeting	123
The consecration-meeting	125
Helpful hints for the consecration service	127
Think on these things	128
A testimony receipt	129

Index of Subjects.

PART VII.
For Leaders of Prayer-Meetings

Hints to leaders of prayer-meetings	132
Helpful hints about leading a meeting	135
Promptness	137

PART VIII.
Officers and Committees

The duties of officers	140
A talk with some of the committees	144
Practical questions concerning the committees	147

PART IX.
The Lookout Committee

The lookout committee and its work	151
Eyes wide open	155
Hints for the lookout committee	157
Something for each of us now to do	159
Suggestion for lookout committees	160
Covenant reminders	161

PART X.
Prayer-Meeting Committee

Hints for the prayer-meeting committee	162
"General utility men"	163
The work of the prayer-meeting committee	164
More hints for the prayer-meeting committee	166
A prayer-meeting letter	169
Some New Year letters	170
Minute men	171
Careful preparation	171
Suggestions for the Christian Endeavor prayer-meeting	172

PART XI.
The Social Committee

Suggestions for the social committee	174
Plans for socials	177
Methods for social entertainment	178

Index of Subjects.

Entertainments suggested	180
Games for social gatherings	192
A good test	194
Practical questions concerning socials	195

Part XII.

Music, Temperance, Missionary and Sunday School Committees

Music —
Music and music committee	197
The ministry of song	200
"Overworking the hymn-book"	203
A Christian Endeavor choir	204

Temperance —
Work of the temperance committee	206
The temperance committee	208

Missionary —
Christian Endeavor and missions	209
How to give	213
Some methods of raising money	216
The Christian Endeavor Society and Young People's Missionary organizations	217
For the missionary committee	219
Missionary work	220
How one mission circle works	220
Practical questions concerning the work of the missionary committee	221

Sunday School —
Hints for the Sunday School committee	222

Part XIII.

Miscellaneous Committees

Good literature committee	224
The "Omnibus Committee"	225
Calling and flower committee	226
Pastor's committee	227
Messenger committee	227
Christian Endeavor classes	227
For the hotel committees	228

Index of Subjects.

Part XIV.

Miscellaneous

A Christian Endeavor parlor for young men and boys	230
An invitation	232
For young societies	232
Correspondence between societies	233
Saving time	234
A good word for the badge	234
Suggestions for anniversaries	235
Hotel invitations	235
A Christian Endeavor savings bank	236
Practical questions	236
Suggestions for summer missionary work	237
Newspaper exchange	238
A prayer-circle card	238
A monthly conference	239
Society visitation	240

Part XV.

Business Meetings

A familiar letter from the President of the United Society	241
Practical questions concerning business meetings	245
Reports of committees	246

Part XVI.

The United Society — Local and State Unions

The United Society	250
Christian Endeavor unions. — Their helpfulness and possibilities	253
Concerning local unions	256
The ideal programme for a local union	260
Concerning the ideal convention	261
How to prepare for a State convention	265
An ideal State convention programme	267
Practical questions concerning united society local unions, etc.	269

Index of Subjects.

Part XVII
Junior Societies

A familiar letter by the President of the United Society	271
Work among children	273
The junior society of Christian Endeavor	277
How one pastor manages his junior society	280

Part XVIII.
Reorganization

Concerning reorganization	282
How to reorganize	284
A practical example	286
Practical questions concerning reorganization	287

Part XIX.
The Society in a Revival

A familiar letter from the President of The United Society	289
Our society and our revival	292

Part XX.
The Society as a Part of the Church

Sustaining the church services	295
Gaining the confidence of the church	298
For the beginning of the church year	301
The alumni of Y. P. S. C. E. — The church of the future	304

Part XXI.
Societies in City and Country

Concerning a large society	308
Christian Endeavor work in the country	312

Part XXII.
Woman's Work

Woman's work in Christian Endeavor	317

Index of Subjects.

PART XXIII.

Familiar Letters on Various Topics

    Doubtful amusements 322
    Concerning interdenominationalism 325
    Concerning anniversaries 328
    Our societies in the vacation season 332
    An infallible touchstone 334
    To young Christians who are not members of the society 336

INDEX OF AUTHORS.

Adriance, S. W.	88
Allen, Jessica Wolcott	85
Amerman, W. L.	75, 225
Baker, Smith	70
Barrows, John Henry	38
Bartlett, C. A.	166
Brandell, Millie E	96
Bruhlman, Otto C.	227
Canfield, James	232
Caswell, Mrs.	216
Childs, W. H.	260
Christy, A. B.	161
Clark, F. E.	1, 15, 44, 51, 54, 72, 79, 82, 100, 104, 111, 117, 120, 132, 140, 151, 174, 197, 209, 213, 241, 250, 256, 261, 271, 284, 289, 295, 298, 301, 308, 322, 325, 328, 332, 334, 336
Colburn, H. E.	178, 192
Creighton, W. S.	39
Cromer, J. C.	206
C. D. S.	129
Dana, Mary F.	273
Darby, W. J.	39
Dumm, Mrs. W. W.	123
Francis, John	187
F. D. G.	183

Index of Authors.

Goodrich, Charles N.	200
Hamilton, J. W.	39
Hamlin, T. S.	38
Helwig, J. B.	40
Hill, James L.	64, 144
Hill, Mrs. James L.	217
Hoyt, Wayland	33, 57
Hudson, M. A.	164
Jackson, J. C.	157, 162
Kinney, H. N.	267
Loomis, E. R.	227
Lowell, D. R.	48
Mitchella	180
Newton, A. F.	238
Niccolls, J. S.	38, 228
Northrop, Charles A.	204
Noyes, E. M.	222
Pepper, H. Howard	226
Plass, Norman	108, 277
Pope, H. W.	127, 160, 280
Pratt, Dwight M.	137
Rand, George A.	90
Robinson, Edward A.	172
Scudder, Mrs. Alice May	317
Sewall, John L.	265, 292
Seymour, Mrs. C. R.	185
Sigma	208
Smith, Albert D.	95
Talladay, Mrs. J. W.	95
Temple, W. H. G.	155
Twitchell, Justin E.	253
Tyler, J. Z.	36, 39
Ward, George M.	282
Wells, Amos R.	125
Wells, Geo. H.	38
Winslow, Mrs. E. M.	312
Yatman, C. H.	128

AIDS TO ENDEAVOR.

12mo, cloth, .75; gilt edges, $1.00.

Selections from standard authors designed for the public and private use of members of the Y. P. S. C. E. It also contains an Introduction and a richly suggestive talk with leaders of meetings by FRANCIS E. CLARK, President of the Y. P. S. C. E. This latter alone makes "Aids to Endeavor" almost as indispensable a part of the Christian Endeavor outfit as Bible, hymn-book and pledge-card.

    A handy and very handsomely published little book, made up of a great number of short, apt selections in prose and verse, from a wide variety of devout writers, containing such bits of Christian wisdom, such bright, pat, kindly and kindling utterances as are fitted to be really helpful to the young Christian. — *Chicago Advance.*

    The book is a good idea, happily conceived and worthily wrought out. The selections are uniformly of a high and uplifting grade, and in the hands of members of Christian Endeavor Societies the book will fulfill a very helpful mission. — REV. CHARLES P. MILLS, Newburyport, Mass.

    It is equally suitable for general reading, an admirable book for the center-table, and one a young man may have in his pocket for leisure reading. — *Herald and Presbyter.*

    These short selections are invariably devotional in spirit, and the book might very well be called "Aids to Devotion." — *Interior*, Chicago.

    It is admirably done and will certainly be found of great help to timid young Christians, especially in connection with the weekly prayer-meetings. — *Detroit Tribune.*

    Our young people will find "Aids to Endeavor" a rich store-house of precious thoughts and inspiring suggestions. — *The Assistant Pastor*, Pittsfield.

    It will be at once a tonic for the live societies and new life for the moribund. — *Albany Journal.*

    Many young members hesitate to express their own thoughts before others, and it was to furnish such with appropriate utterances for the occasion, that the little work before us was compiled. — *Zion's Advocate*, Portland.

    This is a good hand-book for all young Christians, as well as for members of the Y. P. S. C. E. It ought to have a large circulation and do a great deal of good. — *The Occident*, San Francisco.

    The selections are made with excellent taste and care, and cannot fail to be helpful to young Christians. — *Zion's Herald.*

OUR BUSINESS BOYS.

By REV. F. E. CLARK, D. D.
16mo, .60.

This little book contains an amount of valuable truth quite out of proportion to its small compass. . . . It is the condensed testimony of the successful majority as to the qualities which go to the making of success. — *Christian Register*, Boston.

It is not often that a book is packed so full of good sense and the best experience. It is a first-class present for young men, and will afford many valuable hints to those who talk to the young. — *Sunday School Journal*.

This little work comes before the public at a most opportune season, for the reason that the problem of "What shall we do with our boys?" and what methods will best secure their success in life, is one that is engaging the minds of fathers and mothers throughout all this broad land. — *N. Y. Analysis*.

The author stops in his formula for success to remark that every rich man is not by any means truly successful, nor is every poor man unsuccessful; for many things may be bought too dear. — *Philadelphia Ledger*.

OUR TOWN.

By MARGARET SIDNEY.
12mo, $1.25.

Written for and dedicated to all the Young People's Societies of Christian Endeavor.

Margaret Sidney makes interesting the homeliest and most ordinary aspects of daily life, and imparts to duty the glory of doing, and to virtue its own reward. — *Inter-Ocean*.

It is one of those rare stories which teach a lovely lesson without seeming to know it. — *Toledo Bee*.

Like all the stories that come from the pen of Margaret Sidney, "Our Town" evinces the strong love of humanity that must be a heart sentiment, that bubbles over with clarified humor and with a plain common sense that are delightful and fascinating to some besides young readers. — *Home Journal*, Boston.

Some of the methods here followed may serve as suggestions to others who are seeking for practical work for their members. — *Christian Observer*, Louisville, Ky.

New uses and new possibilities for the Y. P. S. C. E. are outlined in this story. — *Northern Christian Advocate*, Syracuse.

"Our Town" illustrates what the Christian Endeavor Society is doing to solve the problem of bettering communities, and the book is full of brightness and action. — *The Morning Star*.

The Mossback Correspondence.

By REV. F. E. CLARK, D. D.

12mo, $1.00.

The book will be a capital one for a parish or Sunday-school library, and would be as great a friend and helper to the preacher, in its way, as the more elaborate and studied "Parish Problems." It is often keen, always kindly, never dull. — *Christian Union.*

There is much solid, practical sense in these brief epistles of Mossback, which it would be well for every one to appropriate. There is a dry humor pervading the whole which dulls the keen edge of his satire and the sharp point of his wit. — *Zion's Herald.*

Its author is as sensible as the late Dr. Holland, but more concise; and what, by this comparison, he loses in grace, he gains in pithiness. — *Sunday School Times.*

Full of sound sense and wholesome advice, and permeated by a most kindly spirit. The style is charmingly direct and crisp, and the frequent "hits" will be keenly appreciated, especially by Christian workers. — *The Inquirer*, New York.

CHRISSY'S ENDEAVOR.

By "PANSY."

12mo, $1.50.

Mrs. Alden could not write a dull or purposeless book if she tried. This will doubtless attain a wide circulation. — *Lutheran Observer*, Philadelphia.

This charming story of Chrissy Hollister's experience in her labors for Christ, the beautiful truths herein illustrated and emphasized, cannot fail to be of great benefit and encouragement to all workers for the cause. — *Portland Transcript.*

The book ought to be in every Sunday-school library. . . . It would leave an indelible impression on all earnest minds as to the duties and privileges connected with membership in the Y. P. S. C. E. — *Weekly Witness*, New York.

There is a great deal in the book which will help those who are trying to start branches of this league, or who are already interested in its methods. — *Watchman*, Boston.

The huge convention in this city proved to the wondering masses who attended that the Christian Endeavor organization had come to stay. "Pansy," in giving this story, does more — gives the purposes of this body represented by so many thousands. — *Philadelphia Methodist.*

It makes a fine distinction between societies of the true and the false kind. — *Christian Secretary*, Hartford.

DANGER SIGNALS.

By REV. F. E. CLARK, D. D.

12mo, .75.

The "signals" displayed are to warn young readers against the perils of intemperance, corrupt and trashy literature, low theatres, gambling, impurity, frivolity and dishonesty. The addresses are strong, pungent discourses with words that go home like arrows. — *Christian Index*, Atlanta, Ga.

Many books of advice have been written for the young, but there are exceedingly few that the young will read. We believe that this volume, like Holland's Letters, is likely to prove an exception. — *The Advance*, Chicago.

There is enough to save a generation of young men if they would give heed thereto. Put this book in the trunk of the young man when he leaves home for business life, or college or even for a summer vacation. — *Christian Union*, New York.

If the young girls would read this book, they would get a better idea of the dangers which beset their sweethearts and brothers, and would get points, too, of dangerous tendencies, which, if they can check, may prevent them speechless misery in future life. — *Seminarium*.

It is a book which should not only be put in the hands of the young, but parents ought to read these thrilling words. The eyes of many may thus be opened to the perils which beset the paths of their children. — *National Baptist*, Philadelphia.

Among the active men who are devoting their lives to philanthropy and Christian work, there is no one more earnest in behalf of the young of our land than the author of this important little book, who is the president of the United Society of Christian Endeavor. — *Journal of Education*, Boston.

Mr. Clark, fearing lest it should be taken for granted that a minister had not enough knowledge of the world intelligently to counsel young business men, asked and received letters from many successful Boston merchants, pointing out the special dangers to which city boys are constantly exposed. — *N. Y. Witness*.

It is very seldom that anything is written more important for our young people. The devil is extremely busy, more busy I fear than some easy-going parents think, and I am glad you have had the courage to speak out so boldly. The book ought to be read by everybody, old and young. "To be forewarned is to be forearmed." — SAMUEL B. CAPEN, *of Torrey, Bright & Capen*.

At the Bookstores, or sent postpaid by the Publishers,

D. LOTHROP COMPANY,

364 and 366 Washington Street, Boston.

www.ingramcontent.com/pod-product-compliance
Lightning Source LLC
LaVergne TN
LVHW091247080426
835510LV00007B/147